The Penguin

HISTORICAL ATLAS of the BRITISH EMPIRE

Nigel Dalziel

Introduction by John M. MacKenzie

PENGUIN BOOKS

Published by the Penguin Group
Penguin Books Ltd, 80 Strand, London WC2R 0RL, England
Penguin Group (USA) Inc., 375 Hudson Street, New York, New York 10014, USA
Penguin Group (Canada), 90 Eglinton Avenue East, Suite 700, Toronto, Ontario, Canada M4P 2Y3
(a division of Pearson Penguin Canada Inc.)
Penguin Ireland, 25 St Stephen's Green, Dublin 2, Ireland
(a division of Penguin Books Ltd)
Penguin Group (Australia), 707 Collins Street, Melbourne, Victoria 3008, Australia
(a division of Pearson Australia Group Pty Ltd)
Penguin Books India Pvt Ltd, 11 Community Centre,
Panchsheel Park, New Delhi – 110 017, India
Penguin Group (NZ), 67 Apollo Drive, Rosedale, Auckland 0632, New Zealand
(a division of Pearson New Zealand Ltd)
Penguin Books (South Africa) (Pty) Ltd, Block D, Rosebank Office Park, 181 Jan Smuts Avenue,
Parktown North, Gauteng 2193, South Africa

Penguin Books Ltd, Registered Offices: 80 Strand, London WC2R 0RL, England

www.penguin.com

First published 2006
6

Copyright © Penguin Books, 2006
All rights reserved

Printed and bound by South China Printing Co. Ltd., China

ISBN-13: 978-0-141-01844-7

Produced for Penguin Books by Haywood & Hall

Preface

The emergence of the British Empire was one of the greatest historical phenomena of modern times. It remained in existence until very recently, and its implications and legacies remain with us today. The study of the British Empire is fundamental to understanding much about both contemporary international relations and the domestic history of many post-colonial societies throughout the world, not least that of Britain itself.

This atlas of more than 50 maps and explanatory texts charts the development of the Empire chronologically and by region, beginning with the extension of political power and control across the British Isles as they gradually fell under English hegemony. British exploration overseas began more than 500 years ago, at a time when other European states were developing the first truly global maritime empires – the means by which European religion, culture and economics were universally disseminated. But oceanic routes were two-lane highways. This work mainly describes the emergence of the British Empire over several centuries in every corner of the world, but it also considers themes such as imperial exhibitions and botanical science, which had a direct and long-lasting influence on British as well as colonial societies and indigenous peoples. It also follows the course of the British Empire through to its ultimate collapse and to decolonization after the Second World War, when a new realpolitik determined Britain's realignment with Europe. The atlas concludes by examining Britain's lingering imperial commitments, and the emergence of the Commonwealth as a force in world affairs.

The subject of the British Empire is a huge one, and in projects devoted to such subjects it is always difficult deciding what to omit or compress and what to include. I believe that the subject matter we have selected for inclusion is sufficiently comprehensive to provide a valuable overview of the world's greatest empire. Many people have had a hand in compiling this work; I would particularly like to thank John MacKenzie, John Haywood, Simon Hall, Fiona Plowman, Veneta Bullen, Darren Bennett, Gerard Hill and Tim Aspden and his team at the University of Southampton Cartographic Unit for their considerable contributions.

Nigel Dalziel
2005

Contents

The Significance of the British Empire

In the long history of empires, British imperialism was unique. It was striking both in its extent and in its diversity, exemplifying all the many ways in which empires have developed in modern times. To start with a definition: empire is a supra-national political entity, involving the imposition of the power and authority of one people over another or multiple others. This power can be expressed through commercial penetration, military conquest, settlement, the imposition of administration or a combination of several or all of these. It can be established gradually and insidiously over a period of time; or it can happen suddenly. Once an administration has been formed, whether of expatriates or of settlers, this is known as 'formal' empire. But sometimes the dominant state can achieve its ends through working with indigenous rulers or through commercial sectors in a manner which has often been described as 'informal'. Empires in modern times have often involved a mixture of these two systems.

Sea Powers

Empires have been a characteristic of human history for almost four thousand years. But most of the empires before modern times were essentially landward in character: this was true of the Assyrians, Persians, Macedonian Greeks, various imperial formations in China and surrounding territory, the Mongols, the Mughals, and others in Africa and Central and South America. The maritime dimension was significantly more important only for the Carthaginians, the Romans and the Ottomans.

But from Renaissance times, the marine dimension became critical. The Portuguese and Spanish empires were essentially seaborne. Their ambition was based upon a growing understanding of the oceans, developing technology in shipping and armaments, and a complex of commercial, religious and political designs. The Dutch, French, and British empires were generated by more

diverse commercial projects, by religious rivalry and by the projection of European political and military hostilities on to a global stage. The Spanish and Portuguese had also set out to 'plant' some of their own nationals overseas, and this theme was also taken up by their successors.

The British, in an imperial period spanning almost five centuries, created several empires in one. For the Tudors, an English empire meant a polity that was free from other authority, notably that of Rome. Various parts of the British Isles had been subordinated or invaded by other empires and peoples (Romans, Normans, Vikings, Angles, Saxons). As the English

A view of ships on the Thames in 1761. Mastery of the seas has played a crucial part in the development of a number of the world's great empires. The Royal Navy has been a key asset in Britain's history as an island nation in terms of defence, trade and scientific discovery, and was central in establishing Britain's global empire.

lost their territories in France, they became more conscious of the possibility of establishing a single political entity within the British Isles. But this was achieved only gradually, with the Unions of English and Scottish crowns (1603) and parliaments (1707), and the forced Union with Ireland in 1801. Thus a regional empire was only established at the same time as the British Empire was progressively established overseas.

By the beginning of the 20th century, many British politicians, intellectuals and educational and other propagandists saw these developments as revealing the true meaning of British history. The coming together of a romantically idealised 'island race' (which was of course ethnically diverse) had provided the opportunity for the establishment of overseas power. This involved settlement of colonists in North America and the Caribbean from the 17th century, in Australia and New Zealand from the late 18th and early 19th, and later in southern Africa and other African colonies. But it also involved extensive commerce, which was jointly organized by indigenous producers and merchants and by expatriates temporarily deposited in colonies around the world to manage the trading flows. As naval and mercantile power grew, influenced by new technologies, the British recognized the need for strategic outposts to protect trade routes and supply their navy. These included Gibraltar, Malta, Cyprus, Ascension, St Helena, Aden, Singapore, Hong Kong and others. From the 17th century, under the aegis of the East

Illustration of a British officer being carried on a palanquin in 1828. European traders in Bengal during the 17th and 18th centuries often used palanquins and even lowly East India Company employees could afford to use this mode of transport. Britain maintained a presence in India for more than two centuries and it became the most impressive element in its empire.

India Company, the British embarked upon the grandest of all their exploits. Begun tentatively, and partly unintentionally, this was no less than the conquest of one of the great pre-European empires, the Mughal, and its surrounding territories, a process that took almost two hundred years. India demonstrates the compulsive expansiveness of empire: conquest demands more conquest, the addition of territorial buffers to protect gains already made.

Globalization

Some see the British Empire as an early exercise in globalization, spreading a single language and common cultural elements, political, legal and educational systems as well as commercial patterns, transport infrastructures and currency flows. From the 19th century, the telegraph, the steamship, railways and an extensive ports system, with docks rather than anchorages, confirmed these globalizing tendencies. Missionaries also set about expanding Christendom, with varied degrees of success, in non-European territories. All these operated both within the territories of formal empire (where power was directly imposed) and in areas which remained theoretically independent.

Empire also instigated much violence, extensive destabilization of indigenous systems, and the movement of black and brown peoples as well as whites around the globe. The slave trade and plantation slavery remain the major crimes of the imperial era, a black Holocaust of frightening proportions. Non-European peoples also indulged in slavery, but seldom so brutally or in such stark numbers. Other peoples, including Indians, Chinese and Pacific Islanders, were moved around the globe in what has been called a 'new system of slavery', indentured labour. Economies everywhere were re-orientated towards the imperial economy, notably through the restriction of non-European lands to raw material production while end-product industries were built up in the metropolitan country. Nonetheless, some notable industrialization had taken place in the wider empire by the 20th century. The balance sheet of empire is still debated, but it is clear that by the era of decolonization, aspects of modernization, however ill-balanced and disruptive, had been spread around the world.

Whatever else may be said about the British Empire, it is clear that we need to understand its history in order to comprehend much of the present. This atlas is devoted to spreading such an understanding, offering insights in cartographic form into the scale of empire, as well as its economic and demographic, technological and environmental, political and military, cultural and religious dimensions. Ultimately, empire was a joint enterprise between the dominant and subordinate peoples, with elements of co-operation as well as conflict ebbing and flowing in imperial territories. The results are still very much with us. Thus, the 50 map spreads that follow offer many informative routes into the history and character of British imperialism.

John M. MacKenzie
2005

Timeline 1150–1783

BRITAIN AND THE AMERICAS	AFRICA, MEDITERRANEAN AND MIDDLE EAST	ASIA, AUSTRALASIA AND THE PACIFIC	INTERNATIONAL EVENTS
1169 Start of English expansion in Ireland			
1497 John Cabot claims region of Newfoundland for Henry VII			
1536 Union of England and Wales			
	1562 John Hawkins inaugurates the English transatlantic slave trade		
1577–80 First English circumnavigation of the globe by Francis Drake			**1584–1604** Anglo-Spanish War
1585 First (abortive) settlement of Virginia at Roanoke	**1585** Drake's expedition to the West Indies		
1588 Defeat of the Spanish Armada			
		1600 East India Company chartered	
1603 Union of the Crowns of England and Scotland			
1607 First permanent English settlement in North America, at Jamestown, Virginia	**c.1607** John Davies starts redwood trade with Sierra Leone	**1608** First East India Company ship arrives to trade at Surat	
1609 Plantation of Ulster begins			
	1618 English traders active on the Gold Coast		
1620 Plymouth Plantation established, New England			
1624 Settlement of Barbados			**1642–6** English Civil War
1651 Navigation Act provokes the First Dutch War	**1661** Acquisition of Fort James at the mouth of the Gambia River	**1661** Bombay ceded by Portugal (effective 1665)	**1652–4** First Anglo-Dutch War
			1665–7 Second Anglo-Dutch War
1670 Hudson's Bay Company chartered and claims the vast area of Rupert's Land			
1672 Royal Africa Company chartered	**1672** Royal Africa Company chartered		**1672–4** Third Anglo-Dutch War
1690 Victory of Protestant William III at the Battle of the Boyne			**1689–97** War of the League of Augsburg (King William's War)
1707 Union of England and Scotland as Great Britain			**1702–13** War of the Spanish Succession (Queen Anne's War)
1713 Treaty of Utrecht: Britain's territorial gains recognised			**1739–48** War of Jenkins' Ear leading into War of the Austrian Succession (King George's War)
	1750 Company of Merchants Trading to Africa founded	**1750** Robert Clive successfully defends Arcot	
1759 Capture of Quebec by General Wolfe		**1757** Battle of Plassey: Britain becomes the master of Bengal	**1756–63** Seven Years War (French and Indian War)
1760 Montreal falls and New France capitulates		**1760** French defeated at Battle of Wandiwash, Carnatic	
1763 Peace of Paris. Britain gains French North America, Florida, Senegal and Caribbean 'Ceded Islands'.		**1763** War with Nawab of Bengal, defeated with Mughal emperor and Wazir of Oudh at Buxar (1764)	
1763 Proclamation Line limiting westward American settlement			
1765 Stamp Act leads to discontent in the American Colonies	**1765** Senegambia becomes first British colony in Africa	**1765** Treaty of Allahabad: East India Company gains the diwani of Bengal	
1768 Troops used to quell Boston riots		**1768** First Pacific voyage of Captain James Cook	
		1769 New Zealand claimed for Britain by Captain Cook	
		1770 Captain Cook claims eastern Australia for Britain	
1773 Boston Tea Party			
1774 First Continental Congress of American rebels meets in Philadelphia			**1775–83** American Revolutionary War
1776 American Declaration of Independence		**1776** Start of Captain Cook's third voyage to the Pacific	
1778 France enters war against Britain		**1778** Captain Cook charts American NW coast	
1779 Spain enters war against Britain		**1779** Death of Cook in Hawaii	
1781 British surrender at Yorktown		**1781** Nominal control of India passes to the Crown	
1783 End of the American war and territorial adjustments in the Peace of Paris			

1784–1860

BRITAIN AND THE AMERICAS	AFRICA, MEDITERRANEAN AND MIDDLE EAST	ASIA, AUSTRALASIA AND THE PACIFIC	INTERNATIONAL EVENTS
1784 Migration of American Loyalists to Quebec and the Maritimes		**1784** William Pitt's India Act establishes dual system of Company-Government control **1786** First British (East India Company) foothold on Malay peninsula, at Penang	
	1787 First British settlers arrive in Sierra Leone	**1788** First Fleet arrives at Botany Bay and begins the British settlement of Australia	
1791–5 Captain George Vancouver's voyage surveying the coast of NW America **1795** Founding of the London Missionary Society **1798** Irish rebellion	**1795–1803** First British occupation of the Cape **1798** Nelson defeats French fleet at the Battle of Aboukir, Egypt **1801** Defeat of French forces in Egypt	**1795–6** Conquest of Dutch Ceylon by the East India Company	**1793–1802** French Revolutionary War
1801 Union with Ireland creating the United Kingdom of Great Britain and Ireland **1802** Peace of Amiens. Britain retains Trinidad and Ceylon **1805** Battle of Trafalgar			**1803–15** Napoleonic Wars
1807 British slave trade abolished **1812–14** 'War of 1812' with USA **1815** Vienna Settlement: Britain retains Ionian Islands, Malta, Caribbean territory, Cape and Mauritius **1818** British-US border agreed as 49th Parallel west to Rocky Mountains **1821** Merger of Hudson's Bay Company and North-West Company **1823** Anti-Slavery Society founded	**1806** Second and permanent British occupation of the Cape **1821** British government takes control of Gold Coast forts **1823** British traders established in Natal **1824–31** First Asante War	**1819** Singapore ceded to Stamford Raffles **1823–4** First Burmese War **1824** Britain swops Bencoolen for Dutch Malacca **1825** First British occupation of Western Australia, at Albany **1829** The whole Australian continent declared British	
1832 Representative government in Newfoundland **1833** Act for the emancipation of slaves in the British Empire (1st Aug. 1834) **1837** Queen Victoria ascends the throne **1837–8** Canadian rebellions	**1835** The Afrikaner Great Trek begins	**1833** First British Resident to New Zealand **1838–42** First Afghan War **1839–42** First Opium War	
1839 Lord Durham's report on the governance of British North America **1840** Responsible government granted to Canada	**1839** Aden seized **1840** Anti-slave trade treaty with the Sultanate of Zanzibar **1844** Extension of British protection over the southern Gold Coast	**1840** New Zealand annexed **1842** Hong Kong ceded in the Treaty of Nanking	
1845–9 Great Irish potato famine **1846** Settlement of Oregon boundary dispute with USA **1849** Vancouver Island colony established **1849** Repeal of the Navigation Acts	**1849** Bonny (Bight of Biafra) receives its first British consul	**1846** Jammu and Kashmir made a protectorate **1849** Annexation of the Punjab, India	
1851 Great Exhibition in the Crystal Palace, London	**1852** Bight of Benin becomes British **1852** Britain recognises the Afrikaner Transvaal Republic **1854** Afrikaners establish the independent Orange Free State **1856–7** Anglo-Persian War	**1850** Gold discovered in New South Wales **1852** Constitution for New Zealand **1852–3** Second Burmese War. British acquire Pegu **1856** Oudh annexed by Britain **1856–60** Second Chinese Opium, or 'Arrow', War **1856** Responsible government for New South Wales and New Zealand **1857–8** Indian Mutiny/Rebellion	
1858 British Columbia Colony created	**1858–64** David Livingstone's Zambezi Expedition	**1858** East India Company rule ends and India becomes a Crown Colony	

11

1861–1910

BRITAIN AND THE AMERICAS	AFRICA, MEDITERRANEAN AND MIDDLE EAST	ASIA, AUSTRALASIA AND THE PACIFIC	INTERNATIONAL EVENTS
	1861 Lagos annexed, the nucleus of the future Nigeria		
1867 British North America Act creates the Dominion of Canada	**1867** Discovery of diamonds in Griqualand West		
1869 Sale of Hudson's Bay Company territory to Canada	**1869** Suez Canal opens		
	1872 Responsible government granted to Cape Colony		
	1873 Death of missionary explorer David Livingstone		
	1873–4 Asante War		
	1874 Gold Coast Colony created	**1874** Treaty of Pangkor extends British control of Malay peninsula	
	1875 Britain buys 44% of Suez Canal shares		
	1876 Egypt bankrupt. British-French 'Dual Control' begins	**1876** Royal Titles Act makes Victoria Empress of India	
	1877 Transvaal annexed	**1877** Western Pacific High Commission established	
	1878 Cyprus occupied	**1878–80** Second Afghan War	
1879–82 Carnarvon Commission on imperial defence	**1879** Zulu War and British defeat at Isandhlwana		
	1880–1 First Boer War re-gains Transvaal independence subject to British suzerainty		
	1881 Arabi (Urabi) Revolt, Egypt	**1881** British North Borneo Company chartered	
	1882 Battle of Tel el-Kebir and occupation of Egypt		
1884–5 Conference of Berlin accelerates the 'Scramble for Africa'	**1884** Mahdist revolt leads to the evacuation of Egyptian forces from Sudan	**1884** British New Guinea becomes a protectorate	
1885 Transcontinental Canadian Pacific Railway completed	**1885** General Gordon killed by the Mahdi's forces at Khartoum	**1885** Indian National Congress founded	
1885 North-West Rebellion, Canada		**1885** Third Burmese War	
	1886 Transvaal gold rush begins		
	1886 British-German agreement partitioning East Africa		
	1886 Royal Niger Company chartered		
1888 Imperial Exhibition, Glasgow	**1888** Imperial British East Africa Company chartered	**1888** Protectorates extended over North Borneo, Brunei and Sarawak	
	1889 Cecil Rhodes' British South Africa Company chartered		
	1889 Protectorates over Mashonaland and Shire Heights (later Nyasaland)		
	1890 Buganda becomes sphere of influence		
	1893 Responsible government granted to Natal	**1893** Solomon Islands protectorate	
	1893 Conquest of Matabeleland		
1895 Joseph Chamberlain becomes Secretary of State for the Colonies	**1895** Jameson Raid on the Transvaal		
	1895 East African Protectorate		
	1896-7 Shona-Ndebele revolt	**1896** Creation of Federated Malay States	
1897 Klondike gold rush starts	**1898** Battle of Omdurman and renewed control of Sudan		
	1898 Fashoda Crisis	**1898** Lease of Weihaiwei from China	
	1899 British-Egyptian condominium over Sudan		
	1899–1902 Second Anglo-Boer War		
	1900 Relief of Mafeking	**1900–1** Britain and other powers suppress the Boxer Rebellion, China	
	1900 Protectorates of Northern and Southern Nigeria		
1901 Death of Queen Victoria	**1901** Annexation of Asante (Gold Coast)	**1901** Australian Commonwealth established	
1902 British global telegraph system completed	**1902** Treaty of Vereeniging ends the Boer War	**1902** Delhi durbar, India	
1904 Anglo-French Entente		**1902** British-Japanese alliance	
1906 HMS Dreadnought begins a new arms race	**1906–7** Afrikaner colonies granted responsible government	**1905** Partition of Bengal	
1907 Anglo-Russian Entente		**1906** All-India Muslim League founded	
1907 Title 'Dominion' adopted for self-governing colonies		**1907–9** Morley-Minto government reforms in India	
1910 Death of King Edward VII	**1910** Union of South Africa	**1908** British exploit new oil discoveries in Persia	

1911–2005

BRITAIN AND THE AMERICAS	AFRICA, MEDITERRANEAN AND MIDDLE EAST	ASIA, AUSTRALASIA AND THE PACIFIC	INTERNATIONAL EVENTS
1911 First Imperial Conference, London **1914** Irish Home Rule Act	**1913** Afrikaner National Party formed in South Africa **1914** Egypt made a protectorate **1914** Union of Nigeria **1914–15** Conquest of German SW Africa by South African forces **1914–16** Conquest of German Togoland and Kamerun **1915** Unsuccessful Dardanelles and Gallipoli campaign	**1911** George V's Coronation Durbar, Delhi **1914** Australia takes German New Guinea and islands; New Zealand takes German Samoa **1915** Gandhi leaves South Africa and returns to India	**1914–18** First World War
1916 Easter Rising in Dublin **1916** Battle of Jutland	**1916** Arab Revolt against Turks **1916** Sykes-Picot Agreement on the future of the Middle East **1916** Occupation of German East Africa	**1916** Home Rule leagues established in India; Congress-Muslim League Lucknow Pact	
1918 Sinn Fein victory in Irish elections **1919–21** Irish war for independence **1920** Government of Ireland Act	**1918** Allenby's offensive against the Turks forces the Armistice of Mudros **1920** Britain awarded Mandates for Palestine and Iraq **1921** Client ruler Prince Faisal placed on Iraqi throne	**1919** Amritsar Massacre **1919** India Act extends limited responsible government **1920–22** Gandhi launches non-cooperation campaign **1921** End of the British alliance with Japan **1921** Washington Naval Conference	
1921 Irish Free State established as a Dominion; Home Rule in Northern Ireland **1922–3** Irish civil war **1929** Great Depression begins	**1922** Announcement of qualified Egyptian independence	**1929** Viceroy Lord Irwin states Dominion status the goal for India **1931** Round Table Conference on India's future, London	
1931 Statute of Westminster makes explicit the constitutional autonomy of the Dominions **1932** Imperial Preference established at the Ottawa Conference **1932** De Valera heads the Irish government	**1932** Independence of Iraq **1936** Arab Revolt in Palestine **1936** Anglo-Egyptian Treaty	**1935** Provincial self-government for India	
1941–5 Britain at war with Japan	**1941** Conquest of Italian-held Ethiopia and Somaliland **1942** Battle of El Alamein and conquest of Italian Libya	**1941** British and Russian occupation of Iran **1941** Japan captures Singapore **1942** Quit India campaign suppressed **1944** Defeat of Japanese forces at Kohima and Imphal, NE India **1947** Independence of India and Pakistan	**1939–45** Second World War
1944 D-Day invasion of Europe			
1948 Eire leaves the British Commonwealth	**1948** Withdrawal from Palestine and the first Arab-Israeli War **1951** Iran nationalises Anglo-Iranian Oil Company **1951** Egyptian offensive against British Suez Canal Zone	**1948–60** Malayan Communist insurgency **1951** ANZUS Pact	
1952 Accession of Queen Elizabeth II	**1952–9** Mau Mau revolt in Kenya **1955** Creation of anti-Russian Baghdad Pact (CENTO) **1955** Cypriots begin fight for union with Greece **1956** Egyptian nationalisation of Suez Canal and British invasion **1957** Ghana (Gold Coast) becomes the Empire's first independent black African state		
1961 First (unsuccessful) British application to join EEC **1965** Commonwealth Secretariat established in London **1968** Britain decides to withdraw from 'East of Suez' **1968** Beginning of the 'Troubles' in Northern Ireland **1972** End of the British 'Sterling area' **1973** Britain joins the EEC **1982** Falklands War **1994** IRA ceasefire in Northern Ireland **2005** End of IRA campaign	**1961** South Africa leaves the Commonwealth **1965** UDI in Rhodesia **1968–71** Withdrawal from Persian Gulf **1994** Black majority rule in South Africa	**1984** Agreement with China on return of Hong Kong (1997)	

Part I: The Early Empire 1500–1763

John Cabot's voyage to Newfoundland in 1497 can be said to mark the start of England's empire overseas. But the English were slow to embark on international exploration and trade, held back by conflict with France, the Wars of the Roses and the religious turmoil of the early 1500s. In coming late to the fray, however, England benefited from the wider continental experience and new developments in business, finance, shipping and navigation.

The outward-looking European civilization was uniquely placed to dominate world affairs at the end of the Middle Ages. Trade and wealth creation were key to European endeavour and to the wave of international exploration inspired by the travels of Marco Polo (*c.* 1254-1324) and fostered by the new spirit of Renaissance inquiry. Also, it was developing European maritime, not land-based, power that was vital in exploiting world trade. The Italian city-states of Venice and Genoa, with their large trading fleets and maritime empires, showed the way.

In the late 15th century larger, more centralized and powerful nation-states emerged, particularly Spain, France and England, whose rivalry and ambition drove expansion in Europe and overseas. Economic development and war encouraged technological innovation, notably in gun manufacture and ship design. European economies, rebounding after the catastrophe of the Black Death (1348-51), also produced greater state revenues and a new demand for luxury goods, including Eastern spices, precious metals, ivory, slaves, pearls and textiles. Increasingly sophisticated banking systems and business organization, pioneered in Italy, helped deploy large amounts of capital in the search for foreign profit. The desire to bypass the Islamic eastern Mediterranean and find a means of direct access to the riches of the Orient was given impetus by a new religious concern.

Political Union in Britain

In the British Isles the essential prelude to imperial expansion was the political union and consolidation of England, Scotland, Wales and Ireland. Their peoples, who were culturally and ethnically diverse and politically disunited, were combined largely by war and coercion into a powerful, centralized British state

Artist Benjamin West's impression of the Battle of the Boyne which took place on 1st July 1690 near Drogheda on Ireland's east coast. This infamous battle between the deposed King James II of England and VII of Scotland (1633–1701) and William of Orange (1650–1702) for the English and Scottish thrones has great symbolic importance for the Irish. William's victory upheld British and Protestant dominance over the country but also signified a major step to the complete British colonization of Ireland.

under English hegemony, the consequence of the random play of historical events as much as deliberate strategic, economic and social policies. The dynastic politics of Henry VIII (r. 1509-47) and the establishment of an English Protestant national church were crucial in this process. Religion reinforced English nationalism and sharpened differences with Catholic European rivals which threatened the survival of the Tudor dynasty. Ireland became the prime battleground, another victim of England's westward advance that had already absorbed Wales. The consolidation of Britain, culminating in political union with Scotland in 1707, provided valuable experience of colonial conquest and of dealing with tribal societies and kinship groups that were later applied elsewhere on the imperial frontier.

A miniature of Sir Francis Drake (c. 1540–1596). Drake was typical of the daring, but ruthlessly profit-seeking, privateers who boosted Queen Elizabeth I's maritime expansion.

The reign of Elizabeth I (1558-1603) saw a new involvement in world trade based on maritime power. Underlying the English effort, the new national purpose, was the search for riches, prompting schemes of plunder, exploration (primarily in search of a new route to China and the East) and, increasingly, colonial settlement. More immediately desirable were the rich pickings of the Caribbean that developed as the major frontline for competing European countries. Attempts to exploit the wealth of the West Indies and bypass Spain's monopoly of trade began early. In 1562-3 John Hawkins of Plymouth began selling African slaves to Spanish colonists, as he says, 'with prosperous successe and much gaine', but the trade was quickly suppressed. His cousin and protégé Francis Drake sought profitable revenge and led a series of raids on Spanish possessions that were subsumed into the Anglo-Spanish War (1585-1604). His success and daring stirred others, and Drake's ships proved the vanguard of several hundred privateers of various nations – and sometimes none at all – which regularly plundered the Caribbean sea lanes.

The Push for Colonization

From the 1560s there was a growing support in England for colonization as a source of wealth and important commodities, national prestige and strategic security, partly through the spread of Protestantism in a Roman Catholic world. It was also seen as an outlet for social and religious undesirables and surplus population. To influential propagandist Richard Hakluyt in 1584, 'no greater glory can be handed down than to conquer the barbarian, to recall the savage and the pagan to civility, to draw the ignorant from the orbit of reason.'

After the successful Spanish war, in which around 235 ships took part in the privateering offensive, English penetration of the Caribbean continued with renewed vigour. Commercial interest was concentrated on mainland Guiana (and the Amazon) involving the first attempt at colonization, on the Wiapaco River in 1604, soon followed by St Lucia and Grenada in the eastern Caribbean. With the success of tobacco cultivation on the Atlantic colony of Bermuda from about 1620, the economic potential of the West Indies began to be recognized. Several islands in the Lesser Antilles were colonized during the 1620s and 1630s; here settlers cultivated tobacco, cotton, indigo and ginger for European consumption.

Circumstances soon changed with the introduction of sugar, requiring labour-intensive production. West Africa was a rich source of redwood, gold and especially slaves, the scene of intense rivalry among European states until Britain established its mastery of the coast's trade in the early 18th century. Slaves became a vital part of the Atlantic economy (and the infamous triangular trade), essential to the plantation production of sugar and other produce in the Caribbean and Americas which lay at the heart of imperial commerce. It became fundamental to British economic development, promoting new industries and providing lucrative government revenue.

Colonization continued most vigorously in North America. After a number of years of trial and error, an English presence in the continent was assured with the permanent settlement of Virginia from 1607, and New England shortly afterwards. Although they were little regarded in England at first, these colonies developed rapidly. In the 1630s as many as 21,000 settlers arrived in Massachusetts alone, and by 1700 the population of New England stood at more than 90,000. Its economy flourished on the back of mixed agriculture, the North Atlantic cod fishery, overseas trade and shipbuilding. In Virginia the profitable tobacco plantations soon absorbed all available family and indentured labour, leading to the increasing import of slaves from Africa. By 1700 blacks numbered around 13,000 in a population of 98,000.

Growing Colonial Pride

As the 17th century progressed, England gained a new appreciation of its colonies. They were increasingly seen as a growing source of wealth, both directly and through taxation. Maritime commerce and naval power were now vital to national survival, and of all European nations England was best placed to reap the rewards they offered. Sir Robert Mansell's expedition to destroy the Algerine pirates (1620-1), the first venture by a Royal Naval squadron into the Mediterranean, shows that the state was increasingly obliged to follow the commercial flag in the new era of international economic rivalry. From 1651 the Navigation Acts forced colonial economic specialization, confined the imperial carrying trade to English ships and channelled trade through English ports, all part of the new mercantilist philosophy which sought to monopolize economic activity. It was a measure largely aimed at England's Dutch rivals, and led to three wars with the Netherlands between 1652 and 1674. Eventual success in these wars established English mercantile supremacy.

A stained-glass window dedicated to John Smith (1580–1631) at St Sepulchre's Church without Newgate, London. Smith founded Jamestown, the first English settlement in North America. He was responsible for naming New England.

This aggressive commercial and territorial expansion continued from the Commonwealth into the Restoration period under Charles II (r. 1660–86), and Charles also used American land grants to reward family and supporters who had remained loyal during the interregnum. An important feature of these dominions was the measure of self-government allowed to the colonists – which proved in time to be a serious oversight by the English Crown. The long-standing failure to address this problem had serious consequences for the future of British North America. For the time being, however, and in the face of threats from the Indian nations on the frontier and French settlers and traders in the North American hinterland, the British colonists remained firmly attached to the imperial relationship.

With the decline of Spanish (and Portuguese) power and the removal of Dutch competition, France emerged as the main threat to Britain's global interests. Following the early explorations of Jacques Cartier (1534-5) the French were keen to extend their authority in North America. Samuel de Champlain set up permanent settlements in Acadia, founded Quebec on the St Lawrence in 1608 and laid claim to much of the vast hinterland and its rich fur trade.

French rivalry with England began early in the 17th century. The first French colony, Port Royal, was destroyed by an expedition from Virginia in 1613. In the 1620s, French opposition forced the abandonment of Sir William Alexander's colonization of Nova Scotia, granted by James VI and I; and, hoping to capture the lucrative fur trade, the English temporarily occupied Quebec in 1628-32. Following the distraction of the British civil wars and interregnum, Anglo-French conflict returned with the War of the League of Augsburg (1689). New France survived decades of skirmishes and four major wars, but colonial British America's greater resources (including a population of two million in 1750 compared with 60,000 French colonists), increased British military com-

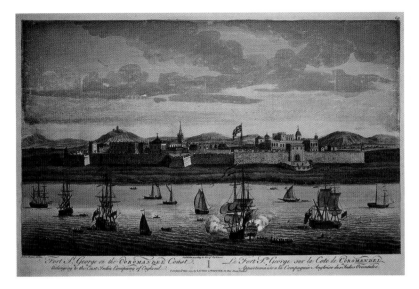

A copper engraving of Fort St George in Madras, on the Coromandel Coast of India. The East India Company purchased Madras, once described as 'the most incommodious place', in 1639 and it later became the main base of the Company. Madras developed into a modern city under the Company; Robert Clive began his career there as a clerk.

mitment and the support of the Royal Navy put ultimate victory for the British colony over its rival beyond doubt. New France was formally annexed to Britain at the Treaty of Paris, 1763, marking the end of the Seven Years War and the culmination of the British Empire in North America.

Empire in India

The Anglo-French conflict was also pursued on the other side of the world. The history of British India effectively began with the royal charter awarded to the East India Company in 1600. Despite early Portuguese opposition to its intrusion, and faced with Dutch hostility in the Spice Islands further to the east, the Company decided to focus on Indian trade. It was a fortuitous decision: textiles, particularly calicoes and muslins, became increasingly popular in Europe and the staple trade of the Company, along with pepper from the Malabar Coast, silk, saltpetre and many other goods.

Based on its main trading factories at Bombay, Madras and Calcutta, the Company formed part of a huge network of regional commerce, and operated in partnership with Indian merchants and bankers. For most of the early years of its existence the Company was primarily a trading organization, plying the eastern oceans, and it became very important to Britain's prosperity and its public finances. Non-intervention in Indian affairs was the general rule in this period, but from the 1740s the British and French were both drawn into Indian politics on the side of friendly rulers and allied merchant interests for commercial advantage, a contest from which Britain emerged victorious in 1761. The East India Company was now a considerable Indian territorial power, poised to bring the whole of the sub-continent under British rule.

Britain's early empire was acquired in the face of intense European rivalry. Spain, the Netherlands and France had been elbowed aside and by the end of the Seven Years War Britain was acknowledged as the world superpower. The war had demolished the colonial pretensions of France and its allies. Despite the Jacobite rebellions of 1715 and 1745-6, Britain was generally a stable state throughout the 18th century, and its population was mostly united. Economically and industrially the country was powerful, London was solidly entrenched as the world's major capital market, and the Royal Navy and Britain's merchant fleet were pre-eminent in the oceans of the world. All these elements provided the basis for future imperial expansion.

English and British

The consolidation of the British Isles

"This realme now called Englande [is] the onely supreme seat of the empire of greate Briteigne."

James Henrisoun, *An Exhortacion to the Scottes* (1547)

England, the largest and wealthiest of the home nations, gradually achieved the political consolidation of the British Isles through coercion and persuasion. The union of the several kingdoms and territories underlay the expansion of Britain's empire overseas.

At the end of the Middle Ages the developing states of England and Scotland were increasingly determined to control the semi-independent tribal and feudal lordships in the northern and western regions, particularly in 'uncivilized' Gaelic Ireland and Scotland. In England, control was exerted through the reform of the state apparatus that began with Henry VII (1485-1509), founder of the Tudor dynasty whose patrimony included the Lordship of Ireland. This process became more urgent in the reign of his son Henry VIII (1509-47), whose break with Rome made powerful new enemies both at home and in Catholic Europe.

Settling Ireland

In attempting to exert royal authority over the feuding Anglo-Irish lords, Henry provoked the Kildare rebellion in 1534-5 and the threat of foreign, Catholic intervention encouraged the long piecemeal conquest of Ireland, in a policy characterized as annihilation or assimilation. Under Thomas Radcliffe, Earl of Sussex (viceroy 1556-65), the plantation of Laois and Offaly was begun as a way of achieving security through Anglicization, in language, culture and religion. Further colonization occurred in rebellious Ulster (alongside informal Scottish settlement) and in Munster after the Desmond War (1579-80).

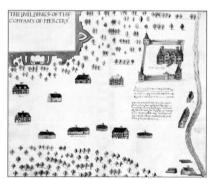

A Survey of the Plantation of Londonderry made in 1624 by Thomas Phillips. The policy of seizing Irish land and granting it to British landlords was aimed at subduing the Gaelic and Catholic population. Derry was granted to the City of London in 1613, populated with new settlers and renamed Londonderry. The plantations reshaped Ireland's demography, creating large communities with a British, Protestant identity.

The loss of Calais in 1558 focused English minds. Under Queen Elizabeth (1558-1603) English intervention helped to consolidate the Protestant Reformation in Scotland and neutralize the Franco-Scottish alliance. Despite the defeat of the Armada in 1588, the Spanish remained a threat and supported the defiant Gaelic lords of Ulster, led by Hugh O'Neill in the Nine Years War (1594-1603), until defeated at Kinsale in 1601.

The English victory permitted union with Scotland in 1603. The new Protestant and anti-Gaelic king, James VI of Scotland (1567-1625) and I of England and Ireland, continued policies of pacification and control. His military campaigns, land expropriation and legal pressure had defeated the over-mighty lords and clans of northern and western Scotland, where control was now exercised by favoured baronial families. After 1603 the Anglo-Scottish border region was ruthlessly subdued and the Statutes of Iona (1609) began to undermine Gaelic clanship, culture and language.

James's support for colonization in Harris, Lewis and the Northern Isles by Scottish Lowlanders was now extended to Ireland and North America. The six forfeited counties of Ulster, together with Wexford, Leitrim, Longford and other areas, were colonized by British settlers, whose total numbers approached 100,000 by 1641 in a population of around 2.1 million. Irish discontent resurfaced in the Confederate Wars of 1641-52, ended with Oliver Cromwell's brutal campaign followed by further colonization and forced clearances. The last hope of the Irish lay in the accession of the Catholic King James II (1685-8), but his overthrow by co-regents William and Mary and his military defeat in Ireland in 1690 confirmed the Protestant ascendancy and Ireland's dependant status.

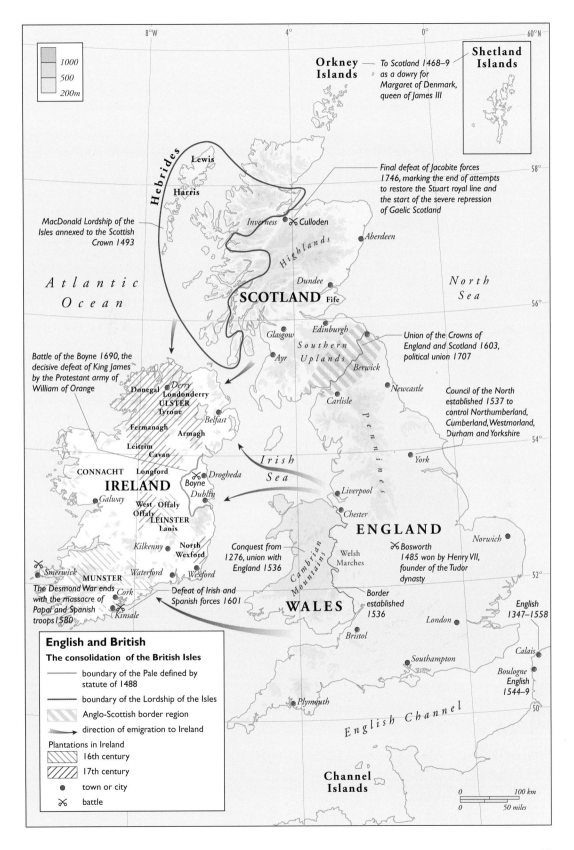

Orkney Islands — To Scotland 1468–9 as a dowry for Margaret of Denmark, queen of James III

Shetland Islands

1000
500
200m

Lewis

Hebrides

Harris

Final defeat of Jacobite forces 1746, marking the end of attempts to restore the Stuart royal line and the start of the severe repression of Gaelic Scotland

MacDonald Lordship of the Isles annexed to the Scottish Crown 1493

Inverness ⚔ Culloden

Aberdeen

Highlands

Atlantic Ocean

Dundee

SCOTLAND Fife

North Sea

Glasgow Edinburgh

Southern Uplands

Ayr

Berwick

Union of the Crowns of England and Scotland 1603, political union 1707

Battle of the Boyne 1690, the decisive defeat of King James by the Protestant army of William of Orange

Derry
Donegal Londonderry
ULSTER
Tyrone
Belfast
Fermanagh Armagh
Leitrim
Cavan

Newcastle

Carlisle

Council of the North established 1537 to control Northumberland, Cumberland, Westmorland, Durham and Yorkshire

Pennines

CONNACHT Longford

IRELAND

Galway

⚔ Drogheda
Boyne
Dublin

Irish Sea

York

Liverpool

West Offaly
Offaly
LEINSTER
Laois

Chester

ENGLAND

Norwich

Kilkenny North Wexford

Conquest from 1276, union with England 1536

Welsh Marches

⚔ Bosworth 1485 won by Henry VII, founder of the Tudor dynasty

⚔ Smerwick Waterford Wexford

MUNSTER
The Desmond War ends with the massacre of Papal and Spanish troops 1580

Cork

⚔ Kinsale

Defeat of Irish and Spanish forces 1601

Cambrian Mountains

WALES

Border established 1536

London

English 1347–1558

Bristol

Calais

Southampton

Boulogne English 1544–9

English and British

The consolidation of the British Isles

——— boundary of the Pale defined by statute of 1488

——— boundary of the Lordship of the Isles

▨ Anglo-Scottish border region

➤ direction of emigration to Ireland

Plantations in Ireland
▨ 16th century
▨ 17th century
● town or city
⚔ battle

Plymouth

English Channel

Channel Islands

0   100 km
0   50 miles

19

Exploring and Exploiting

European expansion to the mid-16th century

Following the expulsion of the Moors and the capture of the North African enclave of Ceuta in 1415, Portugal became the first state to break out of European waters. The global search for wealth, power and territory by Europe's maritime powers had begun.

"[John Cabot] … says he has discovered land 700 leagues away, which is the country of the Grand Khan… The king here is much pleased at this. "

Anonymous Venetian letter, London, 23 August 1497

Portuguese explorers followed the West African coast and rounded the Cape of Good Hope in 1488. Vasco da Gama pioneered the sea route to India, arriving at Calicut in 1498; ruthlessly applied sea power soon gave Portugal dominance of Indian Ocean trade. Portuguese primacy was confirmed with the defeat of the Egyptian-Gujerati Muslim allies at the Battle of Diu in 1509, and the following year Goa became the centre of a new Portuguese eastern empire. With the capture of Malacca in 1511 and the Spice Islands (Moluccas) Portugal attempted to monopolize the European spice trade, whose products were bought with African gold, and within 50 years trade started with China and Japan.

New World Riches

Portugal's success encouraged imitation. Castile dispatched its own explorers westwards in search of Cathay (Asia) and in 1492–3 Christopher Columbus reached the West Indies. The *conquistadores* soon subjected most of Central and South America to Spanish rule; they began to realize the fabled wealth of the New World with the discovery of rich silver deposits, notably at Zacatecas

The Venetian explorers Giovanni and son Sebastiano Caboto (John and Sebastian Cabot). When Portugal and Spain failed to sponsor John Cabot (1450–99), he turned to Henry VII of England for backing. In 1497 he set sail from Bristol in search of Eastern riches, but landed instead on the east coast of North America.

Exploring and Exploiting

European expansion to the mid-16th century

- extent of the Muslim world
- Spanish empire
- Portuguese empire
- • principal Portuguese trading and administrative centres from date shown
- English territory and claims
- Inca empire
- Aztec empire
- Maya empire
- • place and date of foundation
  Panama (1519)
- ✕ battle, with date

Newfoundland *1497*

St Lawrence

Roanoke Island
Discovered by Columbus 1492, occupied 1511

Atlantic Ocean

NEW SPAIN Cuba Hispaniola
Zacatecas *(1548)* Lesser Antilles
Mexico City *(1521)*
Conquered by Hernán Cortés 1519–20
Guatemala *(1524)* Darien *(1510)*
Panama *(1519)* Cartagena *(1533)*
Conquered by Pedro de Alvarado 1524

Pacific Ocean

BRAZIL

Lima *(1535)* PERU

Potosí *(1545)*

Rio de Janeiro *(1565)*

Conquered by Francisco Pisarro 1532–5
Valparaíso *(1536)*
Santiago *(1541)* Buenos Aires *(1536)*

Rio de la Plata first visited by Días de Solís 1516

Treaty of Tordesillas 1494

180°W   160°   140°   120°   100°   60°   40°

in New Spain (1546) and Potosí in Peru (1545), the world's largest source of silver for 100 years. It helped make Spain the superpower of Europe.

Brazil was allowed to Portugal under the Treaty of Tordesillas (1494), whose aim was to establish exclusive Spanish trading rights to what was still thought to be 'Asia'. The understanding that these American territories were in fact a new world was confirmed by the Magellan expedition's circumnavigation in 1519-21 and the discovery of the western Pacific route to Cathay. The Treaty of Saragossa (1529) became necessary to delineate Spanish and Portuguese spheres on the new frontier of European rivalry in the East Indies.

Until the mid-16th century, Spain made little attempt to prevent European expeditions to the more forbidding latitudes of North America. Early English interest, from 1480, was limited to the search for new North Atlantic fisheries, during the course of which Bristol ships probably sighted the American coast. The Venetian explorer John Cabot, searching for a western route to Cathay, made landfall on what was traditionally believed to be Newfoundland in 1497, although it was possibly the coast of Labrador or Cape Breton Island. The new territory was claimed for his royal sponsor, Henry VII of England, but at home there remained little interest in overseas empire, although the search continued for the North-West passage to Asia. For France, Jacques Cartier (1491-1557) discovered the St Lawrence estuary, but its limited economic appeal led to the abandonment of attempts to colonize the area in 1541.

Spain, it seemed, had little to fear. Towards the end of the century, however, the situation was transformed. Economic rivalry, envy, anti-Catholic feeling in England and the Dutch Netherlands, and a growing sense of national purpose led to a renewed assault on the Iberian empires and the re-division of the world's resources.

Routes of European explorers, with dates of expeditions

→ Spanish expeditions

1 Juan Rodríguez Cabrillo 1542
2 Hernán Cortés 1519
3 Cristoforo Colombo (Columbus) 1492–3, 1498–1500, 1502–4
4 Álvaro Saavedra 1527–8
5 Vasco Núñez de Balboa 1513
6 Amerigo Vespucci 1499–1500
7 Fernão de Magalhães (Magellan) 1519–21 and Juan Sebastián del Cano 1521–2

→ English expeditions

8 Giovanni Caboto (John Cabot) 1497, 1498

→ Portuguese expeditions

9 Vasco da Gama 1497–9
10 Bartolomeu Dias 1486–8
11 Pêro da Covilhã 1487–90
12 Diogo Lopes de Sequeira 1509–10
13 Jorge Álvares 1514–16

→ French expeditions

14 Giovanni da Verrazzano 1523–4
15 Jacques Cartier 1534, 1536–7, 1541–2

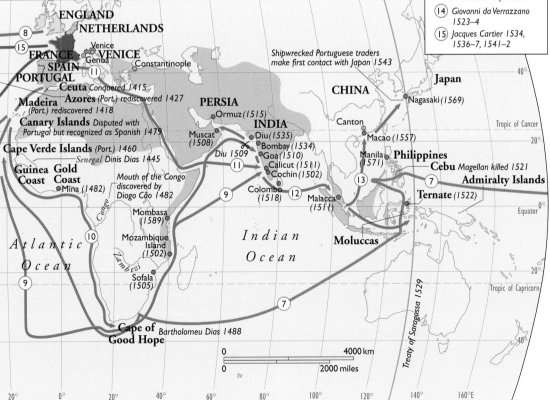

Chasing the Pack English oceanic enterprise to 1630

"The time approacheth ... that we of England may share ... both with the Spaniards and the Portingale in part of America, and other regions as yet undiscovered. "

Richard Hakluyt
Divers Voyages (1582)

From the mid-1500s difficulties selling cloth in the traditional European centres encouraged English merchants to look for new markets. Efforts were made to find a northerly route to Cathay, but areas of Spanish and Portuguese interest proved irresistible.

Merchant enterprise was encouraged by the granting of royal charters awarding monopoly trading rights to investors. Hugh Willoughby and Richard Chancellor, sponsored by the Cathay Company, searching for a North-East passage in 1553, reached Archangel, through which the Muscovy Company established regular trade with Russia. Exploration beyond the North Cape continued to 1608, but the ice formed an impenetrable barrier. Revived interest in a North-West passage led to Martin Frobisher's voyages to Greenland, Baffin Island and Labrador in 1576–8, followed by several other expeditions up to the 1630s.

Meanwhile, in the Mediterranean in 1592, the Turkey and Venice companies combined to form the powerful Levant Company. Its wealth was based on the import of spices and other eastern products, as well as a profitable carrying trade. The Levant

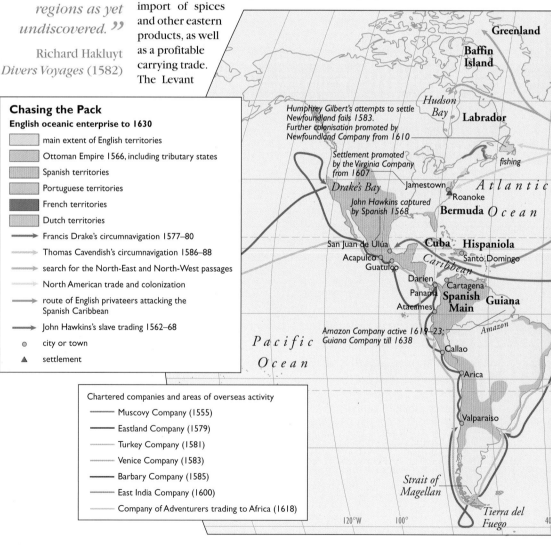

Chasing the Pack
English oceanic enterprise to 1630

- main extent of English territories
- Ottoman Empire 1566, including tributary states
- Spanish territories
- Portuguese territories
- French territories
- Dutch territories
- Francis Drake's circumnavigation 1577–80
- Thomas Cavendish's circumnavigation 1586–88
- search for the North-East and North-West passages
- North American trade and colonization
- route of English privateers attacking the Spanish Caribbean
- John Hawkins's slave trading 1562–68
- city or town
- settlement

Chartered companies and areas of overseas activity
- Muscovy Company (1555)
- Eastland Company (1579)
- Turkey Company (1581)
- Venice Company (1583)
- Barbary Company (1585)
- East India Company (1600)
- Company of Adventurers trading to Africa (1618)

Humphrey Gilbert's attempts to settle Newfoundland fails 1583. Further colonisation promoted by Newfoundland Company from 1610

Settlement promoted by the Virginia Company from 1607

Greenland

Baffin Island

Hudson Bay Labrador

fishing

Drake's Bay   Jamestown   *Atlantic*
John Hawkins captured   Roanoke
by Spanish 1568   Bermuda *Ocean*

San Juan de Ulúa   Cuba   Hispaniola
Acapulco   Santo Domingo
Guatulco   *Caribbean*

Darien   Cartagena
Panama   Spanish   Guiana
Atacames   Main

Amazon Company active 1619–23;   *Amazon*
Pacific   Guiana Company till 1638
Ocean   Callao

Arica

Valparaiso

Strait of Magellan

Tierra del Fuego

120°W   100°   40°

Elizabeth I's reign (1558–1603) was a golden age for English exploration and trade. The growth of the British Empire dates from this era when private companies were backed by the Crown. These companies were associations for foreign trade, exploration and colonization and proved instrumental in empire-building.

Company's commercial skills, maritime expertise and resources were important assets in English expansion.

The First English Circumnavigation

Private enterprise also sought to bypass the trade monopolies of the Spanish and Portuguese in the New World, Africa and the East. Expeditions sent to plunder Spanish ports and sea lanes in the Americas and undertake illicit trade found ready backers, from Queen Elizabeth downwards, the desire for wealth sharpened by religious hostility to the Catholic powers. In 1551 trade began with Morocco (later pursued by the Barbary Company) followed by direct voyages to the Guinea coast, rich in gold, which Portugal guarded closely. In the long struggle with Spain, Francis Drake was prominent among English marauders. On a plundering voyage to the Spanish Pacific in 1577 he discovered the route to the East Indies via the Straits of Magellan and was responsible for the first English circumnavigation, the start of a new English maritime vitality.

By the end of the Anglo-Spanish War (1585–1604) the east coast of North America was increasingly seen as an English preserve. It became an important focus of commercial and colonial endeavour, pursued initially through the Virginia Company (1606). Bermuda was settled from 1609, plantations appeared in Guiana from 1604 and on the Amazon in 1611–20, before the colonization of West Indian islands. The East India Company (1600) began direct trade with the Orient and soon acquired a new focus on India; in West Africa there was a renewed interest in gold, slaves and tropical products. The pattern of future exploitation was established.

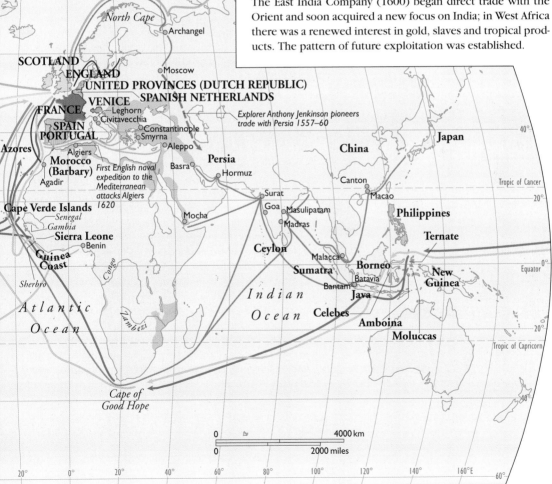

The New World I Virginia

Early attempts at the colonization of the Atlantic seaboard of North America ended in failure. With the end of the Anglo-Spanish conflict in 1604 a powerful combination of interests were ready to support new ambitious but risky schemes to extend English dominion across the Atlantic. It was the beginning of a new imperial future.

"If Virginia had but Horses and Kine in some reasonable proportion, I dare assure my selfe being inhabited with English, no realme in Christendome were comparable to it."

Ralph Lane, letter to Richard Hakluyt, 3 September 1585

In 1578 Sir Humphrey Gilbert, experienced in the colonization of Ireland, was granted a charter to settle lands in North America 'not possessed of any Christian prince or people'. His squadron arrived at St John's, Newfoundland, in 1583 where the island was annexed to England, but his scheme was aborted and the expedition foundered at sea. Between 1585 and 1587 a sustained attempt was made to occupy Roanoke Island on the coast of later North Carolina. Sir Walter Raleigh, Gilbert's half-brother, chose the inadequate site, intended as a base from which to attack Spanish shipping and search for precious metals. Lack of sustained commercial and state support made the venture equally unsuccessful and links with England became even more unreliable during the war with Spain.

Renewed interest in American colonization led to the creation of the Virginia Company (chartered in 1606) by investors in London and South West England. In 1607 the Company's London branch, allocated 'South Virginia', established England's first permanent colony in North America at Jamestown, west of Chesapeake Bay, although for a while its survival was uncertain. Many of the disputatious settlers were again more interested in the search for gold than in cultivating enough food for their own survival. By the end of 1609–10, the 'starving time', famine, disease and conflict with the local Indian population had reduced their numbers from 500 to a mere 60.

Tobacco

The colony managed to survive precariously because of the imposition of strict discipline and a new emphasis on food production begun under the leadership of John Smith, elected president of the Jamestown colony in 1608. Economically, it was saved as a result of John Rolfe's experiments with tobacco, smoked by Indians, as a commercial crop in 1612. Exports to England became the basis of the Chesapeake economy as output rose from 20,000 pounds (weight) in 1620 to 15 million pounds by the late 1660s. Although by 1618 only 600 colonists survived out of the 1800 who had originally travelled to Jamestown, increasing numbers of new settlers helped to offset the high mortality rate.

Sir Walter Raleigh (c. 1552–1618). Raleigh organized and part-financed expeditions to the New World, but once he became one of Elizabeth I's favourites he was not allowed to join them. He is often credited with bringing potatoes and tobacco to Britain, but it was probably Sir John Hawkins who introduced them.

The newly confident colony established its own elected assembly in 1619, a precedent for all subsequent American colonies, and expanded in search of productive land. This led to worsening relations with the Indian population and to their uprising of 1622 under Powhatan, in which 350 settlers and many more Indians were killed in brutal circumstances. The threat helped develop a settler view of racial and cultural superiority and justified, in Sir Francis Wyatt's words, 'expulsion of Salvages [sic] to gaine the free range of the countrey'. The conflict and general mismanagement of the whole colonization scheme by the Company, whose shareholders were also at odds over commercial strategy, led to its dissolution in 1624 and Virginia became a royal colony. Its future was assured.

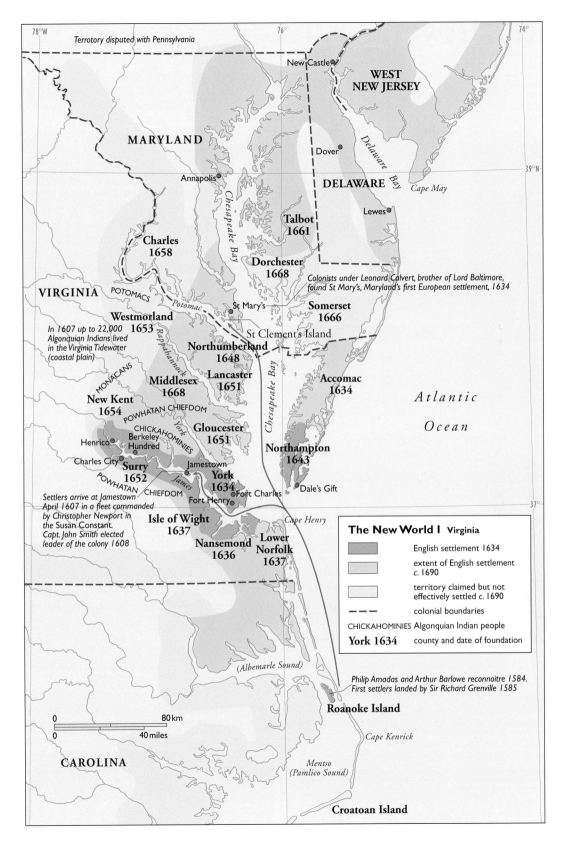

Territory disputed with Pennsylvania

78°W
76°
74°

New Castle

WEST NEW JERSEY

MARYLAND

Dover

Delaware Bay

DELAWARE

39°N

Annapolis

Cape May

Chesapeake Bay

Lewes

Talbot 1661

Charles 1658

Dorchester 1668

Colonists under Leonard Calvert, brother of Lord Baltimore, found St Mary's, Maryland's first European settlement, 1634

VIRGINIA   POTOMACS

Potomac

St Mary's

Somerset 1666

Westmorland 1653

In 1607 up to 22,000 Algonquian Indians lived in the Virginia Tidewater (coastal plain)

St Clement's Island

Rappahannock

Northumberland 1648

Lancaster 1651

Chesapeake Bay

MONACANS

Middlesex 1668

Accomac 1634

Atlantic

New Kent 1654

POWHATAN CHIEFDOM

York

CHICKAHOMINIES

Gloucester 1651

Ocean

Henrico

Berkeley Hundred

Charles City

POWHATAN   CHIEFDOM

Surry 1652

James

Jamestown

York 1634

Fort Charles

Dale's Gift

Northampton 1643

Fort Henry

Settlers arrive at Jamestown April 1607 in a fleet commanded by Christopher Newport in the Susan Constant. Capt. John Smith elected leader of the colony 1608

37°

Isle of Wight 1637

Cape Henry

Nansemond 1636

Lower Norfolk 1637

The New World I *Virginia*

| | English settlement 1634 |
| extent of English settlement c. 1690 |
| territory claimed but not effectively settled c. 1690 |

- - - colonial boundaries

CHICKAHOMINIES Algonquian Indian people

York 1634 county and date of foundation

(Albemarle Sound)

Philip Amadas and Arthur Barlowe reconnoitre 1584. First settlers landed by Sir Richard Grenville 1585

Roanoke Island

Cape Kenrick

0   80 km
0   40 miles

CAROLINA

Mentso (Pamlico Sound)

Croatoan Island

The New World II New England

The Plymouth branch of the Virginia Company, allocated the region of 'North Virginia', initially financed settlements on the coast of what became Maine and New Hampshire. They failed, but events in the British Isles increasingly prompted the search for religious and political freedoms in a 'New England' across the Atlantic, a new focus of empire in North America.

"Great Numbers of [settlers], at all Hazards, transported themselves to New-England, to enjoy there the liberty of conscience refused them at home, which multiply'd this Colony much faster than any other."

John Oldmixon,
The British Empire in America (1708)

While colonists generally emigrated to the New World, in Francis Bacon's words, 'for gold and silver and temporal profit', a significant number were also religious dissenters and objectors to constitutional developments under both James VI & I (1603–25) and Charles I (1625–49). Many of these English men and women chose to colonize New England, the region named by Captain John Smith on his voyage to explore the coast for the Virginia Company in 1614. The putative colonists were better organized than earlier groups. The initial party of 102 Nottinghamshire Congregationalists, London Separatists and others, its menfolk today known as the Pilgrim Fathers, arrived at Cape Cod aboard the *Mayflower* in 1620. Shortly afterwards they founded the colony of Plymouth, the first permanent settlement in the north. Not all were primarily 'religious' settlers, but Protestantism was strong and the Puritan aversion to idleness and luxury made them effective colonists. After early difficulties, they succeeded in creating (with Indian help) a mixed economy based on fishing, farming and fur trading. Within a dozen years they had repaid their investors in England.

In Search of Self-Government

From the start the Plymouth colonists were committed to self-government, based on the Mayflower Compact of 1620, combining together in 'a civill body politick for our better ordering and preservation'. One of its framers was William Bradford, long-standing elected governor of Plymouth, who was influential in nurturing the colony's democratic institutions and a wider New England tradition of self-government.

Religious policies and economic difficulties in England provoked further bouts of Puritan emigration, notably through the Massachusetts Bay Company. In 1630 the Company founded a community of 1,000 at Boston and it soon enjoyed a measure of prosperity that marked out the colony of Massachusetts. It sought religious freedom but also tried to limit as far as possible its dealings with the authorities in England. The Massachusetts charter and centre of government were transferred from London, and its isolation and remoteness bestowed a quasi-independence.

The departure of a Puritan family for the New World. Suffering from religious persecution in England, Puritans and other Nonconformists set off for the Protestant colonies of New England. Many enjoyed freedom of worship, but in these new communities the devout could be as intolerant and ungodly as their erstwhile persecutors.

The region continued to attract a stream of colonists. As many as 20,000 arrived during the course of the 1630s, encouraged to create godly communities free to practise their religion according to conscience, although dissenters also went elsewhere. In 1632 the Crown awarded a charter for the colonization of Maryland to Lord Baltimore, seeking a haven for his Catholic co-religionists and Anglicans. Religious fragmentation, population expansion and frontier opportunity led to the establishment of new settlements along the eastern seaboard and by 1650 New England had more than 40 towns, notably Boston, Charles Town, Salem and Cambridge. A steady flow of settlers from theocratic

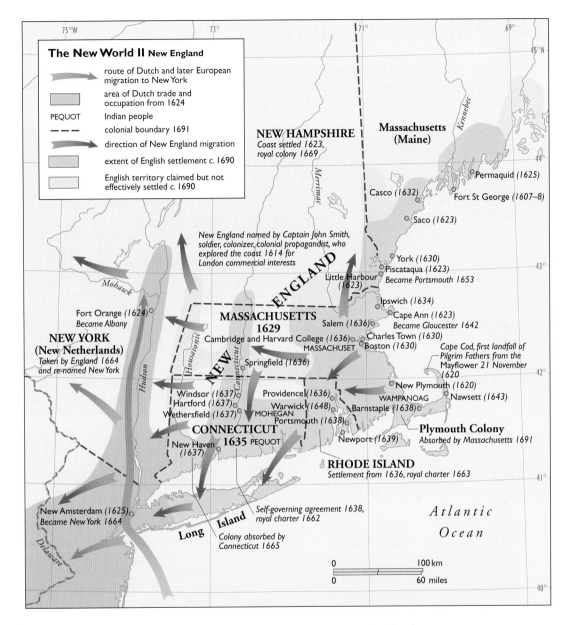

The New World II New England

route of Dutch and later European migration to New York

area of Dutch trade and occupation from 1624

PEQUOT   Indian people

– – –   colonial boundary 1691

direction of New England migration

extent of English settlement c. 1690

English territory claimed but not effectively settled c. 1690

75°W   73°   71°   69°   45°N

NEW HAMPSHIRE
Coast settled 1623, royal colony 1669

Massachusetts
(Maine)

Kennebec

44°

Permaquid (1625)

Casco (1632)   Fort St George (1607–8)

Merrimac

Saco (1623)

New England named by Captain John Smith, soldier, colonizer, colonial propagandist, who explored the coast 1614 for London commercial interests

ENGLAND

York (1630)
Piscataqua (1623)
Little Harbour   Became Portsmouth 1653
(1623)

43°

Mohawk

Ipswich (1634)

Fort Orange (1624)
Became Albany

MASSACHUSETTS
1629

NEW   Cape Ann (1623)
Salem (1636)   *Became Gloucester 1642*

NEW YORK
(New Netherlands)
Taken by England 1664 and re-named New York

Cambridge and Harvard College (1636)   Charles Town (1630)
MASSACHUSET   Boston (1630)

Housatonic

Connecticut

Springfield (1636)

Cape Cod, first landfall of Pilgrim Fathers from the Mayflower 21 November 1620

42°

Hudson

Windsor (1637)
Hartford (1637)   Providence (1636)
Wethersfield (1637)   Warwick (1648)   MOHEGAN   Barnstaple (1638)
Portsmouth (1638)

New Plymouth (1620)
WAMPANOAG   Nawsett (1643)

CONNECTICUT
1635 PEQUOT   Newport (1639)

New Haven
(1637)

Plymouth Colony
Absorbed by Massachusetts 1691

RHODE ISLAND
Settlement from 1636, royal charter 1663

41°

New Amsterdam (1625)
Became New York 1664

Self-governing agreement 1638, royal charter 1662

Long Island

Colony absorbed by Connecticut 1665

*Atlantic
Ocean*

Delaware

0   100 km
0   60 miles

40°

Massachusetts helped build new colonies, including Connecticut, Rhode Island and New Hampshire.

Principles of Christian harmony were not automatically extended to indigenous peoples. As in the south, territorial expansion was achieved through the subjugation of local Indian populations, notably the Pequot, many of whom were killed in battle, massacred or sold into slavery by colonists in 1637. Colonization was made easier by the estimated 90 per cent decline in Indian numbers between 1608 and 1620 due to the spread of European diseases.

The Crown would find it increasingly difficult to rule such a diverse region of settlement and a population of such determinedly independent outlook. Some came to regard New England as a troublesome liability, and its origins partly help to explain the breakdown of relations between Britain and the colonies in the following century.

The Thirteen Colonies

From the early 17th century Britain's first American empire began extending along the eastern seaboard. Few could have predicted its rapid development or the strained relations that eventuated on the road to independence from Britain.

"The several Nations or Tribes of Indians ... who live under our Protection, should not be molested or disturbed in the Possession of ... Territories ... reserved to them ... as their Hunting Grounds."

Royal Proclamation,
7 October 1763

In 1664 the strategic colony of New Amsterdam, including former Swedish territory on the Delaware acquired by the Dutch in 1655, was taken and re-named New York, awarded to the King's brother James, Duke of York. Shortly afterwards the territory of New Jersey was acquired by two royal favourites who were also among the eight cavaliers awarded the vast Carolina territory by the king in 1663. Proportionately larger numbers of Scots and Scots-Irish arrived from the late 17th century, especially in the Mid-Atlantic colonies, together with English Quakers who found a home in West New Jersey and later Pennsylvania, granted to William Penn in 1681. The colony was tolerant, sought cooperation with local Indian peoples and prospered.

The French proved more of a threat than the Dutch as European rivalry spread to North America. They laid claim to the whole Mississippi river basin in 1682 and established a series of forts and trading posts to the west of the English possessions, reaching the Gulf of Mexico by the early 1700s. England realized its obligation to defend the colonies, while at the same time attempting to end their unruliness, evasion of trade regulations and restrictions on Anglican worship, by bringing them further under royal control. Their charters bestowing self-government were annulled and in 1685 James created the Dominion of New England, which grouped several colonies into a viceroyalty intended partly to bolster colonial defence. The colonists, who felt their rights infringed and were affronted by James's Roman Catholicism, supported the 1688 revolution that ended the Dominion and restored their rights.

Conflict with the Indians

By the 1690s the political geography of the eastern seaboard was broadly settled, although boundary disputes remained. New Hampshire was re-established as a royal colony in 1691, Plymouth was absorbed into Massachusetts and, with the founding of Georgia in 1733, the Thirteen Colonies stretched some 1,200 miles along the east coast and 200 miles inland. The growth of newly-emboldened colonies and the great post-Restoration influx of land-hungry settlers led to renewed conflict with the Indian peoples along the frontier. Between 1660 and 1700 some 38,000 Britons arrived in New England, a region where nearly all the Algonquin tribes under Metacom of the Wampanoag rose up against the oppressive colonial presence in 'King Philip's War' (1675–6). Conflict hardened attitudes towards the Indians, and the settlers' own independent success in war was widely seen as an affirmation of their traditional autonomy.

The colonists' fear of the Indians was perpetuated with their recruitment into the wars between Britain and France from 1689, fought to allay French expansion in Europe and North America. Apart from the English-leaning Iroquois confederation, most tribes in the north allied with France, and fighting erupted from Maine to upper New York (1703–7). At the same time, the South Carolina militia and Creeks defeated Spanish Florida, ally of France, and its Indian irregulars, the Apalachee; and in 1711 the Choctaw, the main French ally. Franco-Spanish raids on the coast of South Carolina had limited effect.

The Seven Years War (1756–63) marked the fall of the French empire in North America and Britain's acquisition of virtually all French territory down to

An 18th-century engraving of an Iroquois Indian setting out on an expedition. The Iroquois were united in a league of six tribes and became the most powerful Indian force in eastern North America. Their animosity towards the French made them natural allies of the Brtish. However, the decision of some tribes to side with the latter during the American Revolutionary War proved to be disastrous. Many were killed, dispersed or forced to flee north to Canada.

the Gulf of Mexico east of the Mississippi. Florida was acquired from Spain in exchange for Havana. Indian tribes, fearful of British control and the settler threat to their lands, now combined to capture settlements between Lake Superior and the lower Mississippi in Pontiac's War (1763–4). British policy tried to placate the Amerindians by limiting westward colonial expansion to the Proclamation Line of 1763. The British-Americans, who had fought both the French and Indian threat, felt cheated of the spoils of victory. In their disregard of Indian rights and elevation of their own freedoms and opportunities lay the breakdown in relations with Britain, which culminated in 1776.

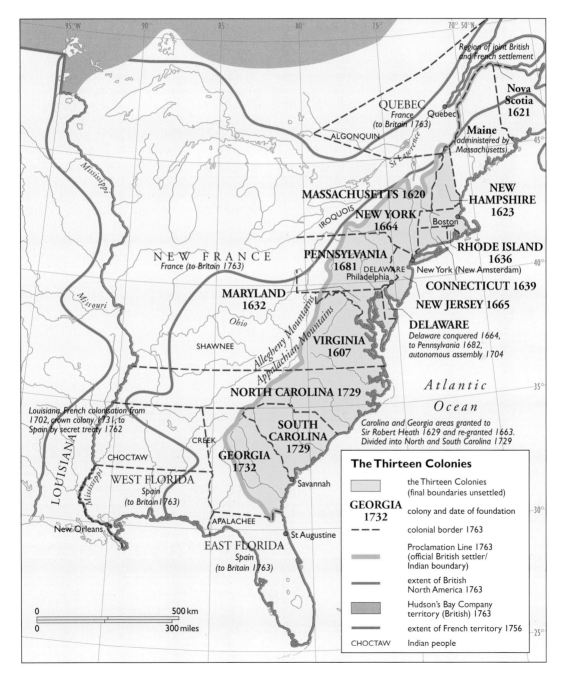

The African Impact Britain and the slave trade

"The first object which saluted my eyes was … a slave ship…. [This] filled me with astonishment, which was soon converted into terror when I was carried on board. "

The Interesting Narrative of the Life of Olaudah Equiano (1789)

The first English trding links with West Africa struggled in the face of intense international competition in the transatlantic trade. From later 17th century, however, new companies concentrated on the slave trade, in which Britain became a major force.

In 1660 the English chartered the Company of Royal Adventurers to trade in gold, ivory and slaves. It occupied Fort James on the Gambia River, took command of the English forts on the Gold Coast, and slaving began east of the Volta River as far as Old Calabar. Losses in the Anglo-Dutch War of 1664–7 ruined the Company but in 1672 it was re-established as the Royal Africa Company, focusing on the lucrative slave trade. The English became the chief transatlantic slavers and by 1700 slaves were the region's most valuable export, growing from an annual average of 6,700 in the 1660s to over 42,000 by the 1760s.

By the 1690s the Company was heavily in debt, and its monopoly rights were removed by Parliament in 1698. By 1730 the Company's commercial activities had ceased, but government subsidies enabled it to maintain its coastal forts in the national interest. As European rivalries subsided, France was left to exploit the Senegal area, Portugal the region of Cacheu and Britain the Gambia and Sierra Leone. Fortified trading posts soon became irrelevant as European shipping collected slaves and goods independently along the coast, forging contacts with African merchants and agents of local rulers.

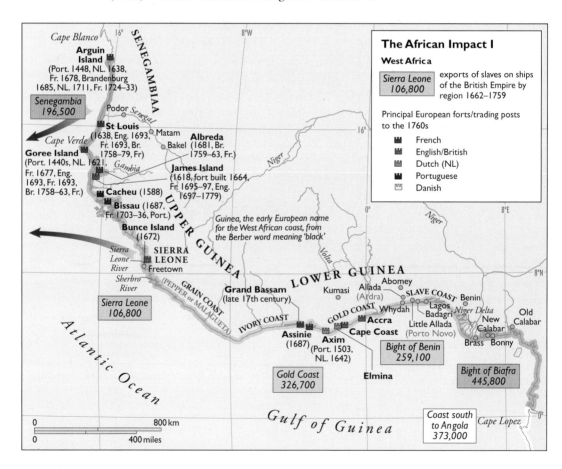

The African Impact I

West Africa

| Sierra Leone 106,800 | exports of slaves on ships of the British Empire by region 1662–1759 |

Principal European forts/trading posts to the 1760s

🏰 French
🏰 English/British
🏰 Dutch (NL)
🏰 Portuguese
🏰 Danish

Guinea, the early European name for the West African coast, from the Berber word meaning 'black'

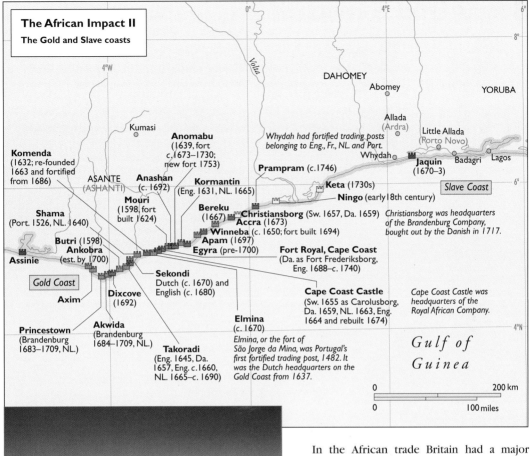

The African Impact II

The Gold and Slave coasts

DAHOMEY

Abomey

YORUBA

Kumasi

Komenda
(1632; re-founded
1663 and fortified
from 1686)

Anomabu
(1639, fort
c.1673–1730;
new fort 1753)

Whydah had fortified trading posts
belonging to Eng., Fr., NL. and Port.

Allada
(Ardra)

Little Allada
(Porto Novo)

Whydah

Jaquin
(1670–3)

Badagri

Lagos

ASANTE
(ASHANTI)

Anashan
(c. 1692)

Kormantin
(Eng. 1631, NL. 1665)

Prampram (c.1746)

Keta (1730s)

Ningo (early 18th century)

Slave Coast

Mouri
(1598, fort
built 1624)

Shama
(Port. 1526, NL. 1640)

Bereku
(1667)

Christiansborg (Sw. 1657, Da. 1659)

Accra (1673)

Christiansborg was headquarters
of the Brandenburg Company,
bought out by the Danish in 1717.

Butri (1598)

Ankobra

Winneba (c. 1650; fort built 1694)

Apam (1697)

Assinie

(est. by 1700)

Egyra (pre-1700)

Fort Royal, Cape Coast
(Da. as Fort Frederiksborg,
Eng. 1688–c.1740)

Gold Coast

Sekondi
Dutch (c. 1670) and
English (c. 1680)

Cape Coast Castle
(Sw. 1655 as Carolusborg,
Da. 1659, NL. 1663, Eng.
1664 and rebuilt 1674)

Cape Coast Castle was
headquarters of the
Royal African Company.

Axim

Dixcove
(1692)

Princestown
(Brandenburg
1683–1709, NL.)

Akwida
(Brandenburg
1684–1709, NL.)

Takoradi
(Eng. 1645, Da.
1657, Eng. c.1660,
NL. 1665–c. 1690)

Elmina
(c. 1670)

Elmina, or the fort of
São Jorge da Mina, was Portugal's
first fortified trading post, 1482. It
was the Dutch headquarters on the
Gold Coast from 1637.

Gulf of
Guinea

0   200 km

0   100 miles

Rows of cannon point dramatically out to sea above the pounding waves at Cape Coast Castle in Ghana. The castle was the headquarters of British colonial rule on the Gold Coast (Ghana's colonial name) from 1644 until 1877. Cape Coast was one of the largest trading posts in the transatlantic slave trade and its dungeons would have once held up to 1,500 slaves awaiting shipment to the Americas.

In the African trade Britain had a major advantage over other Europeans of supplying cheaper industrial goods. The demand for slaves, already growing in British plantations, was further inflated by demand in the Spanish colonies and in the French Caribbean islands captured during the Seven Years War. British shipping transported an estimated 3,415,500 slaves up to 1807 (out of a total of 8,368,000 by 1800), two-thirds during the 18th century, although from 1763 slave exports broadly levelled out before the French wars from 1789 began the slow process of decline.

The personal and social effects were catastrophic in West Africa, where slave raiding and war became endemic. Trade brought new diseases but also valuable new food plants from the Americas, such that the overall impact on population numbers is unclear. Some peoples seemed to prosper, including the Ijaw and Efik slave traders on the Niger Delta. The political effect on the region was the creation of new commercially orientated states, such as Dahomey and the Oyo empire, seeking to control trade on the West African coast. On the Gold Coast several states sought to engross trade by military means and were themselves swallowed up into the powerful Asante empire in the early 18th century. Its attack on the Fante, allies of Britain, began the confrontation which later embroiled the British further in Gold Coast affairs.

Sugar and Slaves The conquest of the Caribbean

The economic value of the Caribbean was increasingly obvious in the early 1600s, and European rivalry intensified as Spanish power declined. Encouraged by Dutch traders seeking new export supplies, English colonists introduced sugar as a crop to the English colony of Barbados in 1640, and subsequently to the Leeward Islands. Its labour-intensive cultivation relied on the growing importation of slaves from Africa.

"[The African trade is] the best Traffic the kingdom hath, as it doth ... give so vast an Imployment to our people both by Sea and Land."

John Cary (1695)

England sent a fleet to the Caribbean in 1649 to assert English commercial interests and to enforce trade laws designed to eliminate Dutch interests; this heralded a new national purpose and involvement in the region. In 1655 Oliver Cromwell despatched another expedition intended to capture Hispaniola, which ended up taking Jamaica instead. The island's productive potential was exploited by Sir Thomas Modyford and a party of 800 settlers from the eastern Caribbean in 1664, who set about establishing Jamaica as the primary British sugar producer. Its strategic value in relation to Spanish possessions was demonstrated by Henry Morgan's buccaneering activities from Port Royal, including the capture of Panama in 1671, the year after the Treaty of Madrid had settled English and Spanish differences in the region and confirmed England's Caribbean possessions. But old habits died hard, and buccaneering was only finally suppressed in the 1730s, when adequate naval forces were at last deployed.

Trading in on the Tropics

Despite the years of warfare between England, Spain, France and the Netherlands in the late 17th-century, the process of trade, cultivation and settlement in the Caribbean continued. A Scottish trading company, in true buccaneering style, established the Darien Colony (New Caledonia) in 1698; its failure propelled Scotland into the Union with England in 1707. Soon, British ports began to benefit from the trade in tropical goods. Sugar became the pre-eminent imperial commodity, providing huge profits for influential British planters, traders and shippers, who became ardent supporters of the Navigation Acts which guaranteed them a growing market. British merchants supplied increasing numbers of slaves, the means, as Bristol merchant John Cary commented in 1695, 'whereby ... such great Quantities of Sugar, Tobacco, Cotton, Ginger, and Indigo are raised'. Britain dominated the slave trade and by the mid-18th century some 70,000 slaves were being shipped across the Atlantic, half to Spanish and other European colonies.

Success in war also strengthened Britain's position in the Caribbean. St Kitts, taken from France

An illustration of a mulatto smoking, taken from a 17th-century manuscript on plants and civilization in the Antilles. 'Mulatto' is a term of either Spanish or Portuguese origin used to describe the offspring of mixed African and European parents. The colonial masters of sugar and tobacco plantations regularly took enslaved women as their mistresses.

90°W

Florida
(from Spain 1763)

Gulf of Mexico

Tropic of Cancer

Black River settlements (British Honduras 1638

Belize

1658 Mosquito Coast

0   500 km
0   300 miles

in 1671 and ceded fully in the Treaty of Utrecht in 1713, prospered as a sugar colony. Exports rose from under 1,000 tons in 1700 to 8,789 tons in 1748, making the island, for its size, the richest colony in the British Empire. European rivalries intensified in the early 18th century. In 1713 Britain acquired the formal right to sell slaves to the Spanish colonies (the 'Asiento') – which was also used as a screen for illicit trade. Spanish attempts to suppress this sparked the War of Jenkins's Ear in 1739 (notable for Admiral Vernon's successful assault on Porto Bello), which merged into the War of the Austrian Succession (1740-8) against Spain's ally, France, the greatest threat to the British West Indies.

Successful French competition contributed to recession in the sugar industry after 1720 and encouraged belligerent British determination to eliminate economic rivalry, acquire new territory for sugar production and maintain colonial security. But the means were still not fully to hand, and at the end of the war Britain's Caribbean position remained largely unchanged. When war erupted again in 1756 the ruthless pursuit of British commercial interest, allied with the supremacy of the Royal Navy, led to the easy capture of Martinique, Guadeloupe and other French islands; and in 1762, following the fall of Quebec, several thousand troops were redeployed in the capture of Spanish Havana and domination of Cuba. The final peace in 1763 left Britain with North American territories including Florida, as well as Grenada, Dominica, St Vincent and Tobago. Britain's position in the Caribbean was now secure, and the West Indies and the Atlantic trade entered their period of greatest prosperity.

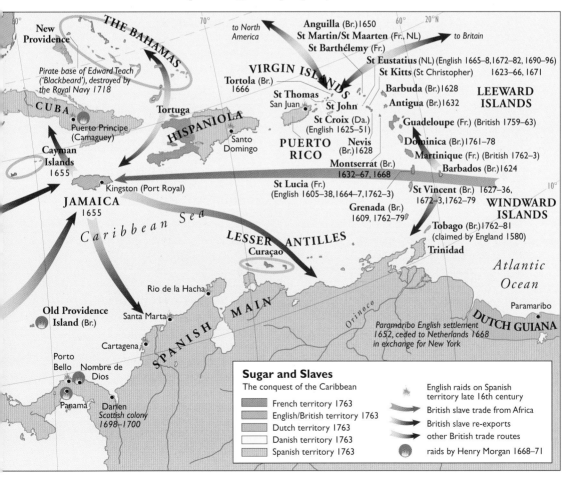

Conflict in Canada Anglo-French rivalry to 1763

During the mid-17th century France consolidated its hold on Canada and set about expanding its empire behind England's Atlantic colonies. It took nearly a century for Britain to mount a sustained and successful campaign for dominance in North America.

"Could they be indulged with a few privileges [the French Canadians could] ... become the most faithful and most useful set of men in this American empire."

Lt. Gen. Sir James Murray, Governor of Quebec (1764)

Coveting the fur trade, Britain claimed the whole of the Hudson Bay region in 1668. Two years later the Hudson's Bay Company was chartered with monopoly trading rights in 'Rupert's Land' (after the company's first Governor, Prince Rupert) comprising 40 per cent of modern-day sub-arctic Canada. In 1689 European rivalries flared into the War of the League of Augsburg: the French captured English trading posts around Hudson's Bay, attacked fishing settlements on Newfoundland, and deployed Indian allies in raids on the English Atlantic colonies. For the first time, Britain's colonial militias were fully mobilized, attacking Quebec, and capturing Acadia and Port Royal.

The status quo was restored at the Treaty of Ryswick in 1697, but when war broke out again in 1702 the result was quite different. France was disadvantaged by the war in Europe, British maritime supremacy and Indian hostility in the vast hinterland beyond Quebec. The whole of Newfoundland, mainland Acadia and the Hudson's Bay territories were ceded to Britain at the Treaty of Utrecht (1713). Yet still, New France remained a formidable opponent. By the time conflict resumed in 1741 the French had built a series of strategically-placed forts from the Gulf of St Lawrence down to New Orleans.

At the end of the War of the Austrian Succession (1748) the major port of Louisbourg, captured by the New England militia, was restored to France, although Halifax was developed as a strategic counterweight (1749). Frontier clashes intensified and

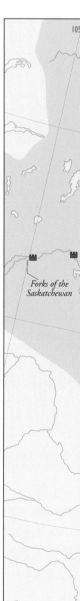

Forks of the Saskatchewan

Fort Garry's Main Street at Hudson's Bay. Fort Garry was founded as a Hudson's Bay Company trading post in 1822. Aside from being a fur trade centre, the fort was a supply centre for leather, crops and dried fish which were shipped out to posts further afield.

in 1754 hostilities were renewed in the French and Indian War, or Seven Years War, (1756–63) which saw the final defeat of France in North America. George Washington and his militia took Fort Duquesne with the aim of opening up the frontier along the Ohio, but it was soon recaptured and a further expedition was ambushed and defeated in 1755. The British, fearing the loyalty of the French population, expelled the Acadians from Nova Scotia.

In 1756 William Pitt the Elder injected new life into the campaign, aiming to conquer New France. In 1758 Fort Duquesne and Louisbourg were recaptured and a series of other forts were taken, culminating in Wolfe's conquest of Quebec in 1759. Montreal surrendered in 1760 and most of the French empire in North America was annexed to Britain at the Treaty of Paris in 1763. Quebec was reduced to a British province, cut off from its fur-trading hinterland, now the preserve of the Hudson's Bay Company or Indian territory under Crown jurisdiction. This was the high point of British North America. The challenge now was to mould a successful colony out of an alienated and divided population in a country with few natural advantages.

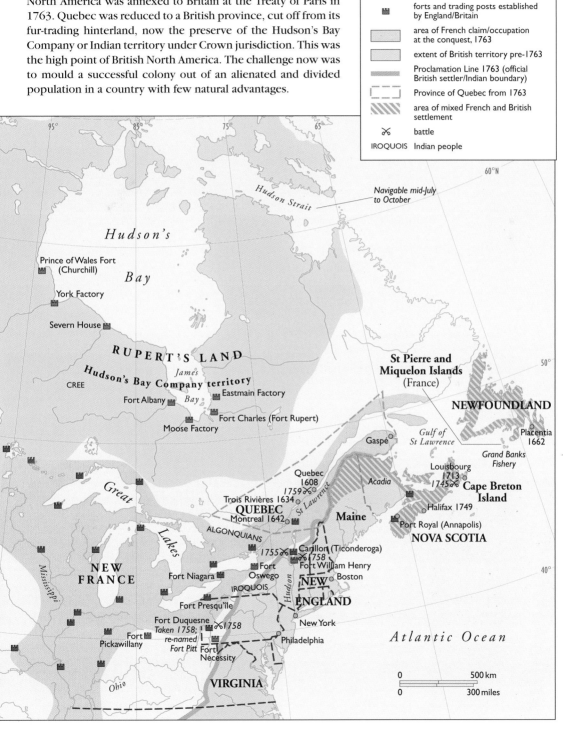

Conflict in Canada
Anglo-French rivalry to 1763

Quebec 1608 — settlement and date of foundation

forts and trading posts established by France

forts and trading posts established by England/Britain

area of French claim/occupation at the conquest, 1763

extent of British territory pre-1763

Proclamation Line 1763 (official British settler/Indian boundary)

Province of Quebec from 1763

area of mixed French and British settlement

battle

IROQUOIS — Indian people

The Infiltration of India British expansion to 1765

The expansion of British influence in India in the 18th century was masterminded by the East India Company. The collapse of Mughal authority and the danger of growing French influence provided the spur for a British infiltration of the subcontinent.

> *"Since the accession of the Company to the Diwani [of Bengal] ... this fine Country, which flourished under the most despotic and arbitrary Government, is verging towards its Ruin."*
>
> Richard Becher, EIC officer, letter, 24 May 1769

The East India Company prospered in conditions of peace and stability, but with the death of Aurangzeb in 1707 the Mughal Empire began to collapse. Feudal subordinates asserted their authority; the Maratha federation emerged to challenge Mughal power in central India; and rival princes fought for control of the Carnatic. Even the imperial capital, Delhi, was sacked by the Persians in 1739.

Around this time the French East India Company emerged as a serious rival to the British, and both companies began exploiting dynastic conflicts in southeast India to gain commercial concessions. Intense rivalry exploded into open hostility in 1744 as part of a wider European war. In 1746 French forces showed their superiority by capturing Madras. The dynamic governor of Pondicherry, Joseph-François Dupleix, continued to plot French supremacy in the south by backing claimants to the thrones of Hyderabad and Arcot, capital of the Carnatic, with some success.

Clive of India

Events began to turn in the Company's favour in 1751 with the seizure of Arcot by the talented former clerk at Madras, Robert Clive. His heavily outnumbered force of 500 British and Indian troops withstood a 50-day siege by the French-backed nawab, whose defeat placed the British-backed claimant, Muhammad Ali, on the throne. In the Seven Years War (1756–63), with a growing army swelled by British government forces, the Company decisively defeated the French at Wandiwash (1761). In addition to the land around the Company's base at Madras, the Jagir, the British gained the Northern Circars and control of the Nawabs of the Carnatic.

In wealthy Bengal political affairs took a different course. In 1756 the British clashed with the ruling nawab, Siraj-ud-Daula, who objected to the Company's growing aggrandisement and to the fortification of Calcutta. The nawab's army stormed the British settlement and around 50 prisoners died in the 'Black Hole' before it was re-taken by the Company's army under Clive. He soon entered a conspiracy organized by discontented Bengali merchants, bankers and disaffected army officers to depose Siraj in favour of his elderly general Mir Jaffa, an alliance which allowed Clive's 3,000-strong army to win the battle of Plassey against ostensibly overwhelming odds in June 1757.

Clive, the East India Company and its agents were handsomely rewarded by the new nawab to the estimated extent of £3 million. A rapaciousness entered British actions as officials – the new nabobs (from *nawab*) – seized the opportunity to become even wealthier. The Company's freedom from internal customs dues was extended to include the private trade of company agents and the lure of reward also encouraged political intrigue. Mir Jaffa was removed in favour of Mir Kassim, who in turn recruited the support of the Wazir of Oudh and the Mughal Emperor against the Company, but they were defeated in battle at Buxar in 1764.

The Company emerged as undisputed master of Bengal, governing a population of 20 million and receiving annual revenues of £3 million, sufficient to finance its large army and to subsidize trading activities. Its position was confirmed in the Treaty of Allahabad (1765) in which the emperor ceded the

Thomas Gainsborough's portrait of Robert Clive, first Baron Clive of Plassey (1725–74), who played a major part in establishing British power in India. Clive began in 1743 as a clerk for the East India Company and joined the Company army as an ensign in 1747. He showed clear military ability, and became one of the great builders of the British Empire.

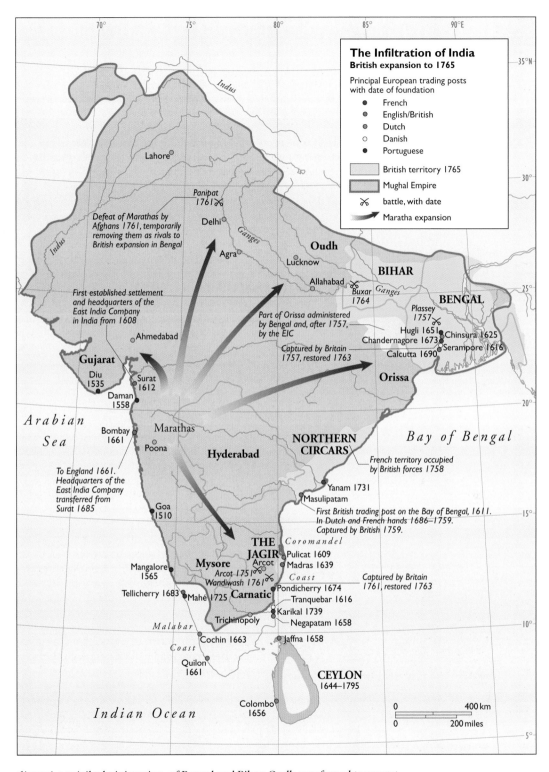

The Infiltration of India
British expansion to 1765

Principal European trading posts
with date of foundation
- French
- English/British
- Dutch
- Danish
- Portuguese

British territory 1765

Mughal Empire

✗ battle, with date

Maratha expansion

Lahore

Panipat
1761 ✗

Defeat of Marathas by Afghans 1761, temporarily removing them as rivals to British expansion in Bengal

Delhi

Agra

Oudh

Lucknow

Allahabad

Buxar
1764

BIHAR

Ganges

BENGAL

Plassey
1757 ✗

Hugli 1651
Chandernagore 1673

Chinsura 1625

Serampore 1616

Calcutta 1690

First established settlement and headquarters of the East India Company in India from 1608

Ahmedabad

Part of Orissa administered by Bengal and, after 1757, by the EIC

Captured by Britain 1757, restored 1763

Orissa

Gujarat

Diu
1535

Surat
1612

Daman
1558

Arabian Sea

Bombay
1661

Poona

Marathas

Hyderabad

NORTHERN CIRCARS

Bay of Bengal

French territory occupied by British forces 1758

To England 1661. Headquarters of the East India Company transferred from Surat 1685

Goa
1510

Yanam 1731

Masulipatam

First British trading post on the Bay of Bengal, 1611. In Dutch and French hands 1686–1759. Captured by British 1759.

THE JAGIR

Coromandel

Mangalore
1565

Mysore

Arcot 1751 ✗
Wandiwash 1761 ✗

Arcot

Pulicat 1609

Madras 1639

Coast

Captured by Britain 1761, restored 1763

Tellicherry 1683

Mahé 1725

Carnatic

Pondicherry 1674

Tranquebar 1616

Trichinopoly

Karikal 1739

Negapatam 1658

Malabar

Cochin 1663

Jaffna 1658

Coast

Quilon
1661

CEYLON
1644–1795

Indian Ocean

Colombo
1656

0   400 km

0   200 miles

diwani, or civil administration, of Bengal and Bihar. Oudh was forced to accept an alliance with Britain and a garrison. The British, whose power now extended to Delhi, became a major contender for supremacy in India.

Part II: The Late Georgian Empire
1763–1837

British success in the Seven Years War (1756–63) marked the start of a new worldwide empire. Territories were acquired in North America, the Caribbean, West Africa and India, largely at the expense of France, and were further augmented during the Revolutionary and Napoleonic wars between 1793 and 1815. These were offset by the loss of the revolutionary American colonies, formally recognized by Britain in 1783. Both elements contributed to the changing nature of the British Empire from a largely self-governing group of white colonies in the Americas to a growing, mainly non-white, dependent empire straddling the globe.

The relentless hunger for land among British settlers along the eastern coast of North America led to a steady march into the interior and a war of attrition with native peoples. The push across the Appalachians, however, had also brought about territorial disputes between colonies and frontier conflict with France. The inadequacies of colonial defence and co-operation together with the cost of the wars and burgeoning administration all required British government intervention. Britain's demand for a fairer financial contribution caused the colonists to fear for their liberties and fuelled a broader discontent that culminated in the American Revolution.

Canada

Strategically there was a price to pay for American independence, for it determined the future shape of Canada and British involvement for years to come. External American hostility added to the internal problem of the large alienated French-speaking community acquired with the conquest of Quebec in 1759–60. Through relatively enlightened policies, Britain was able partially to reconcile the settlers to imperial rule, particularly through the Quebec Act of

1774 which restored autocratic French institutions and affirmed the position of the French language, civil law and Roman Catholic worship. It was a useful lesson for Britain's imperial administrators, who subsequently maintained and adapted local systems of government in other conquered territories with a measure of success.

The equilibrium in Quebec, however, was disturbed following the American Revolution. A new influx of 50,000 British Loyalists arrived from the former Thirteen Colonies (either through choice or through persecution) who desired to live under their own laws and customs based on the old system of representative institutions. The French population felt overwhelmed. Although the old colonial system survived in the Caribbean, Nova Scotia and New Brunswick, the British authorities saw the American Revolution as the consequence of too much democratic freedom and now favoured paternalistic, conservative policies and institutions limiting popular expression. This system of government introduced in the Canada Act (1791) was ultimately a failure, and risked another North American revolution through offering too little freedom rather than too much. By the 1830s the problems of reconciling the English- and

The British siege of Fort Erie, 1814. A British base occcupied by American forces during the 1812 War, Fort Erie was the scene of the bloodiest battle in Canadian history. The 1812 War enhanced nationalist feelings which proved key in Canada's survival as a British colony.

French-speaking peoples and finding a solution to the governance of the northern territories had become urgent.

The revolt of the Thirteen Colonies lost Britain an important part of its early empire, but it was never the most important element. The valuable Caribbean sugar isles, always the priority in imperial defence in the western hemisphere, remained loyal, and ultimately the loss of the American colonies had no detrimental economic impact on Britain. By the end of the Napoleonic War Britain was the world's dominant power and ruled over 200 million people (26 per cent of the world's population). The foundations of this status – which was to continue for a further century – lay in successful industrial development and international trade fostered by a system of imperial economic protection and foreign conquest. It was an age that saw the triumph of mercantilism, combining industrial, commercial and landed interests in a policy of national aggrandisement and enrichment, before the emergence of Free Trade as the prevailing ideology of empire from the 1840s.

Painting of Lord Cornwallis receiving Mysorean hostages in 1792, by Robert Home. The British terms for peace at the end of the Third Mysore War included the surrender of the two young sons of the ruler of Mysore, Tipu Sultan (r. 1782–99). The painting gives some idea of the opulence of the princely state.

Maritime Power

The growing empire was essentially maritime in nature. The prime instrument of conquest and control was the Royal Navy, able to snatch the strategic and economically attractive islands and coastal territories of Britain's rivals and secure the sea lanes for trade and communication. The strategy could also distract enemies in Europe and provide useful bargaining counters in peace talks. Everywhere, trade followed the flag. In the Caribbean, the expansion of Britain's maritime empire was impressive. In the Seven Years War the valuable 'Ceded Islands' of Dominica, St Vincent, Grenada and Tobago were obtained; and although Britain was forced on the defensive during the American war (1775–83) further gains were made from 1793, including St Lucia, Trinidad, Essequibo, Berbice and Demerara. In the Mediterranean, Britain held on to Malta and the Ionian Islands in a region of valuable trade and on the important 'overland' route to India. Remoter islands, too, became desirable real estate on the routes to and from the East, including the Maldives (1796), the Seychelles (1794) and Mauritius (1810). Following the French invasion of the Netherlands in 1795, Britain occupied Ceylon (1796) and the important Cape of Good Hope, strategically situated on the route between Europe, India and the Far East.

The Jewel in the Crown

In the Indian Ocean world the British government and the mighty East India Company co-operated to protect British commercial and strategic interests. In 1765 the Company took control of Bengal, India's richest province, and seemingly by random steps proceeded to subjugate the whole of the subcontinent. It was a process encouraged by the unstable nature of Indian politics after the collapse of Mughal authority, the desire for stable frontiers, and the global rivalry of Britain and France. It was also a consequence of the nature of the Company as a commercial organization with important territorial interests, a powerful army and ambitious officials at its head. The unrestrained actions of local agents were a constant factor in imperial advance everywhere.

At first, the Company's position was politically and economically weak. The capable Governor General Warren Hastings (1772–86) did well to defend British territory while the country was preoccupied with the American war. He kept the administration solvent, using every means to obtain money to support campaigns against the Maratha confederacy in the west and Mysore in the south. To many this seemed more like extortion and breach of trust. Against a background of continuing corruption and maladministration by officials and

the Company's dire financial position (with debts of £20 million), Hastings was summoned home in 1786 to face impeachment. In 1784 Pitt's India Act brought the Company's political activities further under British government supervision, and Lord Cornwallis (Governor General 1786–93) was charged with reforming the Indian administration. He was successful but, like Hastings, found it impossible to maintain peace and curb British expansion.

Britain also consolidated its interests in eastern waters. China was seen as a great commercial prize if the Company, which possessed British monopoly trading rights until 1833, was able to encourage the insular Chinese authorities to liberalize trading relations, but this was a battle to come. To help secure the trade route to the east, the Company acquired the island of Penang (1786) and later Province Wellesley on the Malayan mainland. Malacca was taken from the Netherlands (1795) and although Java (1811) was handed back in 1816, the Dutch commercial threat was keenly felt. The Company's agent Stamford Raffles saw the acquisition of Singapore in 1819 as an effective advance: 'Our object is not territory, but trade; a great commercial emporium, and a fulcrum, whence we may extend our influence politically as circumstances … require…. One free port in these seas must eventually destroy the spell of Dutch monopoly'. The faith placed in Singapore was justified and it became the centre of British power in the eastern seas.

A late-18th century view of Canton harbour, China, showing the *hongs*. During this period of the British Empire the Chinese authorities restricted European trade to the southern port of Canton (Guangzhou). There foreign merchants were required to trade in compounds, known as *hongs*, where they could meet the Chinese traders who had been granted monopoly privileges by the emperor. After the Opium War, which started in 1839 when the Chinese tried to prevent British merchants carrying opium to Canton, four more ports were opened up to British shipping.

Pacific Conquest

The British were also interested in commercial exploitation even further to the east, although its potential never matched expectations. Until the late 18th century the Pacific was the last great unknown and largely unexplored region of the world. Speculation and confusion gave rise to the myth of a great unknown, potentially rich, southern continent – the *Terra Australis Incognita* – and the major prize of Pacific exploration. What Britain did acquire, however, was the much less promising continent of Australia (and New Zealand) arising from the 1768–71 voyage of Captain James Cook. His were the most distinguished of a series of explorations that reflected Britain's maritime pre-eminence, new spirit of scientific enquiry and commercial ambition. With the creation of New South Wales as a penal colony in 1788, the steady influx of British settlers transformed a thinly populated apparently primitive and larely inhospitable land into a thriving colonial asset. To William Gladstone, writing in 1846, 'the energy of the colonists has, without doubt … been the main cause of their singular advancement'. While expanding settler societies gained greater prosperity and political control, the Aboriginal population suffered dispossession, alienation, persecution and, as in the Americas, the ravages of disease. Theirs was the true cost of colonization.

From Sydney the new population not only conquered the continent but also did much to open up the Pacific to British commercial enterprise. But official interest in the remote and economically insignificant Pacific islands waned towards the end of the 18th century. Even the cession of Hawaii obtained by Vancouver in 1794 was ignored. Occasional scientific and technical expeditions culminated in Charles Darwin's voyage to the Galapagos in HMS *Beagle* in the 1830s. Meanwhile, trade and contact with the outside world provoked upheaval in traditional societies in Tahiti, Tonga, the Marquesas and elsewhere, laying the foundation for more direct intervention later in the 19th century.

A similar process also marked British relations with West Africa, an involvement based on the transatlantic slave trade and where Britain assumed responsibility for coastal slaving forts and enclaves from private operators in the Gambia and the Gold Coast. The traffic grew to immense proportions during the 18th century, with an estimated 1,698,400 slaves transported on British Empire shipping to the Americas between 1760 and 1807. Private Christian humanitarian concern led to the founding of Sierra Leone in 1787 as a home for the black poor of England, a means of promoting legitimate commerce at the expense of the slave trade and a beacon of 'civilization' for West Africa. They were joined by rebellious Jamaican Maroons, freed slaves who had fought with Britain in the American War, and others liberated from slave ships by the Royal Navy after the trade was made illegal in 1807. The same year it became a British Crown colony and a focus of future British entanglement in West Africa.

Slavery and Empire

The anti-slavery campaign in Britain culminated in the abolition of slavery throughout the Empire in 1834, although slavery was succeeded by several years of 'apprenticeship' that continued to restrict personal freedom. Preferential British sugar tariffs allowed plantation owners (who were also compensated

A view of Bristol docks and quay in the 1780s. By 1730 Bristol, England's second port, had replaced London as the centre of the transatlantic slave trade. The city's lively trade and wealthy merchant houses were built on the profits of slavery.

to the tune of £20 million) to survive into the 1840s, when the icy blast of Free Trade exposed them to unequal competition from foreign slave plantations. Economic self-interest and humanitarian concern ensured that the worldwide anti-slavery struggle became a key part of British high-Victorian imperialism.

After 1815 the British were able to relax and enjoy the fruits of international military and economic dominance. There were no great power rivals to seriously threaten the Pax Britannica. Success in war was regarded as a mark of divine favour, approval for Britain's virtuous and benevolent system of government and rule of law under the Crown. It contributed to an emerging view of British racial superiority that began to disturb colonial relations. But the pressure for widespread reform was growing, helped along by the Parliamentary Reform Act of 1832 which facilitated the abolition of slavery, the move towards Free Trade economics, and the removal of hitherto autocratic government in the colonies of settlement. Behind the continuing growth of empire lay a powerful confident nationalism, the search for profit, Christian missionary zeal and the activities of ambitious or fearful colonial agents seeking to advance or defend the frontiers. Britons were strongly attached to their empire, widely regarding it as a source of wealth and prestige and a major force for good in the world.

Trade and Enterprise Overseas trade to 1854

Economic success was the main aim of imperial policy, and the exclusion of the rival Dutch from British markets had been the first step in the process. Britain exploited a unique cluster of domestic advantages, including abundant natural resources and early industrialization, that underpinned its burgeoning global trade.

Britain's flourishing economy from the 1780s soon compensated for losses in the American war. New markets were exploited in the East, and Atlantic trade, responsible for around 40 per cent of total British trade, continued to grow after 1782. Although they were now outside the system of imperial commerce, the former Thirteen Colonies (which took 20 per cent of British exports) still required British manufactured goods in exchange for raw materials, the pattern previously enforced by the Navigation Acts.

The French wars from 1793 seriously distorted trade. Britain, excluded from European commerce, became more reliant on imperial trade and also seized several economically valuable colonies from the French and their allies. Although British trade with the Empire expanded during wartime (colonial

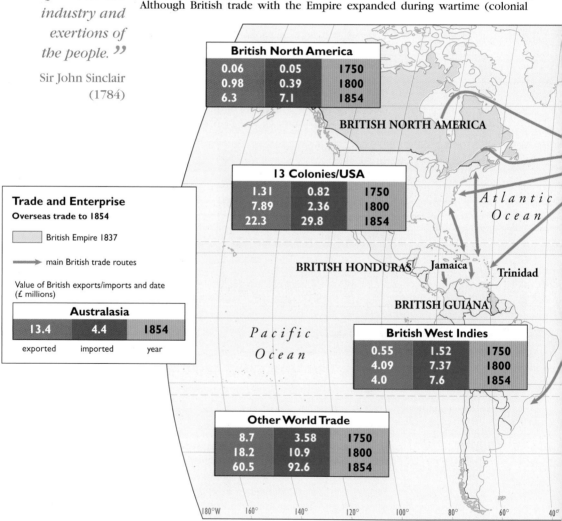

British North America

0.06	0.05	1750
0.98	0.39	1800
6.3	7.1	1854

BRITISH NORTH AMERICA

Atlantic Ocean

13 Colonies/USA

1.31	0.82	1750
7.89	2.36	1800
22.3	29.8	1854

Trade and Enterprise

Overseas trade to 1854

British Empire 1837

→ main British trade routes

Value of British exports/imports and date
(£ millions)

Australasia

13.4	4.4	1854
exported	imported	year

BRITISH HONDURAS Jamaica Trinidad

BRITISH GUIANA

Pacific Ocean

British West Indies

0.55	1.52	1750
4.09	7.37	1800
4.0	7.6	1854

Other World Trade

8.7	3.58	1750
18.2	10.9	1800
60.5	92.6	1854

180°W   160°   140°   120°   100°   80°   60°   40°

imports reaching 35–40 per cent of the total), it fell back slightly afterwards. West Indies imports in particular declined sharply from 18 to 6 per cent by 1845 due to increasing trade competition and the attack on slavery. Overall, however, Britain's volume and share of world trade continued to grow, and imperial trade remained substantial, especially in financial services and shipping. Average exports for the period 1794–6 rose from £21.7 million per annum to £44.4 million during 1814–16.

Difficulties in Europe during the early 19th century encouraged British merchants to seek new overseas markets, especially for cotton goods which accounted for 48 per cent of exports by the mid-1830s. New Mediterranean possessions and the Ottoman Empire provided outlets, together with India and new areas of domination from the Persian Gulf to the Straits of Malacca. Areas of white settlement – especially Canada and Australia – also developed strongly as trading partners, and by 1830 Britain's share of world trade reached 45 per cent.

Meanwhile, London, the world's pre-eminent capital market, developed new institutions to finance expansion and service the National Debt. A new mood of economic liberalization had also developed which would lead to the forcible opening of new markets and the more aggressive imperialism of the early Victorian era. Having won the war in 1815, Britain gradually realized that to succeed in the era of peaceful economic rivalry, cheap food and raw materials (unhindered by tariffs) were the key to international competitiveness. Closed imperial economic systems and the conquest of territory no longer offered a simple solution.

Painting of the Old Custom House Quay in London, c. 1756, by Samuel Scott. First built in 1275, the Custom House in the City of London levied customs duties and processed documents on cargoes. Customs duties were always an important part of government revenue, particularly during the booming trade years of the British Empire.

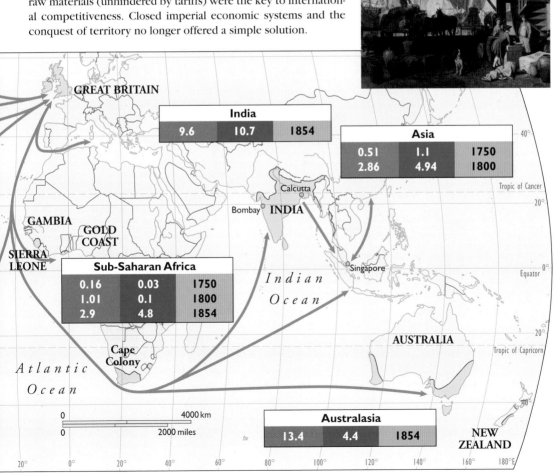

India		
9.6	10.7	1854

Asia		
0.51	1.1	1750
2.86	4.94	1800

Sub-Saharan Africa		
0.16	0.03	1750
1.01	0.1	1800
2.9	4.8	1854

Australasia		
13.4	4.4	1854

GREAT BRITAIN

GAMBIA
GOLD COAST
SIERRA LEONE

Calcutta
Bombay INDIA
Singapore

Cape Colony

AUSTRALIA
NEW ZEALAND

Indian Ocean
Atlantic Ocean

Tropic of Cancer
Equator
Tropic of Capricorn

0 4000 km
0 2000 miles

Conquest of the Cape Southern Africa to 1844

In 1806 Britain re-conquered the strategically important Dutch colony at the Cape of Good Hope. With the territory, as sitting tenants, came a culturally hostile and irreconcilable Afrikaner colonial population of Dutch, German and Huguenot extraction. Conflict with this population determined the course of British expansion in southern Africa and the fate of many African peoples.

"The importance of the Cape ... consists more from the detriment which would result to us if it was in the hands of France, than from any advantage we can possibly derive from it as a colony."

Sir Francis Baring (1795)

The Cape colony was founded by the Dutch East India Company in 1652 and settlers began farming the productive land around Cape Town, the main settlement and port. This Dutch-Afrikaans-speaking white minority, which numbered around 20,000 at the beginning of the 19th century, depended on the tied labour of indigenous Khoi and San peoples, but also on slaves; since too few were forthcoming from the eastern Bantu-speaking areas, they were imported from East Africa and elsewhere. By 1806, when the trade was ended, the Cape slave population numbered some 30,000, and slavery, and the treatment of black people, continued to be the focus of British humanitarian concern throughout the period.

Afrikaner Expansion

With population growth and economic opportunity, the Afrikaners expanded further into the Cape, mainly eastwards on land that was best suited to the running of sheep. During the late 18th century they reached the more densely-populated territories of Bantu-speaking peoples, particularly the powerful Xhosa, who opposed the long process of colonization and dispossession in several Cape Frontier (Kaffir) Wars between 1779 and 1879. Both Dutch and British administrations found they had little control over the Boers, who constantly moved beyond the control of Cape Town yet implicated the administration in their conflicts with Africans over land, labour and cattle.

In the fourth Frontier War (1811–12) British troops were used to support the settlers for the first time. The Xhosa were expelled from the Zuurveld and fort settlements were established at Grahamstown (1812) and sites along the Great Fish River, the new Cape frontier. The war of 1818–19 resulted in the area eastwards to the Keiskamma River being declared neutral (later 'ceded') territory free of occupation. In an experimental project, the Cape government attempted to close and protect the frontier by planting British colonists behind the new *cordon sanitaire* and in 1820 5,000 settlers were established on farmland in the Albany district. It was also intended as a model settlement free of slavery. It was only a partial success (although a similar scheme was tried in 1829 when Khoi families were settled on the Kat River to the north) and intensified conflict with the Afrikaners and indigenous Africans over resources. Increasingly, the British were determined to impose control and tame the unruly and independent-minded Boers in the interests of peace, stable frontiers and economic development, as well as balanced budgets.

From the mid-1820s Britain began to re-shape the colonial order in South Africa. Early reforms had been limited in their effects, but the Afrikaners – still a majority among white settlers – felt threatened. They objected to the growth

A watercolour sketch of Boers returning from hunting in 1804 by Samuel Daniell. The word Boer – Dutch for 'farmer' – came to refer to the Afrikaans-speaking migrating pastoral farmers of the expanding Cape frontier. They were also known as Afrikaners, the early 18th-century term used to describe the white Afrikaans-speaking population who cae to dominate South African politics.

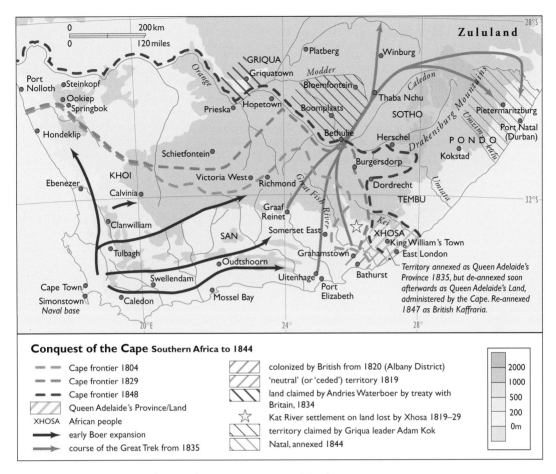

Conquest of the Cape Southern Africa to 1844

- – – – Cape frontier 1804
- – – – Cape frontier 1829
- – – – Cape frontier 1848
- Queen Adelaide's Province/Land
- XHOSA African people
- → early Boer expansion
- → course of the Great Trek from 1835

- colonized by British from 1820 (Albany District)
- 'neutral' (or 'ceded') territory 1819
- land claimed by Andries Waterboer by treaty with Britain, 1834
- ☆ Kat River settlement on land lost by Xhosa 1819–29
- territory claimed by Griqua leader Adam Kok
- Natal, annexed 1844

2000
1000
500
200
0m

Territory annexed as Queen Adelaide's Province 1835, but de-annexed soon afterwards as Queen Adelaide's Land, administered by the Cape. Re-annexed 1847 as British Kaffraria.

of government, to a culture that was becoming more British in character, to constraints on eastward expansion, and especially to the abolition of the slave trade, anti-discrimination legislation and measures for the amelioration of slavery. For many Boers, empire-wide emancipation passed in 1834 prompted the final break with British rule, and Boers like Piet Retief complained of 'the severe losses we have been forced to sustain … and the odium which has been cast on us by interested and dishonest persons, under the cloak of religion'.

The Great Trek

The Boer response was to escape British rule and set up their own republics. In the 'Great Trek' between 1835 and the early 1840s around 15,000 Boers migrated across the Orange and Vaal rivers on to the Highveld, which later became the Orange Free State and the Transvaal. In 1837 Retief himself led 3,000 Boers to southern Zululand where, under Andries Pretorius, they defeated the Zulus at Blood River in 1838 and founded the Republic of Natalia. The exodus widened the conflict and drew Britain further into involvement inland and eastwards to Natal, leading to the extension of British jurisdiction beyond the frontier of the Cape in 1836. Treaties were signed to delineate borders and establish authority: the West Griqua territory of Andries Waterboer was recognized in 1834, followed by other littoral states. Even with the appointment of a Lieutenant-Governor to the eastern frontier, British attempts to contain Boer expansion and protect neighbouring African societies had little effect. British expansion naturally followed this conflict over resources.

Opening up the Pacific

The idea of an unknown southern continent excited many in Europe. To influential writer John Campbell, 'whoever ... discovers & settles it will become infallibly possessed of Territories as Rich, as fruitful, & as capable of Improvement as any ... hitherto found'. Lured by the prospect of wealth and trade, and inspired by Enlightenment interest, British explorers made the Pacific another region of gradual penetration and ultimate takeover.

> *"With the Consent of the Natives ... take possession of convenient situations ... or, if ... uninhabited take Possession for His Majesty."*
>
> Admiralty instructions to Lt James Cook (1768)

Popular interest in the Pacific was fired by the numerous published stories of oceanic travel and adventure. These included the accounts of William Dampier, who led the first Royal Navy expedition to the region (1699–1701), and of Commodore George Anson who embarked on the last of the traditional plundering voyages in 1740. Captain John Byron was sent on a largely fruitless circumnavigation in 1764, the start of a new series of explorations organized by the Admiralty but without any overall grand design. Much of the impetus came from private individuals, commercial groups, and scientific organizations. In 1766 Captain Philip Carteret voyaged through unknown Polynesia and Melanesia, while Captain Samuel Wallis made other discoveries, notably Tahiti in June 1767, just ahead of the French explorer Louis Antoine de Bougainville.

Cook's Voyages

Tahiti – its people in what was seen as an original state of nature – exerted a powerful exotic and erotic influence on the European imagination. It was also affected by a new spirit of scientific enquiry powerfully represented on the first Pacific voyage of Lt (later Captain) James Cook in HMS *Endeavour*, sent to observe the Transit of Venus in June 1769 at the request of the Royal Society. In addition to astronomers, the party included artists and scientists

The English explorer Samuel Wallis (1728–95) being received by Queen Oberea of Tahiti. When Wallis landed there in 1767 it was probably the first contact the island's inhabitants had ever had with Europeans. The native population did not initially welcome the Europeans; peace was only established after some armed conflict. Wallis named Tahiti King George Island after the reigning British monarch, although it was eventually to be colonized by the French in the 19th century.

including the botanist Joseph Banks who all contributed to unveiling the Pacific world to European eyes. Cook himself recorded their encounters and created a new map of the region, charting 5,000 miles of coastline, mostly of Australasia. His circumnavigation of the South Island gave New Zealand geographical identity and established it as separate from any putative southern continent.

Cook's triumphant first voyage was followed by a further expedition aboard HMS *Resolution* in 1772 that finally disproved the existence of the southern continent. In the process Cook became the first navigator to cross the Antarctic Circle. With the benefit of the new accurate Harrison-pattern chronometer he was able to accurately chart many island groups in addition to discovering and naming New Caledonia, Norfolk Island and others. His final expedition in search of a North-West Passage led to the survey of the North American coastline from Nootka Sound to the Bering Sea, and to the discovery of the Cook, Palmerston and Sandwich (Hawaiian) Islands, where he was killed in 1779.

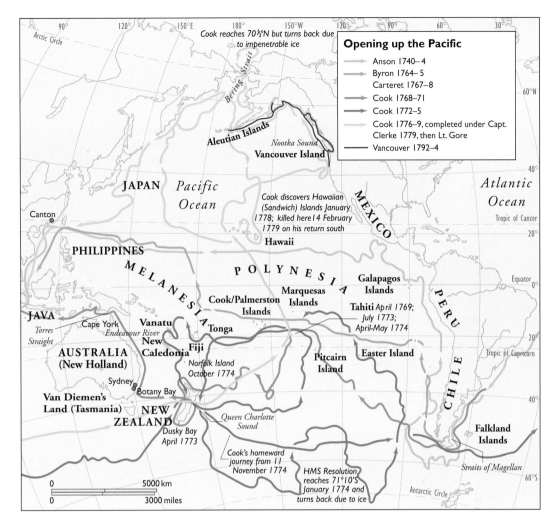

Opening up the Pacific

- Anson 1740–4
- Byron 1764–5
- Carteret 1767–8
- Cook 1768–71
- Cook 1772–5
- Cook 1776–9, completed under Capt. Clerke 1779, then Lt. Gore
- Vancouver 1792–4

Cook reaches 70½°N but turns back due to impenetrable ice

Cook discovers Hawaiian (Sandwich) Islands January 1778; killed here 14 February 1779 on his return south

Tahiti April 1769; July 1773; April-May 1774

Norfolk Island October 1774

Dusky Bay April 1773

Cook's homeward journey from 11 November 1774

HMS Resolution reaches 71°10'S January 1774 and turns back due to ice

Cook's achievements were monumental. He helped establish British interests around the Pacific and cleared the way for commercial penetration and the colonization of New South Wales. By 1793 around 100 British whaling and sealing ships were operating in the southern oceans. Fur traders began exploiting the large sea otter population of North America originally identified by Cook, leading to a confrontation at Nootka Sound in 1789 which forced Spain to recognize British territorial rights in Pacific North America. Captain George Vancouver was despatched to uphold British interests in 1791; his thorough survey of the coast finally disproved the existence of a North-West Passage in temperate latitudes. The glory days of Pacific exploration were over. A new phase of exploitation had begun accompanied by the profound disruption of traditional societies.

A portrait of the explorer, navigator and hydrographer Captain James Cook (1728–79) by Nathaniel Dance. Cook contributed greatly to the exploration and colonization of the Pacific region. He made three voyages to the Pacific Ocean, charting its main shorelines. His last major discovery, the Hawaiian Islands, was also the place of his death in 1779. While investigating the theft of one of his boats, Cook was killed in a skirmish between his marines and the Hawaiian natives.

The Settlement of Australasia

After William Dampier's voyage of 1699, little British exploration of Australasia took place until the voyage of James Cook (1728–79) in HMS Endeavour. *Cook explored the east coast of New Zealand's North Island from October 1769, and the following January it was officially claimed for Britain. In April his party became the first known Europeans to reach eastern New Holland (Australia) and in August 1770 the whole of the 'empty' east coast was formally annexed as far as 38°S. Everywhere, the prior claims of indigenous peoples were disregarded.*

Of all Cook's dazzling achievements, the most significant was the exploration of eastern Australia. Favourable reports of Botany Bay made by members of the *Endeavour* expedition encouraged the British government to choose the site for a convict settlement as an alternative to the lost American colonies. In the broader context of European expansion, the settlement of New South Wales had commercial and strategic advantages, forestalling French claims to the region and securing resources of timber and flax for the Royal Navy.

New South Wales

The First Fleet of 11 ships and over 1,300 convicts, marines and others under Governor Arthur Phillip, founded the colony of NSW in January 1788, but soon decamped from Botany Bay to the more favourable location of Port Jackson (Sydney). A successful agricultural and pastoral economy developed and by 1792 there were 2,500 colonists. They included men of the New South Wales garrison who chose to stay on, such as James Macarthur who was prominent in developing the colony's staple wool trade, joined soon afterwards by a growing number of free settlers who were encouraged by generous land grants and convict labour.

Exploitation and exploration started immediately. Sydney quickly became a centre of trade and exploration for much of the western Pacific. The fisheries, whaling and sealing industries extended to Van Diemen's Land, New Zealand and further afield, providing the primary exports of New South Wales until overtaken by wool after 1834. In 1795 George Bass (1771–*c.* 1802) and Matthew Flinders (1774–1814) set about surveying more of the coast, Van Diemen's Land and the rest of Australia, the name used by Flinders and adopted for the continent by Governor Macquarie in 1817. The first of many explorations into the vast

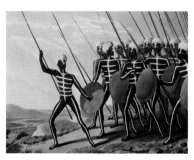

A 19th-century engraving of Aborigine warriors. It is estimated that at the time of the first British settlement of Australia there were 300,000 aboriginal inhabitants. Many were driven away or killed by European diseases; their cultures, deeply integrated with the natural environment, were undermined by its destruction through the introduction of new domestic and feral animals. For most of the 20th century the Aborigines continued to suffer from government restrictions of their rights and attempts to 'Europeanize' them.

Western Australia
1829

*Indian
Ocean*

Perth
Fremantle

King George Sound
(Albany)

interior was begun by John Oxley, Surveyor General of New South Wales, the same year.

By 1815 the number of convicts, guards and settlers in Australia numbered 15,000, concentrated in the temperate south-east. Agricultural investment became significant from the 1820s, when sheep numbers reached 17 million, and soon the settler population began penetrating along the coast and inland across the Great Dividing Range. A similar expansion of (non-convict) settlement took place in western Australia during the 1820s and around Adelaide from 1836. The sale of Crown lands subsidized the passage of new colonists from Britain, and the proportion of free settlers eventually overtook the convict population as transportation itself came under growing attack.

In New Zealand, European settlement, associated with the maritime industries, was just beginning, especially around the Bay of Islands, but lawlessness led to the extension of legal authority from New South Wales and a growing involvement from 1814. The government also laid claim to Van Diemen's Land, which was first settled by a party under Lt. John Bowen in September 1803, followed by the establishment of Hobart and Launceston. The settlers prospered, numbering more than 57,000 by 1840, and many pastoralists and entrepreneurs moved across to the mainland areas of Port Phillip (nucleus of the future colony of Victoria) in the mid-1830s in search of new land and new opportunities.

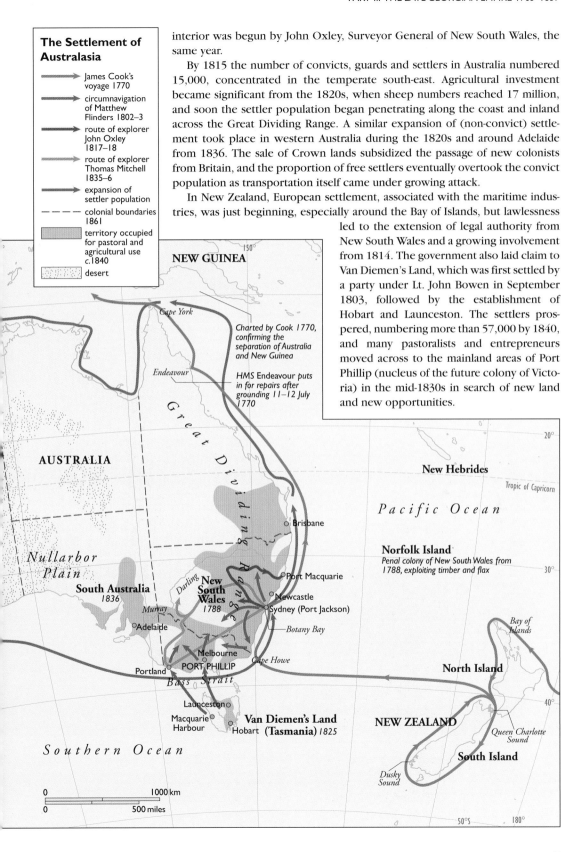

The Settlement of Australasia

- James Cook's voyage 1770
- circumnavigation of Matthew Flinders 1802–3
- route of explorer John Oxley 1817–18
- route of explorer Thomas Mitchell 1835–6
- expansion of settler population
- colonial boundaries 1861
- territory occupied for pastoral and agricultural use c.1840
- desert

NEW GUINEA

Cape York

Charted by Cook 1770, confirming the separation of Australia and New Guinea

Endeavour

HMS Endeavour puts in for repairs after grounding 11–12 July 1770

AUSTRALIA

New Hebrides

Tropic of Capricorn

Pacific Ocean

Brisbane

Norfolk Island
Penal colony of New South Wales from 1788, exploiting timber and flax

Nullarbor Plain

South Australia 1836

Darling

New South Wales 1788

Port Macquarie

Newcastle

Sydney (Port Jackson)

Murray

Adelaide

Botany Bay

Bay of Islands

Melbourne

PORT PHILLIP

Cape Howe

North Island

Portland

Bass Strait

NEW ZEALAND

Launceston

Macquarie Harbour

Van Diemen's Land (Tasmania) 1825

Hobart

Queen Charlotte Sound

Southern Ocean

South Island

Dusky Sound

0   1000 km
0   500 miles

On the Move Early migration to the Empire

"Such numbers of their friends ... have preceded them, more especially to the British North American possessions, that they no longer consider these to be the land of strangers. "

The New Statistical Account of Scotland (1845)

From the early 1600s large numbers of people began to leave the British Isles to populate territories overseas. They did so for a variety of reasons including poverty, official persecution, the opportunity for enrichment and the prospect of greater religious and political freedom. Ultimately, this exodus was important in creating a global economic system and a culturally unified empire.

The Americas superseded Ireland as the early focus of colonization, attracting around 400,000 settlers during the 17th century. Of these some 200,000 headed for the Caribbean, but from the mid-1600s their numbers declined with the growth of sugar plantations using African slave labour. Most of the early settlers were English, but the 18th century emigrant profile became more diverse, comprising 115,000 Irish (including Scots-Irish from Ulster), 75,000 Scots and under 100,000 English and Welsh.

Emigrants benefited from the growing availability of shipping and the declining cost of travel. At home, accelerating industrial and agrarian changes fragmented and dispersed established communities, notably in the Highlands of Scotland. Many of the emigrants headed for the American backcountry, their

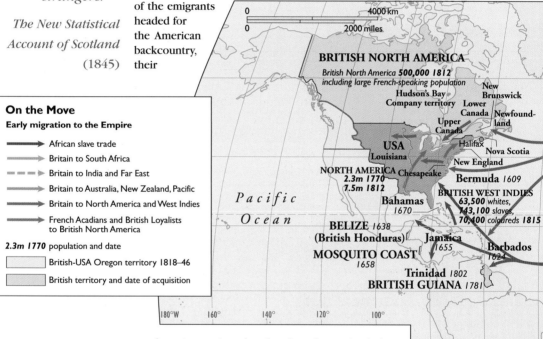

On the Move

Early migration to the Empire

- African slave trade
- Britain to South Africa
- Britain to India and Far East
- Britain to Australia, New Zealand, Pacific
- Britain to North America and West Indies
- French Acadians and British Loyalists to British North America

2.3m 1770 population and date

British-USA Oregon territory 1818–46

British territory and date of acquisition

numbers increasing sharply after the end of the Seven Years' War in 1763, and again after American independence. From 1780 to 1815 as many as 150,000 Irish arrived in North America, and they were accompanied by numerous – more often than not Highland – Scots emigrating to the maritime colonies and Upper Canada.

Generally, the imperial government left matters of emigration to the private sector, but it selectively assisted British settlement for defensive purposes. In

John Nicol's painting *Lochaber No More* (1883). From the late 18th century many Scottish Highlanders were evicted from land to make way for intensive sheep farming. Many of them emigrated to Canada in search of a better life. The sombreness of this painting reflects their feelings about leaving home.

1749 it financed the resettlement of 2,500 Britons to the new strategic port of Halifax in Nova Scotia; and following the second British-American War (1812-14) until 1825 subsidized passages to Canada were introduced along with land grants. Settlement of the eastern frontier of Cape Colony was promoted in 1820. The government was also involved in forced emigration from Britain: felons were transported initially to the American colonies (49,000 1718-75) and from 1787 to the new penal colony of New South Wales (Australia), which received 29,400 men and women by 1820. It also progressively regulated the emigrant carrying trade from 1803.

Incentives to Emigration

After 1815 there was a growing appreciation of colonies as a useful 'safety valve' for surplus population, demobilized troops, the destitute and unemployed. The economic and strategic value of settled colonies was also recognized; the government, especially from the 1830s, approved of colonization although it remained strictly non-interventionist. Australia increasingly demanded free settlers, especially skilled artisans, agricultural workers and young single women, to further develop the colony and, under the influence of Edward Gibbon Wakefield, a powerful advocate of colonization, land sale receipts were used to subsidize passages. Philanthropic societies were also important sponsors.

Towards the end of the 18th century a growing number of individuals in commercial, ecclesiastical, military and government careers settled widely in British territories. They were never as numerous as in the established colonies of settlement, and many of them, as 'temporary emigrants', returned home, often to enjoy their prosperity and consolidate the idea of empire at its heart.

Ulster

Ireland **GREAT BRITAIN**

British population **13m 1815**
Emigration **185,000 1790–1815;
600,000 1815–50**

FRANCE

Ionian Islands
1809

Gibraltar **Malta**
1704   1800

CHINESE EMPIRE

EGYPT

Fort James
1663

GAMBIA
1618

GOLD COAST
1672

SIERRA LEONE
1787

Ascension Is.
1815

St Helena
1651

Calcutta
1696   Canton

Bombay   **BRITISH
1661   INDIA**   **Tenasserim**
           Madras   1826
           1639

*Mostly temporary commercial,
administrative and military officials* **Ceylon**   Penang 1786
                  Maldives 1796   Malacca 1824
                  1802   Singapore 1819
                       Bencoolen
           Seychelles   1685–1824
           1794   **Chagos** 1784   Batavia
                              1811–16

Tropic of Cancer

Equator

I n d i a n   O c e a n

Natal
1824

A t l a n t i c

O c e a n

Cape Colony
1795/1806

42,217 *whites (mainly Afrikaners)* **1819**
Significant British immigration from 1820

Mauritius 1810

AUSTRALIA

Swan River Colony   New South Wales
1825   1788

White population **15,000 1815;
400,000 1851.** *Convicts:* **162,000**
transported **1788–1840**

Tropic of Capricorn

Norfolk Is.
1774

Tasmania
1825

NEW ZEALAND

America Rebels The American Revolution 1775–83

The American Revolution came soon after Britain's triumph in the Seven Years War. The loss of the 'first empire' was a shock, but the danger of a revived French North America was averted in the peace settlement of 1783, and it failed to dent British eonomic fortunes.

"The nation has run itself into an immense debt to give [the Americans] their protection; and now they are called upon to contribute a small share … [they] break out I might almost say, into open rebellion."

George Grenville, Chancellor of the Exchequer, to the House of Commons, 14 January 1766

Relations between the American colonists and the imperial government worsened after the end of the Seven Years War in 1763. Britain was left with a national debt of £150 million (and continuing liabilities) partly accrued in defence of the colonists who were now expected to contribute more in taxation. At the same time the British government, through the Proclamation Line of 1763, attempted to limit aggressive westward expansion by land-hungry colonists to prevent further conflict with Indian populations.

The Boston Tea Party

The Thirteen Colonies united for the first time against the introduction of stamp duty in 1765, and representatives met in New York to plan their opposition. Government-imposed customs duties provoked the Boston Tea Party (December 1773) protest, and also official retaliation through the 'Intolerable Acts'. Suspicion of the government grew in 1774 when much of the territory between the Mississippi and Ohio rivers was placed under Quebec's jurisdiction. New Englanders in particular feared that the French-speaking Catholic population was being groomed as a counterweight to the free English-speaking Protestant colonists, even to the extent of invasion.

Events proceeded quickly. In September 1774 the first rebel Continental Congress met in Philadelphia and asserted the equality of the colonial assemblies with the parliament at Westminster, at which Americans were unrepresented. In April 1775 the first clash took place at Concord, Massachusetts, where British troops attempted to seize rebel arms. The war had started. In May the second Congress, reflecting the growing belief in complete separation, authorized the recruitment of an army (eventually 20,000-strong) to be led by George Washington (1732–99), who was to later become the first president of the United States of America. The Declaration of Independence was made on 4 July 1776, following a year in which the British were forced to evacuate Boston and the Americans undertook a fruitless invasion of Quebec, where they found no support.

William Mercer's dramatic depiction of the Battle of Princeton in 1777. The battle was a turning point in the Revolutionary War. It showed for the first time that the Americans could outmanoeuvre and defeat a British army in the field, thus bringing the British one step closer to expulsion from their North American colonies.

In 1776 the main battles took place in the north. Sir William Howe took New York before Washington counter-attacked at Trenton and Princeton, New Jersey. Howe's failure to prevent Washington's escape from New York was one of a series of blunders that contributed to the eventual American victory. Another was the defeat at Saratoga in 1777 of General John Burgoyne's army from Montreal after it failed to rendezvous with British forces in the Hudson Valley. Despite Howe's capture of Philadelphia, the seat of the American Congress, Saratoga encouraged the French to intervene on the rebel side, with profound consequences for the outcome of the war.

Washington succeeded in creating an effective fighting force and, in the face of many privations, maintaining it in the field. In 1778 Philadelphia was recaptured and serious fighting ended in the north. The following year British strategy concentrated on re-taking the southern colonies as far north as Virginia, but British forces were spread too thinly. In the autumn of 1781 Lord Cornwallis's army of only 7,000 found itself confronted by Washington's Franco-American force of 14,000 at Yorktown and cut off from naval support by a French fleet under de Grasse. There was no alternative to surrender, and when Prime Minister Lord North heard the news he said simply, 'It is all over'. The British political establishment refused to continue the war, and American independence was recognized in the peace negotiations at Paris.

The naval victory of Lord Rodney over de Grasse at the Saints, off Dominica, in 1782 limited British losses in the final peace settlement. Captured West Indies possessions were recovered, although France regained Tobago and Senegal, and Spain kept Florida and Minorca. The terms gained by the new American states were generous, but by relinquishing claims to former French territories south of the Great Lakes they reduced British exposure to conflict with the expansionist Americans. Much of the revolutionary fighting had been between American rebels and loyalists, a large group that included allied Indians and former black slaves, who now began the trek north to British North America, a new life and even new freedoms of their own.

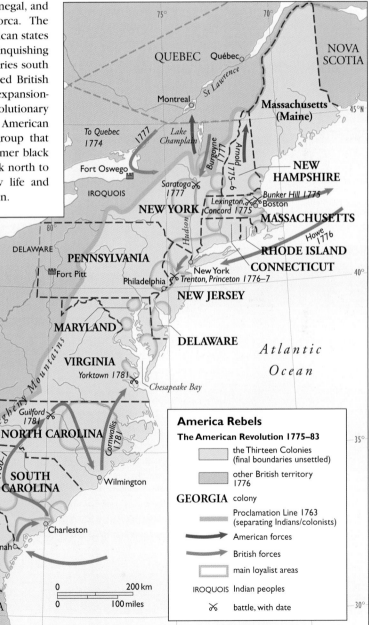

America Rebels

The American Revolution 1775–83

- the Thirteen Colonies (final boundaries unsettled)
- other British territory 1776
- GEORGIA colony
- Proclamation Line 1763 (separating Indians/colonists)
- American forces
- British forces
- main loyalist areas
- IROQUOIS Indian peoples
- ⚔ battle, with date

The Consolidation of Canada

After the American Revolution, the British government set about consolidating its remaining North American territories. But their vast extent, comparatively small population and semi-hostile French-speaking community made the task extremely difficult.

> *"[There exists] a most bitter animosity between the [French] Canadians and the British ... as different races engaged in a national contest. "*
>
> Lord Durham, letter, 9 August 1838

British Loyalists in the newly independent American states migrated north to the maritime colonies and especially to the west of the old province of Quebec, north of Lake Ontario. To accommodate them, New Brunswick was carved out of western Nova Scotia (1784), and Quebec divided into predominantly British Upper and French Lower Canada (1791). In the light of the American Revolution the government was determined to maintain a tight control and ruled through governors and reactionary landholding cliques, allowing virtually no power to the legislative assemblies or to French interests. This became a serious cause of tension.

French Nationalism

The first threat to British North America came with the War of 1812. The USA objected to Britain's attitude towards neutral American shipping during the Napoleonic Wars and desired further territorial conquest. After two years of inconclusive fighting, both sides agreed a peace based on the *status quo ante bellum*, but US aggression fostered a new patriotism among British North Americans. Meanwhile, many in the French community of Lower Canada lent increasing support to nationalist leaders, and to the rebellion of 1837 led by Louis-Joseph Papineau. A similar unsuccessful revolt occurred in Upper Canada under William Lyon Mackenzie. An inquiry by Lord Durham initiated 'responsible government', or partial autonomy, and an Act of Union (1840), which joined Upper and Lower Canada into a single colony with equal representation.

Until the 1840s the region prospered economically, and wheat was becoming a major product of Upper Canada. A significant, mostly Scottish, merchant class emerged in Montreal and was instrumental in establishing the North-West Company (1783) to compete with Hudson's Bay, shipping large quantities of furs from the St Lawrence. It also sponsored exploration to the west, notably Alexander Mackenzie's expedition to the Pacific coast in 1793, the first to cross North America, helping to establish British economic and political interests there.

Aided by large-scale immigration, the population of Upper and Lower Canada increased from 150,000 in 1773 to 600,000 in 1830. Land for set-

The army disperses rebels behind the Church of St Eustache during the Papineau Rebellion in 1837. Louis-Joseph Papineau (1786–1871) and his supporters, the Patriotes, believed that French-Canadians in Lower Canada (Quebec) were being unfairly treated and their culture undermined. During November 1837 riots led to clashes between the rebels and the superior forces of the Canadian government militia aided by British troops. The rebels were easily quashed at St Eustache and order was restored. Papineau fled to the United States before the fighting erupted but returned to politics in Quebec in 1845.

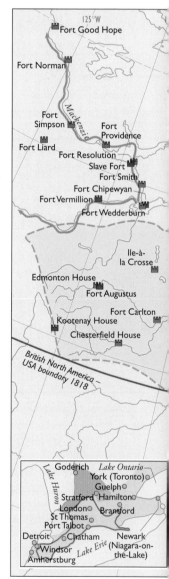

tlement was acquired from individuals and organizations favoured by government, such as the Canada Land Company which bought one million cheap acres adjoining Lake Huron in 1823. Many Scots settled in Rideau district and the area along the strategic Rideau Canal; Irish immigrants around Peterborough; and English colonists on Colonel Thomas Talbot's grant north of Lake Erie.

To the west, the Hudson's Bay Company granted the Earl of Selkirk around 116,000 square miles of territory to establish a colony of Scottish Highlanders in the Red River Valley during 1811–12, the first white settlement on the prairies. It was destroyed in 1816 by the French-Indian Métis, working for the rival North-West Company, who were against the occupation of their traditional hunting lands. Colonization resumed after the merger of the two companies in 1821, creating an imperial outpost that would later be incorporated into the Dominion as Manitoba. Western British North America was further defined in 1819 when the US-Canadian border from Lake Superior to the Rockies was established as the 49th parallel of latitude. Canada was taking shape.

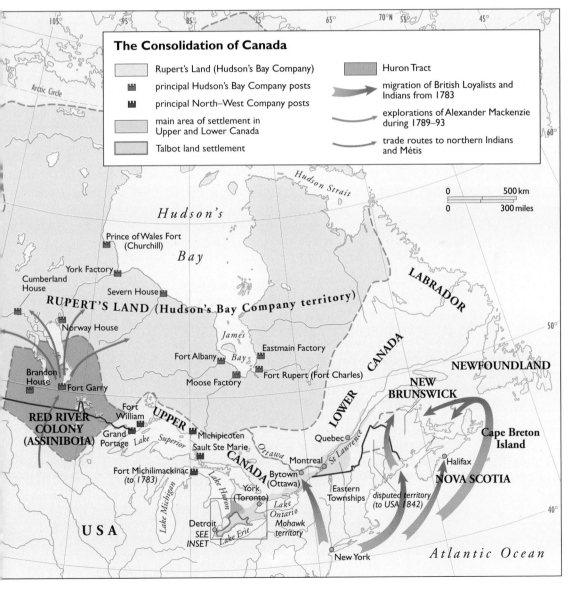

British West Indies Exploitation and emancipation

Economically the West Indian territories were vital to Britain, and by 1815 they achieved their greatest importance, responsible for 20 per cent of British trade. Conflict focused on the abolition of slavery as the region slipped into economic decline. White rule continued, but Britain needed to assume greater direct responsibility.

From the 1750s until the 1820s sugar was Britain's largest single import, fundamental to both the financial system and the Atlantic economy. Between 1795

and 1804 British shipping transported an estimated 242,100 slaves from West Africa to the British West Indies and a further 95,500 to a number of other American destinations. Furthermore, shipping and commerce benefited from reduced North American competition after the Revolutionary War. British goods were also in growing demand, and to promote trade with Spanish and French colonies the government established free ports in the West Indies from 1766. The wartime trade disruption after 1793 and the conquest of Trinidad allowed further commercial penetration of the Spanish territories, and by 1815 the free ports were at the receiving end of half of all Britain's exports to the West Indies.

Slaves cut the sugar on a plantation in Antigua in 1823. Once new slaves went to the plantation they were branded with 'estate marks'. Many did not survive the harshness of plantation life where the slaves existed only for work. Diseases such as dysentery and pneumonia killed many, the diet was poor, the work back-breaking and the discipline hard, if not cruel.

Anti-Slavery Movement

Internally, however, problems multiplied. There were increasing attacks on the wealthy, largely absentee, owners of the sugar plantations and the economic system that favoured them. The most serious threat was the anti-slavery movement championed by William Wilberforce, but reform was seriously checked by the French Revolution, whose libertarian message inspired the successful slave revolt in St Domingue in 1791, and by the war with France.

The region remained of great strategic importance and in the 1790s Britain committed 70,000 troops in several expeditions against French, Spanish and Dutch possessions. The Revolution (and subsequent emancipation of slaves) caused turmoil in the French West Indies and helped the British to capture the most productive sugar islands in 1793–4. The invasion of St Domingue, however, and failure to overcome the Jacobin subversion under Toussaint L'Ouverture led to their own expulsion in 1798. The French encouraged revolts in British Guadeloupe, Grenada and St Vincent (1795–6) and in Jamaica, where the independent Maroons (communities of escaped slaves and their descendants) were defeated during 1795–7. Most British conquests were handed back in the Treaty

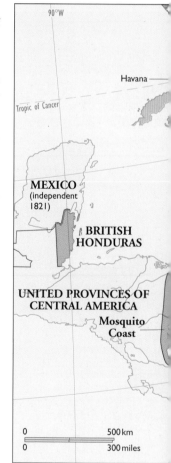

90°W

Havana

Tropic of Cancer

MEXICO
(independent 1821)

BRITISH HONDURAS

UNITED PROVINCES OF CENTRAL AMERICA

Mosquito Coast

0   500 km
0   300 miles

of Amiens (1802) but war resumed the following year and French territory was regained with ease.

In 1807 Britain introduced an empire-wide ban on the slave trade, persuaded by both moral arguments and the view that it was no longer indispensable. There were signs of natural population growth and rising productivity on the plantations, and the British economy was growing fast enough to offset any loss of tax revenue. Furthermore, it looked likely that all of Britain's main competitors would soon follow suit, a mistaken view that helped undermine the economy of the British Caribbean. Faced with growing competition from Brazil, Cuba, the USA and other sugar producers, British plantations struggled with declining income in the post-war deflation after 1815, a tightening labour supply and even soil exhaustion. Free ports also struggled as direct trade developed between Britain and the newly independent South and Central American states.

Yet abolitionist pressure was unrelenting. The Anti-Slavery Society formed in 1823 gave the movement new impetus and regulations to improve the condition of slaves emboldened local communities. Several slave revolts broke out and in western Jamaica (1831-2) a large insurrection caused loss of life and damage of over £1 million. With the vastly preponderant black slave population in Britain's colonies it was clear that slavery could not continue. The reformed House of Commons (1832) was more sympathetic to popular pressure, and against planter privilege, and passed the Emancipation Act in 1833 which saw around 750,000 slaves freed across the British Caribbean on 1 August 1834.

"This infernal commerce is carried on by the humane, the Christian inhabitants of Europe, whose ancestors have bled in the cause of liberty."

Thomas Percival, *A Father's Instructions to his Children* (1776)

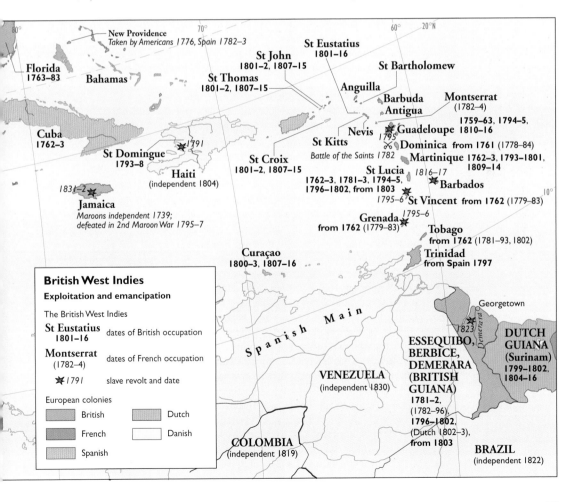

British West Indies

Exploitation and emancipation

The British West Indies

St Eustatius 1801–16   dates of British occupation

Montserrat (1782–4)   dates of French occupation

✳ *1791*   slave revolt and date

European colonies

▨ British		▨ Dutch
▨ French		☐ Danish
▨ Spanish		

Indian Riches The East India Company's conquests

India, the focus of Britain's later empire, was a vast dominion acquired in piecemeal fashion by a company of merchants. Its particular status was matched by the fragmentary and seemingly baffling manner of its creation, less by deliberate design than the dynamic created by local circumstances and the commercial penetration and military power of the East India Company.

> *"Conquests in India are not at all necessary to either our safety or comfort... We must be actuated by a sheer love of gain; a sheer love of plunder."*
>
> William Cobbett, essayist and political commentator, April 1808

In 1772 the British government introduced the Regulating Act designed to restore the East India Company to financial health, exercise some control over its political activities and, particularly, to restrain its urge to conquest. Warren Hastings (1772-86) became the first Governor General, in charge of all the Company's Indian territories and, although he wanted peace, his period in office was dominated by war. In 1778 his armies attacked the powerful Maratha chiefs, anxious to prevent a hostile alliance with the French, whose scattered trading posts were then captured for good measure. In the south Haidar Ali of Mysore, who had previously shown his effectiveness against the British in the first Mysore War (1767-9), joined forces with the Marathas and invaded the Carnatic (1780). Despite French naval and military support his attempt to take Madras was a failure, and Haidar himself died in 1782.

The Dynamic of Expansion

In 1790 Haidar's son and successor, Tipu Sultan, attacked the British protected state of Travancore, thus provoking an alliance between the Company and neighbouring states that felt equally threatened. In 1792 the Marquess of Cornwallis advanced to the Mysore capital, Seringapatam, and received Tipu's surrender, forcing him to pay an indemnity and cede extensive territories to the allies. Even with these gains, British territorial acquisitions during the late 18th century had been modest – but this changed radically from 1798 with the appointment of Richard Wellesley, Lord Mornington (1798-1805), aided by the precocious military talent of his brother Arthur, the future Duke of Wellington.

Wellesley was determined to impose peace, order and the benefits of British rule on the Indian peninsula, and to eradicate French rivalry in the princely states. He immediately introduced a system of 'subsidiary' alliances, subordinating rulers to British power, enforced by sepoy garrisons usually paid for by the cession of territory. Hyderabad became the first of these protectorates in 1798, followed by Mysore, which was invaded again the following year in the course of its fourth and final war with the British. The power of Tipu Sultan was broken at the storming of Seringapatam and half of Mysore's remaining territory was annexed to the Company. The Madras presidency was further enlarged with the annexation of the Carnatic, Tanjore and Arcot, confirming the British as the paramount power in southern India.

In 1801 Wellesley consolidated British control of Oudh, situated on the frontier Bihar adjoining Bengal, with a new treaty involving the cession of Doab and Rohilkhand. This involved closer involvement with the powerful Maratha chiefs and further warfare (and acquisitions) from 1802 to stamp British authority on northern India. The Company was increasingly unhappy at the escalating cost of his policies and Wellesley was summoned home three years later, leaving an even more turbulent political environment and continued opposition to the new British supremacy.

It was left to the Marquess of Hastings (Governor General 1813-23) to complete the subjugation of the Marathas in 1817-19, which brought control over

An engraving of Tipu Sultan from Edmund Scott's *Picturesque Scenery in the Kingdom of Mysore*. Tipu Sultan (1750–99), also known as 'The Tiger of Mysore', was only 15 when he first accompanied his father Haidar Ali into battle. After Haidar's death in 1782, Tipu ruled Mysore until 1799 when he died defending his capital of Seringapatam against the British. Tipu introduced a new calendar and new coinage among other innovations during his reign, which is remembered as an enlightened one.

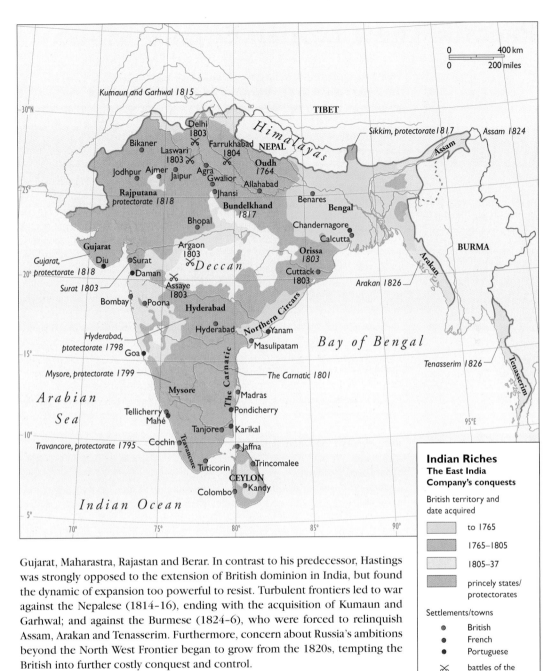

Indian Riches
The East India Company's conquests

British territory and date acquired

	to 1765
	1765–1805
	1805–37
	princely states/ protectorates

Settlements/towns

● British
● French
● Portuguese
✕ battles of the Maratha War 1803–5

Gujarat, Maharastra, Rajastan and Berar. In contrast to his predecessor, Hastings was strongly opposed to the extension of British dominion in India, but found the dynamic of expansion too powerful to resist. Turbulent frontiers led to war against the Nepalese (1814–16), ending with the acquisition of Kumaun and Garhwal; and against the Burmese (1824–6), who were forced to relinquish Assam, Arakan and Tenasserim. Furthermore, concern about Russia's ambitions beyond the North West Frontier began to grow from the 1820s, tempting the British into further costly conquest and control.

Throughout the period from the 1790s changes in the pattern of international trade undermined the Company's economic role and it lost its monopoly of British-Indian trade in 1813 (and with China in 1833). Increasingly, and with growing territorial dominion, it became an organization of government dependent on land and other revenues to fund its activities, pay the shareholder dividend and, in particular, finance the Company's huge army. This was probably more important as a motive for state expansion than the search for new markets and sources of materials. Ultimately, the British success can be ascribed to superior military organization and technology as much as to Indian disunity, and to a widespread desire for the peace and stability it ensured.

Part III: The Victorian Empire 1837–1901

By the 1830s, the British government was increasingly subject to the reforming zeal of free traders, Christian evangelicals and philosophical utilitarians. Gradually tariffs were reduced and the East India Company's monopoly on trade to the East was abolished. The Victorian mind ineluctably linked trade and prosperity with the encouragement of modernization and civilization in the less developed regions of the world. It also demanded reciprocation by other countries, which led to the imperialism of Free Trade.

During the Victorian period British overseas trade and investment grew rapidly. Many held out great hopes for trade with the huge Chinese empire, but it took the two Opium Wars (1839–42, 1856–60) to achieve international economic penetration. The trade of the British Empire continued to prosper, and with India especially. Here Britain's investment in infrastructure was seen to be achieving universal benefits, a vindication of territorial acquisition which, although often necessary for strategic reasons, also ensured British economic access in the face of foreign rivalry and protectionism.

Maritime power and a supervisory consular network supported Britain's desire to open up areas of the world to commerce and 'civilization' through free trade agreements. Unchallenged global naval supremacy, achieved at Trafalgar in 1805, allowed a massive reduction in the Royal Navy's strength at the end of the French wars in 1815. The fleet of more than 200 ships-of-the-line fell to 58 in 1835, sailors and marines to 27,000, and expenditure to £4.5 million. Like the army, however, the navy's commitments grew with the expansion of trade and empire and new threats appeared, increasing naval spending to £8 million and manpower to 45,000 by 1846.

Costs and Reforms

Maintaining Britain's global reach and responsibilities was a costly affair, so that economy and administrative efficiency were important factors behind British imperial reform. The vast distances involved also made centralized government from London impracticable, and British settlers would accept nothing less than the freedoms enjoyed at home. Disturbed conditions in Canada led to the Durham Report (1839) advocating 'responsible government' – representative internal self-government – as an effective and economical remedy eventually applied throughout the colonies of settlement. It revolutionized the British concept of empire and marked the first step on the road to the granting of Dominion and Commonwealth status to former colonies.

These reforms did much to retain the imperial loyalty of the white colonies, which gradually emerged as proto-states emulating Great Britain. Their sense of regional patriotism was developing, but stood alongside a British imperial identity, reinforced by kindred, racial and economic ties, and symbolically led by the Queen and royal family. All of the white colonies continued to rely on British power, investment, expertise and people. Between 1821 and 1911 the population of Britain increased from 14.1 to

Italian satirical cartoon showing the British Empire strangling the world (1878). Britain was sometimes criticized by other countries for its imperial endeavours, but it was not without its critics closer to home. The Scottish economist Adam Smith argued in *The Wealth of Nations* (1776) against the economic enterprise of empire: 'under the present system of management Great Britain derives nothing but loss from the dominion which she assumes over her colonies.' Smith's economic theories, however, also helped advance the Empire's growth.

UMBRE. *Progresso e civiltà riyorano il mondo .Molti credono l'Inghilterra una piccola bestia, e ben vedrasno che é un serpentone*

40.9 million, while that of Ireland declined from 6.8 to 4.4 million. Over the same period, some 17 million people left the British Isles to start new lives in British North America, the USA, Australia, New Zealand and southern Africa, where wage rates were higher and cultural differences minimal. By contrast, the Caribbean colonies fell from favour as a destination for emigrants.

Many other non-white territories were Crown Colonies, adopting British laws and institutions within a system of benevolent autocracy headed by a Governor, where local representation was entirely absent. India, ruled by the East India Company until 1858, and Ceylon were unique in substantially retaining their own laws and customs, but only after a major conflict over imperial policy in Britain itself. Evangelical Christians and radical liberals succeeded in imposing their dogmas on the wider Empire, ensuring the introduction, as William Wilberforce stated, 'of our own principles and opinions; of our laws, institutions and manners; above all, as the source of every other improvement, of our religion, and consequently of our morals' (1813). This civilizing mission – for this is how it was conceived – was also seen as a kind of obligation, the 'white man's burden'.

A procession of elephants of Nawab Muhammad Yusuf Ali of Rampur with units of the Queen's Own 7th Cavalry. How Britain managed to build its empire in India, where many of the states were well-organized and powerful, has been much debated. However, British leaders in India proved particularly shrewd at picking which princes should become their allies.

The millennial vision of brown-skinned Englishmen populating the Indian sub-continent, allowing Britain to discharge its sacred 'trusteeship', never became a reality. Liberal measures designed to transform the sub-continent, particularly associated with Governor General Lord Bentinck (1828–35), included land and law reform, the promotion of Western-style education and English as the official language. A class of Indians educated in the British manner emerged nationwide, and was to exercise a profound influence on the future of all parts of the sub-continent. But these changes also challenged the traditional way of life for both Hindu and Muslim, and the Company's attempts to eliminate social abuses were also seen as an affront to religious and cultural feeling, aggravated by the presence of Christian missionaries from 1813. The Indian Mutiny, or Revolt, of 1856 came as a severe shock to Britain and led to a re-evaluation of policy. The British fell back on practical reforms and a conservative agenda designed to promote material prosperity and stability. Lingering distrust, aloofness and racial prejudice anchored in a belief in British superiority remained.

The West Indies

Similar adjustments were required elsewhere, especially in the Caribbean. The abolition of slavery in 1834, leading to the exodus of former slaves from the sugar estates, bequeathed a labour shortage that was satisfied by indentured workers. It was a system too close to slavery for comfort, but large numbers of Indians, Africans, Pacific Islanders and Chinese were vital to the success of plantations and industries throughout the mainly tropical regions of the Empire.

In the British Caribbean, now suffering economic decline, the ruling white plantocracies remained hostile to black interests (and their church supporters) and pressure was applied to encourage local West Indians to labour on the plantations. Conflict over land and the absence of political representation resulted in the rebellion at Morant Bay, Jamaica, in 1865, brutally suppressed by Governor Eyre. He was subsequently censured and London took the opportunity to abolish the old colonial assemblies of Jamaica and some other West Indian islands in favour of direct Crown control. But white rule continued in another form and removed the threat of ultimate black majority rule that representative government threatened.

Elsewhere non-whites were outnumbered. The Aborigines in Australia, Maoris in New Zealand and Indians in North America were soon swept aside and white dominance assured. In South Africa the extension of British rule was more complicated, part of a three-way conflict between British, Afrikaners and Africans for control of land, labour and mineral resources. The Calvinist, independent-minded Boers were hungry for land and averse to British administrative and humanitarian interference, especially in relation to their slaves and servants. Their migration inland, outside the control of the British at the Cape, resulted in British recognition of Boer independence with the Sand River (1852) and Bloemfontein (1854) Conventions, anticipating the creation of the Transvaal Republic and the Orange Free State. The largely British settlers of the Cape and Natal also formed powerful enough groups to establish their own colonies over the heads of the majority African population.

The Anglo-Boer War

In the late 19th century diamond mining began to galvanize the Cape economy, followed by gold, found unfortunately for Britain in the Witwatersrand area of the Transvaal (1883–6). It provided an annual revenue to the Afrikaner republic of £1.5 million by 1889, regarded covetously by Britain and Cape politicians and business interests. It transformed the economic and political geography of South Africa, placing the Cape and Natal at a disadvantage and threatening Britain's strategic interests in the region. The Cape premier, Cecil Rhodes, the single most important investor in the diamond and gold industries, continued to pursue the idea of South African federation and imperial expansion. His government-chartered British South Africa Company began to annex land between the Limpopo and Zambezi and beyond to prospect for gold and prevent any further Boer expansion northwards. Although the gold mines were largely dependant on British manpower, expertise, capital, and ports and railways connecting the Afrikaner republics with the outside world, the Afrikaners refused economic co-operation with British South Africa and began building a railway line to Portuguese Delagoa Bay, outside British control. The British government, based on their old claim to suzerainty, used the pretext of the denial of rights to largely British mining and related personnel, the Uitlanders, to bring matters to a head.

In the ensuing (Second) Anglo-Boer War the size of the British war effort, which involved 400,000 imperial troops and cost £250 million, was too great for the Afrikaners, who also faced a largely hostile black population. The result was a forced political union to match the essential economic unity of the region. As Britain sought reconciliation with the Afrikaners, the real losers of the war were the Africans who were denied their land and civil rights, and who continued to suffer racial discrimination, later entrenched in the legislation of the Afrikaner-dominated Union government.

The war displayed British vulnerability to European rivalry – with Germany in particular, which gave tacit support to the Afrikaners. British superiority had been at its height between 1815 and 1870, a pre-eminence emphasized by the absence of strong rivals in Europe and America. This imbalance was later reversed, and Britain fell into relative decline, aggravating concerns for imperi-

WITH THE COLOURS.

ASPINALL'S ENAMEL

A magazine advertisement for Aspinall's enamel from the 1890s. From the late 19th century advertising penetrated all aspects of British life as manufacturers sought to reach customers in the new Victorian consumer society. As this period also witnessed the peak of the British Empire, advertising became an important tool for promoting the ideology of empire as well as its products.

al security, prompting demands for trade protection (Tariff Reform) and stimulating a more aggressive 'new imperialism'. To ensure the future of the British 'race', in the Earl of Rosebery's words, 'we should … grossly fail [if we] decline to take our share in a partition of the world which we have not forced on, but which has been forced upon us' (1893).

The most dramatic partition took place in Africa. The reasons are complex, reflecting a desire to promote economic and strategic interests in an atmosphere of exaggerated hope and anxiety, and different in each part of the continent. The short sea route to and from Britain to India and the East, involving the overland crossing between Alexandria and Suez, assumed great strategic importance, even more so after the opening of the Suez Canal (1869). Overarching interests in Egypt and the Nile Valley, where Britain faced down a French challenge at Fashoda in 1898, and South Africa, still an important route to the East, were an important factor. In little more than a decade from 1880, over 100 million people and 10 million square miles of territory were brought under European rule, partitioning the continent in its modern form.

The Great Game

Rivalry with Russia was also coming to a climax. From the Black Sea to Siberia, Britain was determined to oppose any Russian threat, both to India and to the imperial lines of communication through the Ottoman Empire. Propping up this 'sick man of Europe' became an axiom of British foreign policy. Between the 1820s and 1907 the 'Great Game' was played by governments and armies spanning the Asian landmass, using diplomacy, influence, financial support, subversion and force to protect their interests and obtain mastery of the East.

Britain's military and economic resources in India were formidable. In 1850 the Crown and Company's armed forces in India numbered 275,000, paid for by Indian taxpayers. By 1910 the Indian Army strength was 226,700 plus 88,000 volunteer and reserve troops, costing £20 million annually. India and its immense military power – unhindered by democratic constraints – acted as a stimulus to expansion both within the subcontinent against the Russian threat from the north; and, as Britain's oriental army, further afield in wars and expeditions from Malta to China.

At the time of Queen Victoria's Diamond Jubilee in 1897, in the words of Clement Attlee, 'nearly a quarter of the globe owed allegiance to the widow of Windsor', the head of a 'great empire ruled by the people of a little island, safe behind the guns of the British fleet'.

An illustration of the colonial armies made in celebration of Queen Victoria's jubilee in 1887. Unparalleled imperial expansion took place during Victoria's reign, with territories gained in almost every quarter of the globe.

But Britain was finding the cost unsustainable. From 1889, German rivalry provoked a vast increase in naval estimates, to £23.8 million in 1898 (287 ships and 97,000 men) and on to the First World War. At the same time, pressure was growing for costly social reform at home. The Anglo-Boer War exposed diplomatic, military and economic weaknesses which Britain's government was now determined to remedy. But the new opposition to empire that emerged gave credence to the view, attributed by Attlee to Field Marshall Smuts, that 'the South African War was the beginning of the end of imperialism'. The British Empire had turned a corner.

Heyday of Empire

In the early Victorian period Britain was generally content with informal control of overseas territories. Markets were more important than territorial title and authority and economic access were achieved without the need for expensive administration. But gradually the Empire expanded and by the end of the century the new challenges to British supremacy resulted in vast new acquisitions in defence of British interests.

"Each one of us ... is a working part of this world-shaping force. How small you must feel in face of this stupendous whole, and yet how great to be a unit in it! "

G. W. Steevens,
Daily Mail,
23 June 1897

The key to British power was remarkable economic development. The profits of agriculture and trade financed the Industrial Revolution that began in Britain, and by the mid-19th century the country was producing 40 per cent of world manufactured goods. Merchants sought out new markets in the Ottoman Empire, South America and especially India, where British textile imports rose from 253 million yards in 1830 to 3,562 million yards in 1875. By 1900 India consumed almost one-fifth of British exports at a time when the Empire as a whole accounted for one-third of British trade, absorbing manufactured goods in exchange for foodstuffs and raw materials.

As Europe and North America industrialized countries increasingly traded

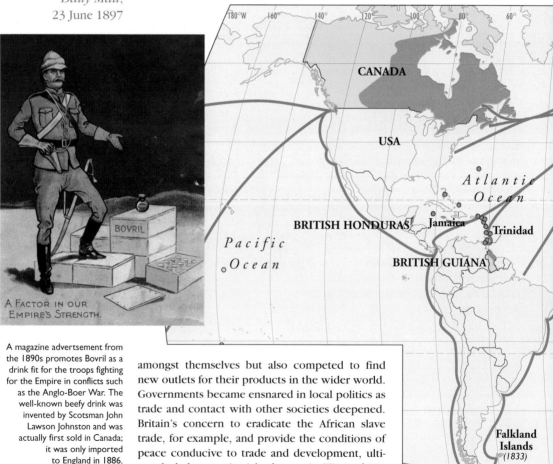

A magazine advertisement from the 1890s promotes Bovril as a drink fit for the troops fighting for the Empire in conflicts such as the Anglo-Boer War. The well-known beefy drink was invented by Scotsman John Lawson Johnston and was actually first sold in Canada; it was only imported to England in 1886.

amongst themselves but also competed to find new outlets for their products in the wider world. Governments became ensnared in local politics as trade and contact with other societies deepened. Britain's concern to eradicate the African slave trade, for example, and provide the conditions of peace conducive to trade and development, ultimately led to territorial advance in West Africa.

Political instability, often the result of the impact of western industry and politics, was seen as a threat to British interests and led to further involvement.

Although ambitious local agents had always encouraged imperial 'creep', the dynamic of territorial acquisition gained pace in the late 19th century as governments moved to protect their colonies and economic interests. British motivations can be seen most clearly in Egypt, where financial investments, concern to protect the route to the East, political instability and rivalry with France all contributed to the British conquest in 1882. Similar issues were at play in South Africa, where control of mineral wealth was a powerful incentive.

Challenges to Empire

The 1880s witnessed the start of the great power rivalry that carved up the whole world by 1914, an aggressive 'new imperialism' that was a response to the threatening international situation. These new territorial gains were a recognition of imperial weakness just as Germany was overtaking Britain as the world's main industrial power, and challenging for naval predominance. The second Anglo-Boer War (1899–1902) made clear that Britain could not maintain a policy of splendid isolation nor the expense of global domination. In 1902 the Anglo-Japanese alliance helped Britain confront Russia in the East, followed by agreements with France and Russia leading to the Triple Entente in 1907, relieving much of their imperial rivalry. The era of unalloyed supremacy was over.

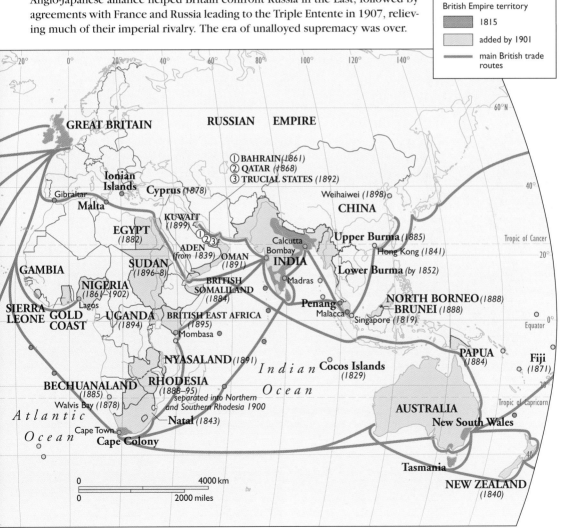

Heyday of Empire

British Empire territory

- 1815
- added by 1901
- main British trade routes

Naval Power and Gunboat Diplomacy

*"A British
subject, in
whatever land
he may be, shall
feel confident that
the watchful eye
and the strong
arm of England
will protect him
against injustice
and wrong. "*

Lord Palmerston,
Foreign Secretary,
25 June 1850

*By the mid-19th century increasing numbers of Royal Navy ships
were stationed overseas (63 in 1817, 129 in 1848) to maintain
the* **Pax Britannica***. They were reliant on a chain of strategic
bases, themselves centres of local power and control, and coaling
stations which accompanied the gradual adoption of steam by the
navy from the 1820s, a revolutionary technology which reinforced
Britain's maritime supremacy.*

Many of the new steamers were small, shallow-draught, iron- (later steel-) hulled
gunboats, able to penetrate coastal areas previously inaccessible; these vessels
became characteristic of the Victorian navy. Their speed, reliability and powerful new armaments made them a potent tool of imperialism. The East India
Company was the first to use steamers in warfare (against the Burmese in
1824–6) but the gunboat was developed further and adopted in large numbers
by the Royal Navy during the Crimean War (1854–6). The new technology was
especially associated with the high-handed diplomacy and blunt use of naval
and military force of Lord Palmerston (Foreign Secretary 1830–41 and 1846–51,
Prime Minister 1855–8), most notably to open China's huge market to western
trade in the Opium Wars from 1839.

Minor displays of naval power were equally impressive, whether chastising

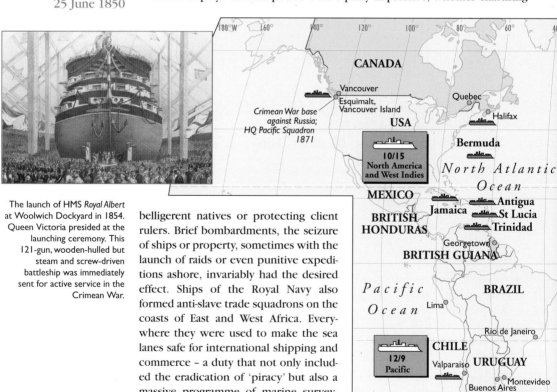

The launch of HMS *Royal Albert*
at Woolwich Dockyard in 1854.
Queen Victoria presided at the
launching ceremony. This
121-gun, wooden-hulled but
steam and screw-driven
battleship was immediately
sent for active service in the
Crimean War.

belligerent natives or protecting client
rulers. Brief bombardments, the seizure
of ships or property, sometimes with the
launch of raids or even punitive expeditions ashore, invariably had the desired
effect. Ships of the Royal Navy also
formed anti-slave trade squadrons on the
coasts of East and West Africa. Everywhere they were used to make the sea
lanes safe for international shipping and
commerce – a duty that not only included the eradication of 'piracy' but also a
massive programme of marine surveying. It all contributed to further imperial
entanglements.

Overwhelming naval power not only
allowed Britain to create a vast territorial

empire but also an informal empire of domination, including protectorates and spheres of influence. In the Persian Gulf, British India's intervention against what it termed Arab 'piracy' led to agreements with the sheikhdoms of the Trucial Coast, Qatar, Bahrain and later Kuwait. The maritime peace and British interests were enforced by an Indian Navy squadron, superseded by the Royal Navy in 1871, supporting the British Resident at Bushire. Elsewhere, as in Latin America, the Royal Navy applied selective pressure to aid commercial penetration which itself gave considerable influence in local political affairs. Between 1850 and 1913 South America was responsible for around 10 per cent of British exports and imports; and by 1865 investment in the region had reached £81 million. A similar process occurred in the Ottoman Empire and Egypt to protect British strategic interests.

From the 1850s, Britains leaders became concerned that a widely scattered navy of small ships existed at the expense of a strong main fleet. Worries about French and Russian invasions in the 1840s and 1850s were heightened by the perceived weaknesses exposed in the Royal Navy during the Crimean War. The country put its faith in the development of the new powerful steam ironclads (and telegraphic communications) together with a concentration of forces in home waters, which also permitted reduced fleet numbers and expenditure. Only in the mid-1880s did concern about naval weakness lead to a re-ordering of naval priorities and a large shipbuilding programme from 1889. The big-gun battlefleet now superseded the gunboat navy; this process obscured the relative decline of British naval power and its maritime domination.

Naval Power and Gunboat Diplomacy

British Empire 1901

naval bases

(1852) new naval bases acquired after 1848, with date

14/4 South America

naval station, with numbers of ships in 1848/1898

Peopling the Empire Imperial migration 1815–1924

Emigration from Britain to the colonies was driven by wider changes in industrial and agricultural organization, by personal poverty and by the prospect of better opportunities abroad. Many emigrants successfully found new homes and modest prosperity. This huge movement of population was essential to imperial development.

"This is what England must do or perish: she must found colonies as fast and as far as she is able, formed of her most energetic and worthiest men. "

John Ruskin, inaugural lecture, Oxford (1870)

Large numbers of reluctant emigrants left Ireland in the Great Famine of the 1840s and the Scottish Highlands in the wake of the land clearances. A drift from the British countryside to the towns continued throughout the 19th century, but agricultural and other skilled workers were in constant demand in the colonies. Emigration was further encouraged by cheaper and speedier steamship passages and better communications, and assisted by a growing number of societies with charitable and religious aims. Some of these societies sought to build a new Jerusalem, like the Free Church of Scotland which

Peopling the Empire
Imperial migration 1815–1924

Numbers of migrants, dates and destinations

British
1. **4,213,362** 1815–1914 (Canada)
2. **13,714,007** 1815–1914 (USA)
3. **2,359,961** 1815–1914 (Australia & NZ)
4. **761,504** 1871–1914 (Cape and Natal)

Indians
5. **39,437** 1895–1922 (East Africa)
6. **455,187** 1834–1910 (Mauritius)
7. **152,932** 1860–1911 (Natal)
8. **c.440,000** 1837–1918 (British Caribbean)
9. **1,754,000** 1844–1910 (Malaya)
10. **2,321,000** 1843–1924 (Ceylon)
11. **1,164,000** 1852–1924 (Burma)
12. **61,015** 1879–1916 (Fiji)

Chinese
13. **63,695** 1904–1907 (northern Chinese to Transvaal gold mines)
14. **123,734** 1854–1880 (Chinese from Hong Kong to Australia and New Zealand)
15. **186,109** 1855–1880 (Chinese from Hong Kong to SE Asia)

Pacific Islanders
16. **89,000** 1863–1911 (Fiji and Queensland)

liberated African slaves ('Recaptives') post 1840
17. **40,000** 1834–1920 (British Caribbean)

established a colony in Otago, New Zealand, in 1848. Later, shipping and railway companies encouraged emigration for commercial reasons and the trade became more sophisticated with propaganda and professional agents.

Colonial governments, using subsidized passages and land grants, also became heavily involved in attracting settlers; the British government too was increasingly inclined to finance emigration, for example providing £10,000 to re-settle Hebridean families in Canada in 1888 to avert social unrest. North America was the most popular destination, being closer to Britain and cheaper to reach than the

Antipodes, although the 1837 Canadian rebellions and gold strikes in the 1850s heightened the appeal of Australia. Similar discoveries boosted the popularity of South Africa from the 1860s. Temporary career migrants were found throughout the colonies.

After the abolition of slavery in the British Empire in 1834 alternative supplies of labour were required for the tropical plantations. A small number of Africans liberated from slave ships by the Royal Navy went to work in the Caribbean, but Indian indentured labourers were increasingly employed on the sugar plantations of Mauritius, the Caribbean (from 1845), Natal (1860), Fiji (1879) and in other plantations throughout the East. From 1895 they were also recruited to build the Uganda Railway in East Africa. In the last quarter of the century annual migration from India rose to over 425,000 per annum.

The Chinese were also widely recruited for the plantations and mines of South East Asia, the Caribbean, the Antipodes and South Africa, and played a major role in the building of the transcontinental Canadian Pacific Railway in the 1880s. Pacific islanders from Melanesia and Micronesia also worked in the sugar plantations of Queensland (to 1904) and Fiji (to 1911).

An advertisement enticing potential emigrants to Canada for new farming opportunities. British migration to Canada was to rise to 65,000 per year by 1905.

Policies of white preference, increasing indigenous populations, the decline of the

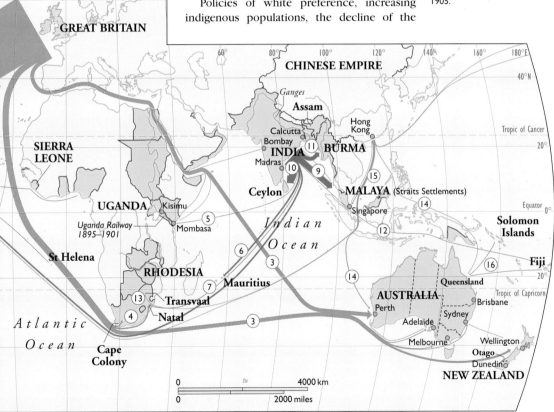

plantation sugar economies and nationalist opposition to the indentured labour system began to restrict these flows of population in the period up to the First World War. Apart from continued British emigration to the white colonies, the age of mass migration to the Empire was over.

Eastern Promise Imperial trade and the Far East

Towards the end of the 18th century British interest grew in trade with China, initially monopolized by the East India Company. Although the trade never flourished as expected, Britain established a dominant position in the Far East, acquiring territories on the strategic routes between India and China to satisfy the demands of security, trade and economic exploitation.

" You come to [China] merely to covet profit....You use opium to injure our common people, cheating us of silver and cash. "

'Placard of the patriotic people of Kwangtung denouncing the English barbarians' (1841)

Apart from the early trading base at Bencoolen in Sumatra, the first British footholds in the Far East were the Malayan way-stations, notably Penang, Malacca and Singapore (founded by Stamford Raffles in 1819), consolidated as the Straits Settlements in 1826. Economic interest, turbulent frontiers and the attack on piracy guaranteed a creeping British control of the peninsula. Abolition of the East India Company's monopoly of China trade in 1833 introduced a flood of new merchants demanding access to Chinese markets. China's desire to suppress the lucrative trade in Indian opium sparked the first Opium War (1839-42), in which Britain acquired Hong Kong and the opening of five treaty ports to international trade. Further concessions followed the second Opium (or Arrow) War (1856-60). More threatening to China were several internal revolts, notably the Taiping Rebellion (1850-64) suppressed with the aid of foreign military officers, notably Major (later General) Charles Gordon, as Britain now sought to create conditions of stability.

Siam and Malaya

Although the value of British trade with China was comparatively low (exports were worth £5 million out of a total of £70 million in 1869 and proportionately less by 1900) Britain dominated foreign trade and investment. A similar influence developed in Siam, which judiciously signed free trade agreements from 1855 and relinquished territory to France in the east and Britain in the Malayan peninsula. European rivalry in the Far East grew from around 1870. Britain signed the Pangkor Engagement with Perak in 1874, inaugurating a series of protectorates across the Malayan peninsula, a region of growing value as a source of tin and, later, rubber and coffee. In 1896 four sultanates were joined into the Federated Malay States in the move towards a unified Malaya. Siam formally recognized British influence in the region (1896) and ceded more territories in 1909.

China remained near collapse in the late 19th century, and drew further foreign demands for economic and territorial concessions. In 1898 Britain acquired Weihaiwei as a naval base to match Russia's Port Arthur. At the same time, China was partitioned into spheres of economic interest which left Britain with supremacy across most of the south. The anti-foreign Boxer Rising of 1900 led to international intervention, but the cost was increased Chinese hostility and the dilution of British influence by 1914.

Elsewhere British power was consolidated. In Burma King Thibaw, with French encouragement, provoked a British invasion in 1885 which resulted in the complete annexation of the country, and in 1888 Britain exerted a protectorate over North Borneo. It combined Sarawak (patrimony of the 'white rajah' James Brooke and his descendants from 1841), the territory of the British North Borneo Company (chartered 1881), and the Sultanate of Brunei which had already ceded the island of Labuan as a coaling station in 1846. Britain's eastern empire was complete.

An illustration of the 1900 Boxer Rising in China. The Boxers were a secret society which grew out of the anti-Western feeling sparked by the increasing commercial influence of foreign powers in China in the late-19th century. In June 1900 the Boxers occupied Beijing for eight weeks, attacking foreigners and Chinese Christians. The siege was broken by an international force that included British, American and Japanese troops.

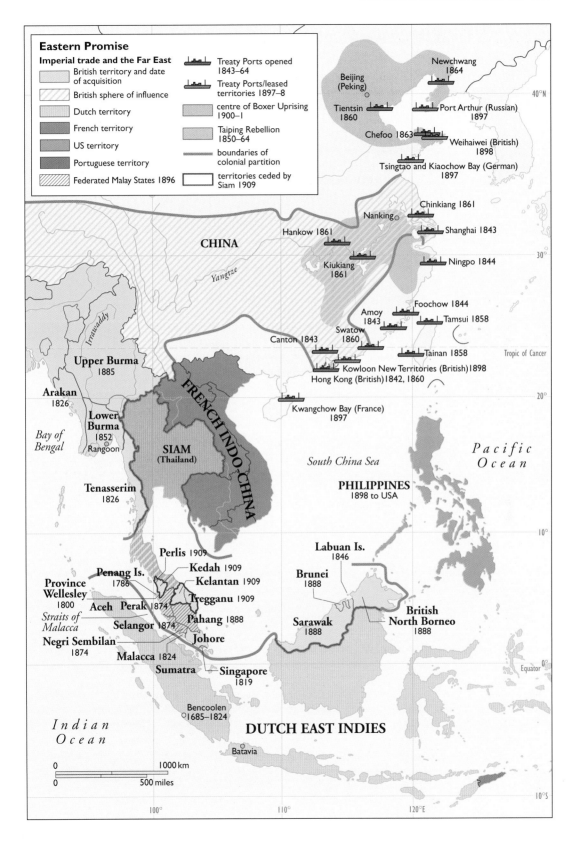

Eastern Promise

Imperial trade and the Far East

- British territory and date of acquisition
- British sphere of influence
- Dutch territory
- French territory
- US territory
- Portuguese territory
- Federated Malay States 1896
- Treaty Ports opened 1843–64
- Treaty Ports/leased territories 1897–8
- centre of Boxer Uprising 1900–1
- Taiping Rebellion 1850–64
- boundaries of colonial partition
- territories ceded by Siam 1909

Newchwang 1864

Beijing (Peking)

Tientsin 1860

Port Arthur (Russian) 1897

Chefoo 1863

Weihaiwei (British) 1898

Tsingtao and Kiaochow Bay (German) 1897

40°N

CHINA

Nanking

Chinkiang 1861

Hankow 1861

Shanghai 1843

Kiukiang 1861

Ningpo 1844

30°

Yangtze

Foochow 1844

Amoy 1843

Tamsui 1858

Swatow 1860

Canton 1843

Tainan 1858

Tropic of Cancer

Irrawaddy

Upper Burma 1885

Kowloon New Territories (British)1898

Hong Kong (British)1842, 1860

Arakan 1826

Kwangchow Bay (France) 1897

20°

Lower Burma 1852

Rangoon

Bay of Bengal

SIAM (Thailand)

FRENCH INDO-CHINA

Pacific Ocean

Tenasserim 1826

South China Sea

PHILIPPINES 1898 to USA

10°

Perlis 1909

Labuan Is. 1846

Kedah 1909

Penang Is. 1786

Kelantan 1909

Brunei 1888

Province Wellesley 1800

Aceh Perak 1874

Tregganu 1909

British North Borneo 1888

Straits of Malacca

Selangor 1874

Pahang 1888

Sarawak 1888

Negri Sembilan 1874

Johore

Malacca 1824

Sumatra   Singapore 1819

Equator

0°

Bencoolen 1685–1824

DUTCH EAST INDIES

Indian Ocean

Batavia

0   1000 km

0   500 miles

10°S

100°   110°   120°E

71

The Scramble for Africa

Towards the end of the 19th century European imperial rivalry reached fever pitch in the 'Scramble for Africa'. In the last two decades of the century, European rule was extended over all parts of the continent except Ethiopia and Liberia. The impetus to colonial expansion was as often a desire to forestall European rivals as to gain economic or political benefits.

"We have been witnesses of one of the most remarkable episodes in the history of the world."

Sir John Scott Keltie, *The Partition of Africa* (1893)

European interest in Africa deepened in the early 19th century. Demand grew for African commodities such as groundnuts and palm oil, and Europeans increasingly explored the interior of the continent, aided by the discovery that quinine greatly reduced deaths from malaria. Pressures increased for European governments to intervene, and in this missionaries were highly influential, especially David Livingstone (1813–73), who was devoted to bringing 'civilization' through Christianity and commerce and an end to the slave trade.

In West Africa British anti-slave trade patrols, agreements and resident consuls brought further entanglement. British intervention in Yoruba affairs led to permanent rule in 1861, just as palm oil exports reached £1 million annually. Asante attacks on Britain's coastal forts and allies led to the Third Anglo-Asante War (1873–4) and the creation of the Gold Coast Colony. After a long period of creeping imperialism, the partitioning of sub-tropical Africa was under way.

By the 1880s Britain was becoming increasingly vulnerable to international competition. France, Germany and King Leopold of Belgium extended their

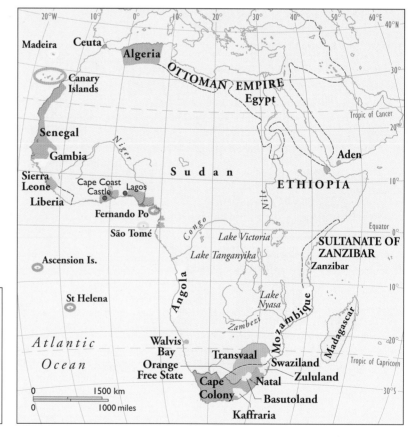

The Scramble for Africa I

European-controlled territory c. 1870

- British
- French
- Spanish
- Portuguese
- Afrikaner

The Scramble for Africa II

European-controlled territory, 1914

- British
- French
- German
- Portuguese
- Spanish
- Belgian
- Italian

Mahdist state 1881–98

✗ battle and date

African empires, while Britain occupied Egypt. The Berlin Conference of 1884 established the ground rules for European expansion in Africa but also intensified the process. Britain chartered the Royal Niger Company (1886) as the main vehicle of expansion in the future Nigeria, and the Imperial British East Africa Company (chartered 1888) laid claim to the territory now comprising Kenya and Uganda. To the north, French expansion towards the Nile Valley was halted by the Fashoda Crisis (see page 76).

Empire in Southern Africa

In southern Africa the British and Boer contest over resources was intensified by the discovery of diamonds (1867), and gold (1885). Concern at prospective rival European alliances with the Afrikaner republics led to a comprehensive British annexation of south-eastern coastal territory and Bechuanaland. Cecil Rhodes, pre-eminent among the Cape imperialists, set out to exploit gold resources north of the Limpopo through the agency of his British South Africa Company (chartered 1889). Its territorial claims confined the Boers, prevented the union of Portuguese Angola and Mozambique and halted King Leopold's expansion into Central Africa. The incorporation of the rich Transvaal territories into the Empire came only with the second Anglo-Boer War (1899–1902).

The impact on Africans, apart from loss of freedom, was profound. Traditional cultures were undermined by new economic demands for labour and taxes. Sometimes Europeans were invited in as protection against rivals or other European predators, but were then impossible to evict. African attempts to regain their independence were mostly short-lived, though the Mahdist revolt in the Anglo-Egyptian Sudan (1881–98) endured longer than most.

South African Supremacy The Anglo-Boer wars

The British concern to protect the Cape was frustrated by Boer expansion and African opposition to European encroachment. Only after the second Anglo-Boer War did British power finally become a reality across the whole of South Africa.

"We had the delusion ... that the ... clique of financiers in Johannesburg stood for freedom and democracy, and we cheerfully joined up to fight. "

Earl Attlee on the Second Anglo-Boer War, *Empire into Commonwealth* (1960)

The Cape government struggled to achieve stability on the frontier. Migrant *voortrekkers* defeated a Zulu army in 1838 and established the Republic of Natalia, annexed by Britain in 1843, and once again the Afrikaners departed northwards. British conflict with the Xhosa led to the annexation of Queen Adelaide's Land (British Kaffraria) in 1847 and to further acquisitions. In the north, treaties were made with the Griqua people, and in 1848 Britain created the Orange River Sovereignty. But ongoing conflict was a costly burden, and Britain recognized the independent Boer republics in the early 1850s.

This imperial retreat left allies vulnerable to Afrikaner expansion, but the discovery of diamonds on the lower Vaal River in 1867 galvanized the British. Diamond-rich Griqualand West was annexed, followed by the impoverished Transvaal republic itself in 1877 in order to achieve stability and forestall rival European involvement. The refusal of the Zulus to submit to the *Pax Britannica* led to a British invasion and disastrous defeat at Isandhlwana (1879) before the Zulus were vanquished at Ulundi. The episode undermined British authority and when Gladstone dashed hopes of renewed Transvaal independence in

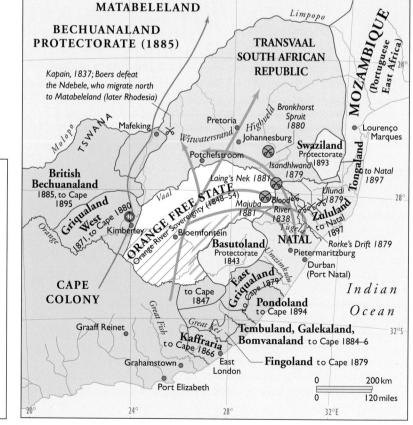

South African Supremacy I

- ✂ battle and date
- ⊗ First Anglo-Boer War battle
- ◉ diamond field
- → the Great Trek 1835–40
- TSWANA African people
- ▢ Cape Colony
- ▢ Natal
- ▢ Orange Free State
- ▢ Transvaal
- ▨ Adam Kok's Land
- ▧ conquered by Orange Free State from Basuto 1866
- → route to the north

The Afrikaners, armed with their efficient bolt-action Mauser rifles, taught the British some hard lessons during the Second Boer War.

1880, the Afrikaners rebelled and defeated Britain in the First Anglo-Boer War. Their independence was restored in 1881 and once again Britain struggled with the problem of containment. Boer encroachment on Tswana territory and the strategic route to the north led to the annexation of what became British Bechuanaland in 1885 and a protectorate was established over the remainder.

The discovery of gold in the Transvaal (1885) emboldened Afrikaner nationalists opposed to co-operation with British South Africa. In 1896 Cape imperialists backed the Jameson Raid to overthrow the Transvaal government; its failure soured relations further. Transvaal cultivated the support of Germany and France, while Britain encouraged the territorial consolidation of the Cape and Natal, culminating in the outbreak of the Second Anglo-Boer War in 1899. Some 35,000 Boer militiamen overran large areas of territory, defeated British forces at Magersfontein, Colenso and Stormberg, and invested Ladysmith, Mafeking and Kimberley. After Generals Roberts and Kitchener reversed the initial shock and invaded the two republics, 15,000 Boers switched to a guerrilla war. New British tactics included a 'scorched earth' policy, in which thousands of farms were destroyed and concentration camps were established for Boer sympathizers. The war was ended by the Treaty of Vereeniging in 1902.

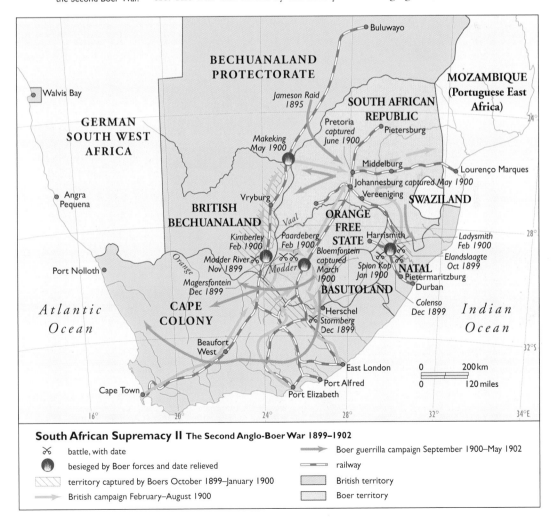

South African Supremacy II The Second Anglo-Boer War 1899–1902

- battle, with date
- besieged by Boer forces and date relieved
- territory captured by Boers October 1899–January 1900
- British campaign February–August 1900
- Boer guerrilla campaign September 1900–May 1902
- railway
- British territory
- Boer territory

Egypt and the Route to the East

The 'overland' route to India across Egypt, and trade with the eastern Mediterranean, were increasingly important to Britain from the early 19th century. The opening of the Suez Canal (1869) further emphasized the significance of Egypt. Its defence lay at the heart of much of Britain's imperial policy in both Africa and the Middle East.

> *"[Egypt] is on the high road to the far East. It can never cease to be an object of interest to all the Powers of Europe, and especially to England."*
>
> Lord Cromer,
> *Modern Egypt*
> (1908)

To counter perceived French and Russian ambitions, Britain sought to maintain the territorial integrity of the Ottoman Empire, of which Egypt was a nominal part. Here, Britain opposed the separatist ambitions of the Khedive (governor) Muhammad Ali (ruled 1805–48) who set about modernizing the Egyptian state and economy with the aid of French advisers. Burdened with European demands, Egypt's economy remained weak and foreign loans were wasted on the imperial ambitions of Khedive Ismail (1863–79) in Sudan and elsewhere. A large proportion of the cost of building the Suez Canal, primarily a French scheme, had also been passed off onto the Egyptian government.

By 1875 Egypt was virtually bankrupt and the Khedives' ambitions were in ruins. To raise cash, Ismail sold his shares in the Canal to Britain, but the following year Britain and France jointly took control of Egypt's finances, and increasingly its administration too. Nationalist unrest led to a British naval bombardment of Alexandria in July 1882. France stood back, and Britain, concerned for the safety of the Canal and fearing an alliance of French and nationalist forces, invaded and defeated the Egyptians under 'Urabi (Arabi) Pasha at Tel el-Kebir in September.

The British had intended a temporary occupation, but a lack of reliable collaborators, and events in the south, made this impossible. Ismail's assault on the Sudan and the slave trade, employing Christian Europeans (notably Sir Herbert Baker and General Charles Gordon) provoked revolt in Kordofan province in 1881, led by an Islamic holy man, Muhammad Ahmad, the 'Mahdi'. It spread rapidly and an Egyptian army under Colonel William Hicks was annihilated at Omdurman in September 1883. The British decided on withdrawal, but Gordon, who was sent to direct an orderly retreat, dug in at Khartoum instead and endured a siege of ten months. The relief expedition arrived two days after his death during the Mahdist capture of the city (26 January 1885).

The Fashoda Incident

Egypt, effectively ruled by the British Consul-General, was returned to solvency in 1889. The Sudan was left to Mahdist rule, and Britain took steps to ensure that other European powers did not exploit Anglo-Egyptian weakness. Agreements with Italy (1891) and King Leopold II of Belgium (1894) fixed Sudan's borders with Eritrea and Congo Free State. In the south, Uganda was declared a protectorate in 1894, and work began on constructing the strategic Uganda Railway the following year. But the main threat came from French territories to the west. The French government retained ambitions for expansion through the Sudan, perhaps ultimately to unite French West African territories with French Somaliland on the Red Sea. With control of the Upper Nile, France would also be able to threaten the British position in Egypt.

Britain decided to reconquer the Sudan, and in 1898 Sir Herbert Kitchener's Anglo-Egyptian army defeated the Sudanese at Atbara (April) and Omdurman (September), where 11,000 followers of the Khalifa were slaughtered. Kitchener continued up the Nile to Fashoda to intercept Jean-Baptiste Marchand's small expeditionary force asserting French claims in the Nile Valley. The con-

Portrait of Major General Lord Kitchener (1850–1916). In 1892 he became commander-in-chief of the Egyptian army. He earned national fame and a knighthood in 1898 when he overwhelmed the Mahdi's forces in Sudan. As Military Governor and then Governor General he initiated the rebuilding of Khartoum, began large-scale irrigation schemes and established a modern government administration.

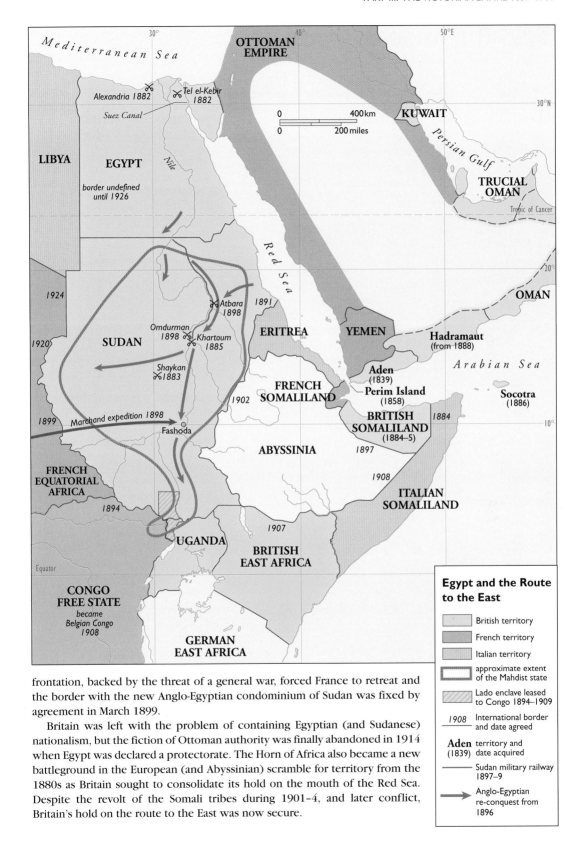

Mediterranean Sea

OTTOMAN EMPIRE

30°

40°

50°E

Alexandria 1882

Tel el-Kebir 1882

Suez Canal

30°N

KUWAIT

0   400km

0   200 miles

LIBYA

EGYPT

Nile

border undefined until 1926

TRUCIAL OMAN

Persian Gulf

Tropic of Cancer

Red Sea

1924

1891

20°

OMAN

1920

Atbara 1898

Omdurman 1898

Khartoum 1885

ERITREA

YEMEN

Hadramaut (from 1888)

Arabian Sea

SUDAN

Shaykan 1883

Aden (1839)

FRENCH SOMALILAND

Perim Island (1858)

Socotra (1886)

1899

Marchand expedition 1898

1902

BRITISH SOMALILAND (1884–5)

1884

10°

Fashoda

FRENCH EQUATORIAL AFRICA

ABYSSINIA

1897

1908

ITALIAN SOMALILAND

1894

UGANDA

1907

Equator

BRITISH EAST AFRICA

CONGO FREE STATE

became Belgian Congo 1908

GERMAN EAST AFRICA

Egypt and the Route to the East

British territory

French territory

Italian territory

approximate extent of the Mahdist state

Lado enclave leased to Congo 1894–1909

1908 International border and date agreed

Aden territory and (1839) date acquired

Sudan military railway 1897–9

Anglo-Egyptian re-conquest from 1896

frontation, backed by the threat of a general war, forced France to retreat and the border with the new Anglo-Egyptian condominium of Sudan was fixed by agreement in March 1899.

Britain was left with the problem of containing Egyptian (and Sudanese) nationalism, but the fiction of Ottoman authority was finally abandoned in 1914 when Egypt was declared a protectorate. The Horn of Africa also became a new battleground in the European (and Abyssinian) scramble for territory from the 1880s as Britain sought to consolidate its hold on the mouth of the Red Sea. Despite the revolt of the Somali tribes during 1901–4, and later conflict, Britain's hold on the route to the East was now secure.

The Raj The heyday of British India

The conquest and control of the Indian subcontinent by the East India Company acquired its own momentum in the early 19th century and by the 1850s British dominion was largely complete. Perhaps more difficult were the decisions about how to govern and defend India under the Raj (British rule).

"We shall respect the rights, dignity and honour of native princes as our own, and we desire that they … should enjoy that prosperity and that social advancement … secured by internal peace and good government."

Queen Victoria, speech to the princes and people of India (1858)

The British in India remained a tiny European minority in an alien environment, threatened by internal sedition and external powers. Fear of Russia prompted the first Anglo-Afghan War (1838–42) and in 1843 Sind was conquered, followed by the two bitter Sikh Wars (1845–9) which led to the annexation of the Punjab. These wars were costly and destabilized societies struggling to adapt to British 'modernization'. Traditional government continued in the princely states under British paramount authority, but under the Governor General Lord Dalhousie (1848–56) more such states were brought under direct Company control, including the Maratha states of Satara (1848), Jhansi and Nagpur (both 1853). The subsidy paid to Nana Sahib, the adopted heir to the last Peshwa (paramount leader) of the Marathas, was also cancelled, and Dalhousie refused to recognize the heir to the Mughal emperor, Bahadur Shah II, unless he renounced his imperial title.

The Indian Mutiny

In 1856 the British annexed the state of Oudh, the home of many of the Company's sepoys (native soldiery) serving in the Bengal Army, where the Indian Mutiny, which developed into a wider rebellion, first began. The annexation compounded other discontents but the military revolt was finally provoked by the introduction of ammunition cartridges greased with animal fat, which offended the religious sensibilities of both Hindus and Muslims. On 10 May 1857 three cavalry regiments mutinied at Meerut and set out for Delhi to restore the emperor, who became the titular head of the revolt. The British were expelled from the imperial capital, besieged at Lucknow, and massacred at Cawnpore (Kanpur), causing outrage across the Empire.

The army's grievances surmounted a wider dissatisfaction with the economic and social changes brought by British rule, which affected some groups more than others. The Indian response to the rebellion was therefore patchy. Dispossessed rulers, notably Nana Sahib, were prominent in the revolt, along with the traditional landed aristocracy and their followers who sought a restoration of the old order. Disaffection was concentrated in the north, but the recently-conquered Punjab remained largely quiet, as did Bengal and the presidencies of Bombay and Madras. This allowed the British to deploy military forces from the rest of India as well as hurriedly reinforced European troops. Sir Henry Havelock and Sir Colin Campbell recaptured much of the lost territory through the autumn and winter, and Sir Hugh Rose re-took Central India in spring the following year. Retribution was severe and peace was declared on 8 July 1858.

The Company itself was the last casualty. It was widely blamed for provoking the rebellion, and in 1858 the government of India was transferred to the British Crown. Policy now sought to attach native princes (who ruled a quarter of India) to the British cause, the army was re-organized to prevent any future

1893 to Britain

PERSIA

Baluchistan
(1877)

Engraving from 1851 of sepoys in the East India Company's service. In India in 1857 there were 45,000 European soldiers and 250,000 sepoys.

rebellion, and although public works proceeded apace, further social and religious reforms were largely avoided. The conservative-minded elite of the Indian Civil Service (and the British community generally) remained aloof, but were forced to rely on increasing numbers of Indian bureaucrats, part of a growing middle class that demanded a greater say in the administration of the country. British refusal drove them towards nationalism and support for the Indian National Congress, established in 1885, which became the vehicle for India's eventual independence. The days of the Raj were numbered.

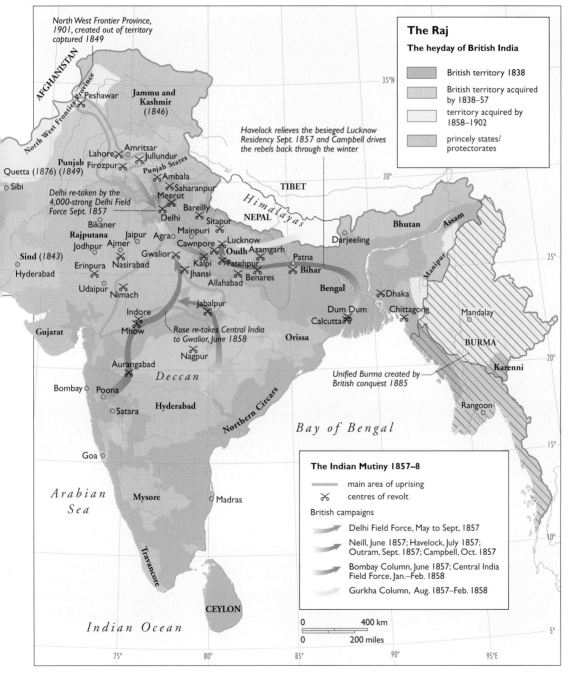

The Great Game Russia and British India

The growing Indian empire was Britain's most important overseas possession. From the 1820s, Russia's designs on the Ottoman Empire, gains in Persia and gradual territorial advance in Central Asia towards Afghanistan and India caused acute British concern. Countering the Russian threat – conceived as the 'Great Game' – became a fundamental aim of British Imperial policy.

"For close on 200 years Russia's dream has been to gain possession of India. "

Lord Roberts, Commander-in-Chief India, 22 May 1885

In the west, Britain acted to avert a Russian threat to Anglo-Indian communications through the eastern Mediterranean and Egypt, or via Mesopotamia and the Persian Gulf, by supporting Turkey in the successful Crimean War (1854-6). Subsequently, Russia concentrated on advances in Central Asia, and by the mid-1880s had absorbed Kazakhstan and the khanates to the south. Much Russian energy was also expended in the East: developing Siberia, matching Britain's commercial concessions in China and annexing Chinese Amur (1858) and Ussuri (1860), which secured a new naval base at Vladivostok.

British fears of a Russian descent on the north-west frontier of India helped prompt the acquisition or control of Sind (1843), Jammu and Kashmir (1846), the Punjab (1846-9) and Baluchistan (1876). It also led to two wars in Afghanistan: the first (1838-42) to install a client ruler, led only to the annihilation of a 4,500-strong British army during the retreat from Kabul; the second (1878-80) was caused by the Amir's agreement to Russian representation but refusal to admit a British envoy. Gladstone's Liberal government settled for the maintenance of Afghanistan as a buffer state, agreed with Russia, and the Durand Line of 1893 defined the respective Indian and Afghan spheres of influence on India's north-west frontier. In the west, Russia's war with Turkey (1877-8) led to the British acquisition of the Mediterranean island of Cyprus as a naval and military base from the Ottoman Sultan in exchange for promises of aid.

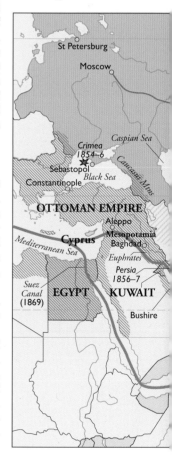

Renewed Russian advances

Persia finally lost its Caucasian territories to Russia with the Treaty of Turkmanchai (1828), which sparked an intense period of Anglo-Russian diplomatic rivalry in the country. Concern that Persian territorial claims on western Afghanistan, and their capture of Herat, were inspired by Russian influence led to the Anglo-Persian War (1856-7), which ended the Shah's expansionist designs.

By the mid-1880s Russia had succeeded to a large extent in Central Asia, and exerted great influence over Turkey, Persia, Afghanistan and China. Nevertheless, India's borders remained free of threat and, after the Pandjeh incident (in which Afghan-occupied territory was taken by Russian forces in 1885) both powers lapsed into a policy of consolidation. But the paranoia remained. Russia looked to railway development for strategic advantage, allowing troops, in the words of Russian general Prince Baryatinsky, to 'descend like an avalanche on Turkey, Persia and the road to India'. The British also feared Russian incitement of the Indian population and that any military attack on the north-west frontier would encourage potential rebels. New protective agreements in the Persian Gulf were made with Bahrain (1880), the Trucial sheikhdoms (1887), Muscat (1891) and Kuwait (1899) – the latter against a revitalized Ottoman Empire now allied to Germany.

At the end of the 19th century, British military reorganization accompanied a growing feeling of vulnerability and over-stretch, not allayed by the more aggressive frontier policy of Lord Curzon (Viceroy of India 1898–1905), who supported the creation of a new base for the Royal Navy at Weihaiwei in northern China in 1898 (to counter the Russians at Port Arthur) and dispatched an expedition to Tibet in 1903. The British government began to look instead to diplomatic alliances, with Japan (1902), France (1904) and Russia itself (1907) fresh from a crushing naval defeat by Japan at Tsushima in the war of 1904–5. The new entente formalized Russian and British spheres of influence in Persia, consolidating Britain's Persian Gulf hegemony, and defined both powers' attitudes to Tibet and Afghanistan. Fears of Russian intentions remained, but the Great Game was over.

An illustration of the storming of Kabul Gate at Ghazni in 1839. The fortress city was considered impregnable but intelligence revealed that the Kabul Gate had not been walled up from the inside. Henry Durand, a lieutenant of the Bengal Engineers, blew up the gate and the British went on to defeat the Afghans in less than an hour.

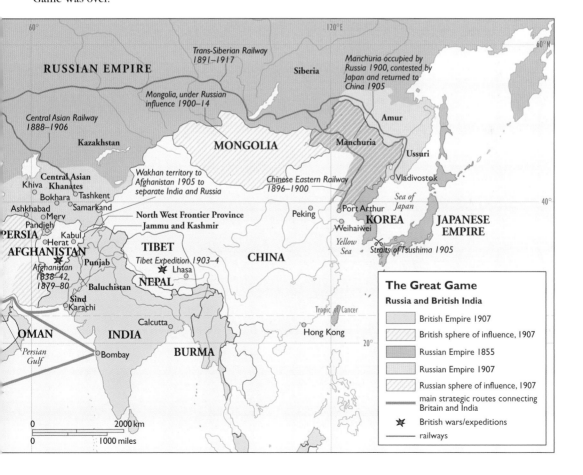

The Great Game
Russia and British India

- British Empire 1907
- British sphere of influence, 1907
- Russian Empire 1855
- Russian Empire 1907
- Russian sphere of influence, 1907
- main strategic routes connecting Britain and India
- ✹ British wars/expeditions
- railways

The White Dominions Canada and Australasia

In the Victorian age, Britain's white colonies developed spectacularly. Scattered agricultural communities coalesced into coherent proto-states emulating the social, political and economic characteristics of 'home'. They shared a British imperial identity, but as they expanded they also began to develop new identities of their own.

"It is in order to keep colonies ... that we would insist on their being allowed to manage their own internal affairs. "

Charles Buller, *Responsible Government for Colonies*, 1840

In the early 19th century Canada was the most significant of these territories, with agricultural and industrial development in the St Lawrence valley aided by railway building from the 1850s. The Durham Report (1839) into the rebellions of 1837 recommended the granting of autonomous representative self-government – which revolutionized the British concept of Empire and led to the assimilation of mutually-hostile Francophone Lower Canada and Anglophone Upper Canada as Canada East (Quebec) and Canada West (Ontario), respectively, in 1840. Pressure to promote further economic growth, eliminate a constitutional imbalance in favour of Quebec and provide more protection from the USA led to the British North America Act (1867), uniting Quebec, Ontario, Nova Scotia and New Brunswick.

The new federal Dominion of Canada focused on west-

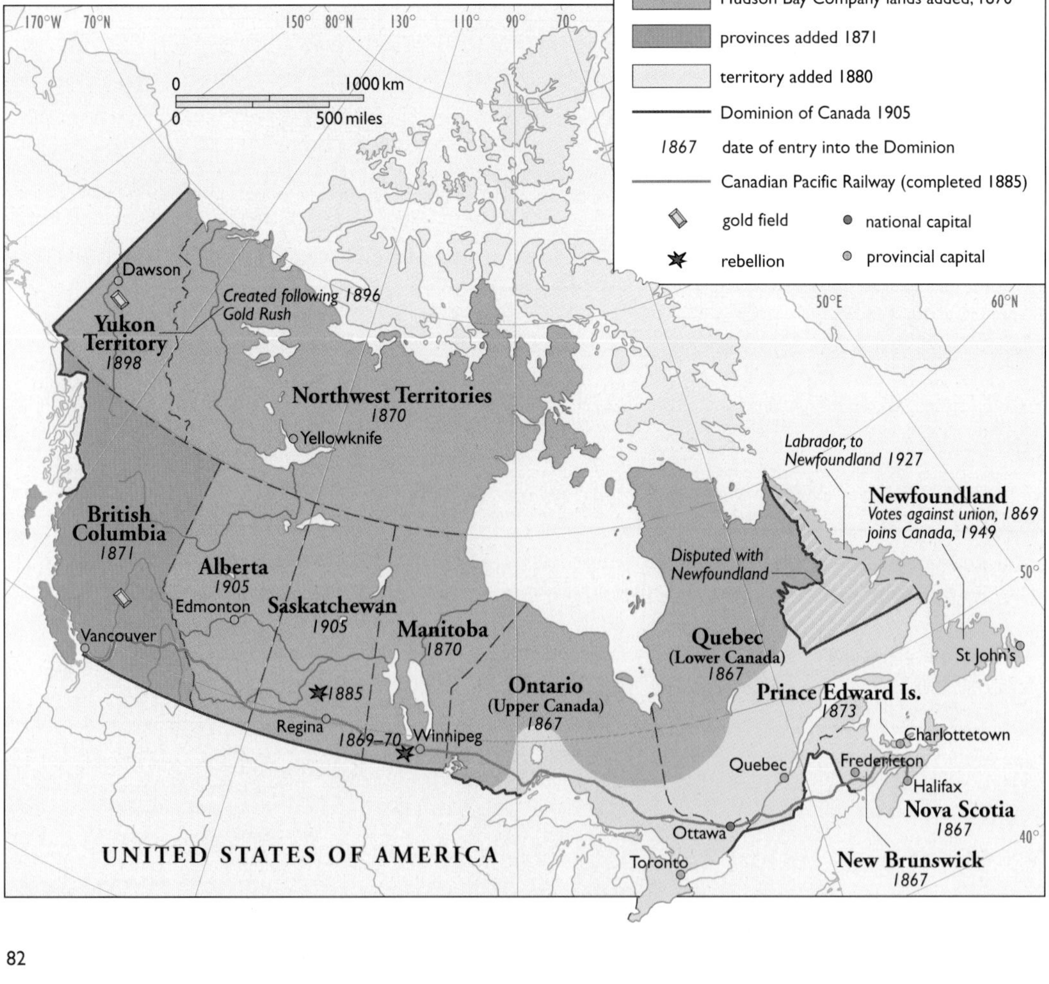

The White Dominions I Canada

- Dominion of Canada 1867
- Hudson Bay Company lands added, 1870
- provinces added 1871
- territory added 1880
- Dominion of Canada 1905
- *1867* date of entry into the Dominion
- Canadian Pacific Railway (completed 1885)
- ◇ gold field
- ● national capital
- ✳ rebellion
- ○ provincial capital

Dawson

Created following 1896 Gold Rush

Yukon Territory 1898

Northwest Territories 1870

○ Yellowknife

Labrador, to Newfoundland 1927

Newfoundland
Votes against union, 1869 joins Canada, 1949

British Columbia 1871

Alberta 1905

Edmonton ○

Saskatchewan 1905

Vancouver

Disputed with Newfoundland

Manitoba 1870

✳1885

Regina ○   1869–70 Winnipeg ✳

Ontario (Upper Canada) 1867

Quebec (Lower Canada) 1867

St John's

Prince Edward Is. 1873

Charlottetown

Quebec ○   Fredericton

Halifax

Nova Scotia 1867

UNITED STATES OF AMERICA

Ottawa ●

Toronto ○

New Brunswick 1867

0 1000 km
0 500 miles

ward expansion and state-building, purchasing the vast territories of the Hudson's Bay Company in 1870 and quashing Indian and Métis resistance. The drive to the west was made possible by railway building which aided economic growth and migration, extended Ottawa's writ to the remotest frontier and staked Canadian claims to territory north of the 49th parallel of latitude, the border agreed with the USA in 1846. Completion of the transcontinental railway was also a condition agreed for the accession to the federation of British Columbia (1871).

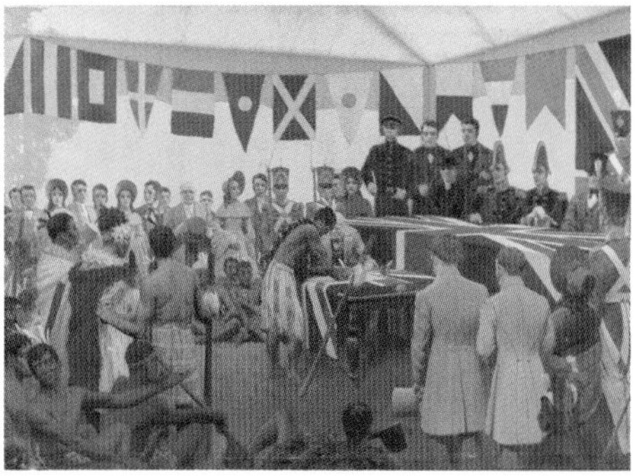

A painting showing the signing of the Treaty of Waitangi by Captain Hobson and the Maori chiefs in 1840, by Marcus King. The treaty established British sovereignty over New Zealand, but provided no legal basis for the subsequent seizure of large areas of Maori land by white settlers. Colonial development proceeded only after resulting wars between settlers and Maori tribes that were both morally and politically awkward for the Imperial government in London.

Development in Australasia

A similar process of development took place in Australia, where sheep farming in particular drove settlers - squatters - in search of new pasture. New breakaway colonies emerged, led by Van Diemen's Land (Tasmania), and obtained self-rule from the 1850s. After the Victoria goldrush of 1851 and the end of convict transportation from Britain in 1852 (to Western Australia, 1860) colonial-born Australians predominated. In the developing white dominions identity was partly defined by racial antipathy to non-white populations. From the 1880s Australia was also increasingly united in the face of European and American designs on the Pacific and perceived British indifference. The federal Commonwealth of Australia was created by democratic vote on 1 January 1901.

A desire for ordered emigration led to the British annexation of New Zealand in 1840, an event marked (at least from the British point of view) by the Treaty of Waitangi with prominent North Island Maori leaders. Settler land-hunger led to a series of short wars with the militarily formidable Maoris, but British immigration and agricultural development continued apace. The colony was reorganized in a federal basis in 1851, gained self-rule in 1856, and became a unitary state in 1876.

By the end of the century, many of the white dominions were on their way to becoming independent states within a British family of nations.

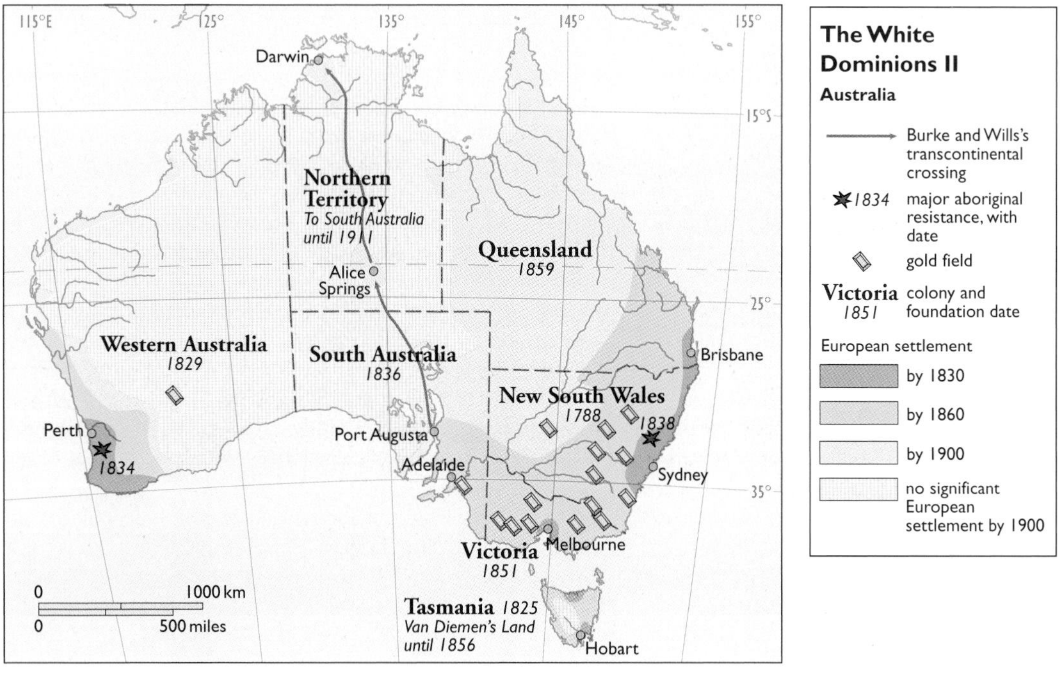
115°E
125°
135°
145°
155°
15°S
25°
35°
Darwin
Northern Territory
To South Australia until 1911
Alice Springs
Queensland
1859
Western Australia
1829
South Australia
1836
Brisbane
New South Wales
1788
1838
Perth
1834
Port Augusta
Adelaide
Sydney
Melbourne
Victoria
1851
Tasmania 1825
Van Diemen's Land until 1856
Hobart
0 1000 km
0 500 miles
The White Dominions II
Australia
Burke and Wills's transcontinental crossing
1834 major aboriginal resistance, with date
gold field
Victoria 1851 colony and foundation date
European settlement
by 1830
by 1860
by 1900
no significant European settlement by 1900

Part IV: Imperial Themes

Behind the huge growth of the Empire in the 19th century lay a deep transformation of British state and society. Industrialization, trade and the accumulation of wealth were catalysts for developments in science, technology, politics and religion, helping to redefine Britain's view of itself. Perceived superiority justified imperial expansion as part of a divinely-inspired civilizing mission. In ruling others, Britain shaped the modern world, but British society itself was also changed.

European interest in the rest of the globe intensified in the 18th century. In Britain, scientific exploration of the wider world was at first seen as a duty of the Royal Navy. It worked closely with learned societies, including the Royal Geographical Society (founded in 1830) which came to dominate the field after the mid-19th century, with a new concentration on acquiring both scientific and commercial data. Knowledge and exploitation went hand in hand. Explorers were the vanguard of imperial penetration, and by the end of the 19th century most of Africa, Asia and the Pacific, which they had helped map, was partitioned between the European powers and the USA.

Saving Souls

The most notable of the new explorers was the African missionary, medical man and natural scientist David Livingstone (1813–73). He neatly represented the

Book cover for *The Life and Explorations of Dr. Livingstone* (c. 1875). Livingstone was the first Briton to cross the African continent. He was an active explorer whose aim was the opening up of Africa to commerce and Christianity, and came to be regarded as the model of a Christian hero.

intellectual interests of the Victorian age and the strong Christian religious impulse: the white man's 'civilizing' destiny identified with the spread of commerce underlying British imperial expansion. It was a convenient justification for the subjugation and exploitation of peoples throughout the world and reflected the confident outlook of a nation reaching the peak of its industrial and commercial power. Although their interests sometimes diverged, Christianity was regarded as an ally of empire and imperial control.

Proselytization, especially by Protestant religious organizations, was pursued everywhere from the remotest Pacific to the sophisticated cultures of China and the Muslim world. The first British missionary societies were founded in the 1790s by lay communities of the Anglican, Baptist and Congregationalist churches. The Wesleyan Methodists founded their own organization in 1818, as did the Presbyterian Church of Scotland in 1825. They were joined by foreign societies, including the (Lutheran) Moravians, founded in Denmark in 1732, the Plymouth Brethren, and by North American and Continental European missions, and were later followed by many others, including the interdenominational China Inland Mission (1865); all were spurred on by the periodic religious revivals of the 19th century. In representing the external world to the British public, however, agents of religion both wittingly and unwittingly inculcated racial attitudes and stereotypes based on white superiority.

Botanical science was another area of imperial penetration. Foreign plant collecting by British institutions and individuals continued throughout the world's climate and vegetation zones: David Douglas (1798–1834), for example, travelled widely in North America for the Royal Horticultural Society and introduced 50 new trees and around 100 herbaceous plants to Britain. From the mid-19th century botanical research and the dissemination of plant material increased dramatically and the exploitation of world botanical resources had a major impact on the economic significance of the Empire and global development. Research by Saharanpur and Peradeniya botanic gardens laid the foundation of the prosperous tea industries of India and Ceylon respectively. Other Indian botanical centres promoted cinchona (to produce anti-malarial quinine) obtained from South America via Kew and widely distributed from 1861, and the prophylactic was soon cheaply available throughout the subcontinent. Many colonies promoted commercial forestry.

Hunting and Wildlife

Exploitation of plants was matched by the exploitation of wildlife for meat, horns, tusks, skins and other products. Their commercial value encouraged European involvement in Africa, the Indian subcontinent and North America in

Hunters posing for the camera after a successful hunt in early-20th-century British India. The attraction of a perceived elite activity for many Britons in India coincided with a rising demand for trophies and other exotic products in Britain and elsewhere. The consequences for the local indigenous people were sometimes even more devastating than for the prized stocks of game.

particular and also subsidized imperial penetration. As an elite sport, hunting was a traditional source of prestige and a bond with aristocratic rulers, especially in India. It took on a romantic allure and was represented as vital military training for British manhood, partly reflected in Robert Baden-Powell's injunction: 'Every boy ought to learn how to shoot and to obey orders, else he is no more good when war breaks out than an old woman' (*Scouting for Boys*, 1908). But so excessive was the slaughter of animals and birds that hunting was banned altogether in the protected reserves that emerged in the 20th century. The British impact on the natural world and subsequent environmental policy was profound, and so too was the British sense of dominion over the natural world.

The developing firearms technology that made hunting so devastating was naturally most apparent in the British Army (and Royal Navy). Despite periodic failures and reverses in the Crimea (1854–6) and imperial campaigns in the 19th century, the prestige of the army increased with its capability, efficiency and worldwide responsibilities enforcing the *Pax Britannica*. It had developed as one of the foundations of the Empire but a reappraisal of military priorities at the start of the 20th century led to a new concentration on home defence, facing a more potent threat from Europe. The Indian army was also a major component of British military power, although it was never completely trusted after the Indian Mutiny of 1857–8. To reduce any future threat, the number of British Army soldiers serving in India was increased to 60,000 and native troops reduced from 250,000 in 1870 to 120,000 from the mid-1860s. This new ratio of around 1:2 became standard in the reconstructed Indian army of the Crown (1858), which continued to provide a relatively cheap and effective pool of forces for campaigns and other duties around the Indian Ocean.

Technology and Communication

The effectiveness of British military and naval forces as the essential tools of imperial defence and annexation was further enhanced by developing communication and transport technology. British governments were particularly keen on rapid communication with the scattered Empire, promoting steamships and telegraphs, developed further from the 1860s by the submarine cables which connected land lines into a worldwide telegraphic network, providing virtually instant communication. The land telegraph, invented for practical use in 1837, was quickly adopted at home and in the Empire, and proved its worth by assisting the suppression of the Indian rebellion of 1857, when 4,500 miles of line were in use across the subcontinent. The British regarded science and technology as a mark of superiority and a justification of empire; but the information explosion it encouraged also benefited peoples on the periphery of the Empire whose loyalties would increasingly diverge.

Steamships

Maritime steam technology gave Britain an equally powerful economic and naval advantage. The development and refinement of iron shipbuilding and steam propulsion for ships were key advances, pioneered in Britain. By 1890, British Empire steam shipping amounted to 5,414,000 tons (and sail 4,274,000), compared with a combined total of 2,293,000 (and 4,865,000) tons for all other leading maritime nations. Between 1890 and 1914, Britain's merchant marine carried up to 60 per cent of the world's trade, and built two-thirds of its ships – mostly on the Clyde slipways that made Glasgow the international centre of shipbuilding. Steam also increased the speed of sea journeys: for example, between 1857 and 1893 the journey by sea from England to Cape Town fell from 42 to 19 days.

Huge coal resources, used to fuel British ships and provide a valuable source of exports and return cargoes, gave Britain a great natural advantage in the steam age. By 1885, 21 million tons of coal were exported for steamer use alone, destined for the bunkering stations around the world that crucially supported the network of British trade. Textile and other manufacturing exports (and emigration) rapidly increased, along with imports of food, raw materials and luxury goods, all providing work for a growing merchant marine. Growing trade and shipping also encouraged the extension of British naval power and the acquisition of strategic territories on the world's sea lanes. It also allowed faster reinforcement of overseas territories in an emergency.

Free Trade

All these developments contributed to British self-confidence, and enhanced Britain's power and international prestige. They were reinforced in the early 20th century by major technological advances encompassing, for example, wireless communication and the development of aeroplanes and air power, used to great effect after the First World War in the control of the Middle East and elsewhere. But the basis of British power was economic and financial strength. Advances in industrial and scientific technology brought declining manufacturing costs and cheaper raw materials, while new shipping and railway technologies made transportation more efficient. Discoveries of gold in California (1848), Australia (1851), Canada (1858) and South Africa (from 1886) increased the money supply and guaranteed finance through the gold standard. By the mid-19th century, Britain was producing 40 per cent of the world's manufactured goods, and from 1870 the pound sterling was the main international trading currency.

A 19th-century print illustrating the launch of the steamship *Great Britain* in 1843. Built by Isambard Kingdom Brunel, *Great Britain* was the world's first iron-hulled, steam-powered ocean liner. It set new standards in engineering, speed and luxury transatlantic passenger travel. Its maiden voyage to New York took only 14 days. The ship typified the technological ingenuity of the Victorian age.

Towards the end of the 19th century, however, Britain's economic pre-eminence began to disappear, and cycles of economic boom and bust added to a sense of foreboding. The free trade that had been so beneficial when the British economy was strong now began to work against it.

Britain's foreign investment in the 19th century was also impressive. British capital was used to develop the mining industries in South Africa, particularly after the diamond and gold discoveries of the 1870s. British settlers and finance opened up the Canadian prairies and other areas of food production throughout the world. Plantation commodities such as tea and rubber were established, as in Malaya where the value of investments reached £25 million by 1914, though this also included a significant contribution to the funding of the dynamic trade, finance and shipping sectors in the peninsula. Overseas investments increasingly paid for exports of British industrial machinery and equipment to the colonies, such as jute-manufacturing machinery to Bengal and sugar-processing machinery to the West Indies. This was especially true of the settler colonies, where basic manufacturing and the processing of raw materials were soon introduced. Yet, the investments that aided the development of the imperial territories – as well as foreign rivals – also contributed to a gradual divergence of interests with Britain. Britain itself, although dependent for roughly one third of its trade on the Empire, chose not to regard imperial loyalties as paramount when economic interests were at stake. Free trade remained the mantra, and comprehensive schemes of 'Imperial Preference', or protectionism, failed to win support until the Depression of 1931.

Selling the Empire

At home, Britain's imperial policies enjoyed widespread support, both for the benefits (especially economic) attributed to empire and because of the advantages British rule apparently bestowed on others. It was reflected in popular culture, including newspapers, printed matter, music, theatre, youth organizations, the church and education. It was most obviously reflected in the series of popular exhibitions devoted to Britain and the Empire. These events came to have a strong funfair element but also combined musical performance and educational displays on art, natural history, science, exploration, naval and military power, engineering, transportation, media developments, anthropology and folk culture, emigration and even pageant and panorama, all on a single site. They reflected imperial global control, exemplified not only by the presence of exotic wild animals but also 'pacified' subject peoples, displayed in 'native villages' such as Somalis at the Bradford Exhibition in 1904. They were used to illustrate the onward march of civilization and confirmed a European racial superiority. British exhibitions continued into the 1950s, but were now smaller, more mobile affairs designed by government departments and addressing new post-war imperial realities.

Developing industrial technology, religion and the search for knowledge exerted a powerful influence on imperial development. They helped boost British economic and political influence and for good and ill brought the country into closer contact with the imperial territories and the wider world. By the end of the 19th century the Empire dominated British culture and ideas, and it remained central to British attitudes until the middle of the 20th century. But to peoples on the periphery of the Empire development and the intrusion of the modern world were not always consistent with British aims and interests.

A poster issued by the Empire Marketing Board. The Board was set up in 1926 to promote trade with the colonies and to encourage consumers to buy Empire goods.

World Wide Web Telegraphic communications to 1902

The advantages offered by telegraphic communication – more effective government and better intelligence gathering, business information and imperial security – were widely appreciated as Britain set about encircling the globe. Fast and efficient communication lay at the heart of imperialism.

"Telegraphy can do much ... to stimulate commercial activity ... [and] strengthen that sense of unity ... on which the cohesion of the Empire ... depends."

The Quarterly Review (1903), in reference to the 'All-Red' Route

India was the main focus of telegraph construction in the Empire, particularly following the rebellion of 1857–8. The first successful submarine cable was laid for the Government of India in 1863–4, linking Karachi with the head of the Persian Gulf and by land line to western Europe in 1865. It was followed by the first successful transatlantic cable, laid from Ireland to Newfoundland in the course of the following year.

A second line was built across Mesopotamia and another via the Mediterranean and Red Sea to Bombay in 1870, transmitting messages that took only five hours. Submarine telegraphy was now established, and in the 1870s further cables were laid connecting India with the Far East, Australia and New Zealand; Aden with South Africa; and Europe with both sides of South America.

Numerous telegraph companies emerged from the 1860s, and by 1900 British firms owned 72 per cent of the world's 190,000 miles of submarine cable, much of it belonging to the Eastern Telegraph Company. British and colonial governments paid large amounts of money to create and maintain cable and

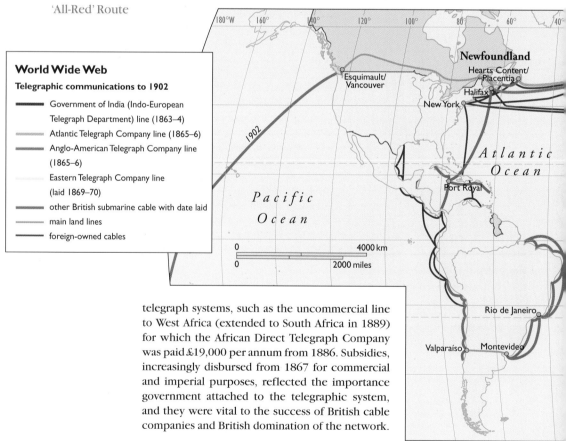

World Wide Web

Telegraphic communications to 1902

▬▬▬ Government of India (Indo-European Telegraph Department) line (1863–4)

▬▬▬ Atlantic Telegraph Company line (1865–6)

▬▬▬ Anglo-American Telegraph Company line (1865–6)

▬▬▬ Eastern Telegraph Company line (laid 1869–70)

▬▬▬ other British submarine cable with date laid

▬▬▬ main land lines

▬▬▬ foreign-owned cables

telegraph systems, such as the uncommercial line to West Africa (extended to South Africa in 1889) for which the African Direct Telegraph Company was paid £19,000 per annum from 1886. Subsidies, increasingly disbursed from 1867 for commercial and imperial purposes, reflected the importance government attached to the telegraphic system, and they were vital to the success of British cable companies and British domination of the network.

A royal party including the Prince of Wales observes the coiling of a telegraph cable in the hold of the *Great Eastern*. Brunel's huge ship was a commecial failure as a liner, but successfully laid four transatlantic telegraph cables and others from Bombay to Aden between 1865 and 1872. The Prince visited the cable manufacturer at Greenwich and the ship itself at Sheerness on 24 May 1865. The cable had to be coiled – and laid – with extreme care to avoid kinks that would impair its performance.

The impact of the telegraphic system on Britain and the colonies was mixed. Faster, more urgent news contributed to public agitation whenever an imperial crisis emerged, as in the Anglo-Boer War (1899–1902), and more widely to imperial propaganda and the course of diplomacy, although its precise impact is hard to assess. More immediate information about markets and prices boosted economic activity and helped to tie the Empire together. Governments received more information about conditions on the imperial frontier, but found events no easier to control. Although the telegraph helped to restrain local officials, it also assisted imperial expansion, as in Zululand in 1879 and Egypt in 1882.

The technology was also valuable in Imperial defence. In the Empire, the telegraph enabled local officials to summon police, military and gunboat assistance quickly, and it ordered up the men and *matériel* required for wars of empire and the conflict in Europe in 1914. It allowed closer supervision of colonial districts, and contemporaries believed the telegraph quelled local disturbances before they could escalate; and it permitted a reduction in imperial garrisons (and therefore cost) because reinforcements could be sent almost immediately. In the very short life of the 1858 cable to Canada, the government's instruction to cancel the redeployment of two regiments to India saved £50,000. But the strategic telegraph relay stations located in remote regions of the world, such as Norfolk Island, Rodrigues, St Helena and the Cocos Islands, and telegraph lines crossing foreign territory, also created defence liabilities. The solution was the creation of the so-called 'All-Red' Route, built entirely across Imperial territory, completed when a trans-Pacific cable was laid between Vancouver and Australasia in 1902. Imperial communications were at last secure.

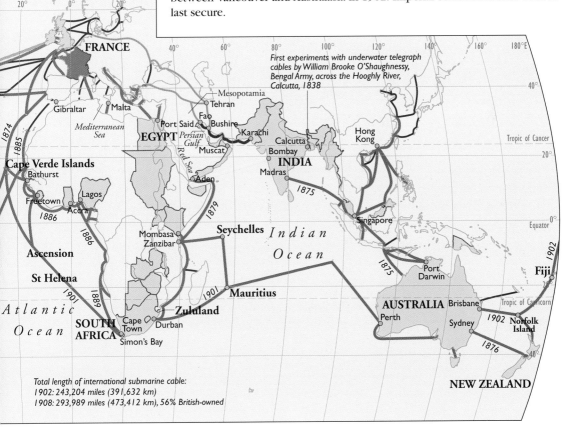

Total length of international submarine cable:
1902: 243,204 miles (391,632 km)
1908: 293,989 miles (473,412 km), 56% British-owned

The Ties that Bind Britain's steamship network

Britain's international supremacy was vitally underpinned by a powerful merchant marine. Sailing vessels were superseded by steamships during the 19th century and provided regular and increasingly rapid communication with every corner of the Empire.

"We have the power in our hands, moral, physical and mechanical; the first, based on the Bible; the second, upon the wonderful adaptation of the Anglo-Saxon race to all ... circumstances ... the third, bequeathed to us by the immortal Watt. "

MacGregor Laird,
Narrative of an Expedition into the Interior of Africa
(1837)

Britain's dominance of world shipping at the end of the age of sail was increasingly challenged after 1815, especially by the USA on the North Atlantic. This dominance was renewed with iron shipbuilding and the adoption of steam propulsion during the 19th century, notably the more fuel-efficient compound engine and high-pressure boilers widely introduced from the 1860s. The pioneers, Alfred Holt's Blue Funnel Line, trading to the Far East, could now travel 8,500 miles without refuelling.

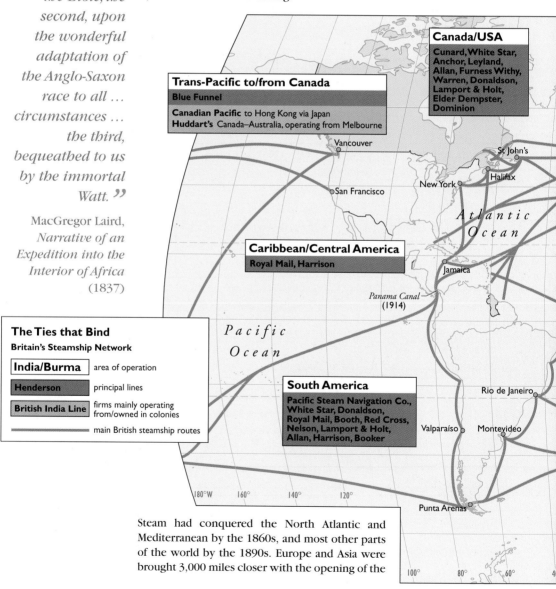

Canada/USA
Cunard, White Star, Anchor, Leyland, Allan, Furness Withy, Warren, Donaldson, Lamport & Holt, Elder Dempster, Dominion

Trans-Pacific to/from Canada
Blue Funnel
Canadian Pacific to Hong Kong via Japan
Huddart's Canada–Australia, operating from Melbourne

Caribbean/Central America
Royal Mail, Harrison

South America
Pacific Steam Navigation Co., White Star, Donaldson, Royal Mail, Booth, Red Cross, Nelson, Lamport & Holt, Allan, Harrison, Booker

The Ties that Bind
Britain's Steamship Network

India/Burma	area of operation
Henderson	principal lines
British India Line	firms mainly operating from/owned in colonies
————	main British steamship routes

Vancouver
San Francisco
St John's
Halifax
New York
Jamaica
Panama Canal (1914)
Rio de Janeiro
Valparaíso
Montevideo
Punta Arenas

Atlantic Ocean
Pacific Ocean

180°W 160° 140° 120° 100° 80° 60° 40

Steam had conquered the North Atlantic and Mediterranean by the 1860s, and most other parts of the world by the 1890s. Europe and Asia were brought 3,000 miles closer with the opening of the

Suez Canal in 1869, and steamships flooded the East. The efficiency of steamships improved with the introduction of the triple-, later quadruple-, expansion engine in the 1870s, steel construction and other refinements. Thousands of highly economical steamers were built in the following half-century.

Dozens of steamship lines were set up by British entrepreneurs, and the government was quick to identify steam transportation as a key to prosperity, national defence and imperial communications. Mail contracts were used to subsidize shipping lines on strategic routes from 1834, starting with P&O for services to the Iberian Peninsula (1837), later India and the Far East. The advantages of subsidized steam communication were summed up by a Parliamentary committee in 1853: 'The ocean has been traversed with ... precision and regularity... commerce and civilisation have been extended, the colonies have been brought more closely into connection with the Home Government, and steamships have been constructed of a size and power that, without government aid, could hardly ... have been produced'.

Steamships were used as tools of imperial policy, to extend free trade and promote national interests in the face of foreign rivalry. Along with economic and naval power, they were fundamental to Britain's 19th-century supremacy.

Postcard showing the *Buluwayo* passenger liner. The diamond funnel marks point to the company's South African links.

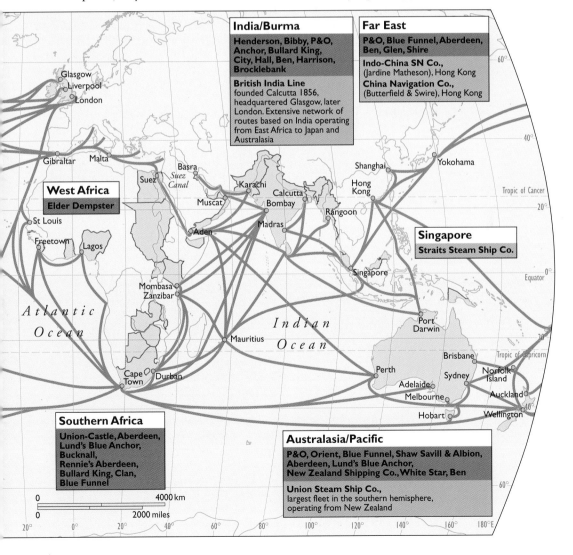

India/Burma

Henderson, Bibby, P&O, Anchor, Bullard King, City, Hall, Ben, Harrison, Brocklebank

British India Line founded Calcutta 1856, headquartered Glasgow, later London. Extensive network of routes based on India operating from East Africa to Japan and Australasia

Far East

P&O, Blue Funnel, Aberdeen, Ben, Glen, Shire

Indo-China SN Co., (Jardine Matheson), Hong Kong
China Navigation Co., (Butterfield & Swire), Hong Kong

West Africa

Elder Dempster

Singapore

Straits Steam Ship Co.

Southern Africa

Union-Castle, Aberdeen, Lund's Blue Anchor, Bucknall, Rennie's Aberdeen, Bullard King, Clan, Blue Funnel

Australasia/Pacific

P&O, Orient, Blue Funnel, Shaw Savill & Albion, Aberdeen, Lund's Blue Anchor, New Zealand Shipping Co., White Star, Ben

Union Steam Ship Co., largest fleet in the southern hemisphere, operating from New Zealand

Creating Countries Overseas investment to 1914

An important feature of British economic growth during the 19th century was the phenomenal and sustained investment of surplus capital abroad. Financial power gave Britain an economic hold over many other countries and contributed to its global hegemony. Investment was highly profitable and just as effective as military power in maintaining control.

"Contemplating the enormous expenditure ... by which modern Governments seek to extend their territorial powers ... Cui bono?... The investor. "

J. A. Hobson,
Imperialism: A Study
(1902)

Britain invested an estimated £195–200 million overseas prior to 1850, and this climbed rapidly thereafter to £4.2 billion in 1914. Investment helped develop the Empire as well as rival states, and the income it provided offset Britain's increasingly weak balance of payments. British investment went mostly to European-type economies, namely the USA, Canada, South Africa, Australia, New Zealand and South American countries. South America became a favoured destination for capital investment, increasing from £30 million in 1826 to £1,180 million in 1913. Argentina took the largest proportion (41 per cent), and British interests came to dominate Argentinian economic activity.

From 1870 to 1914 38 per cent of British overseas investment went to the Empire, and two-thirds of that to the colonies of settlement. British exports of capital, technical expertise and manpower brought goods and raw materials in exchange, in addition to the required financial return.

Creating Countries
Overseas investment to 1914

British Empire 1901

£62 British overseas investments 1914 (£ millions)

main Imperial waterways developed for navigation

developing industrial regions of the Empire

main international railway network 1914

CANADA £576

Vancouver

Quebec

St Lawrence

USA £874

Pacific Ocean

Atlantic Ocean

MEXICO £103

BRITISH HONDURAS

Jamaica

Trinidad

Georgetown

BRITISH GUIANA

BRAZIL £144

Lima

Rio de Janeiro

CHILE £62

Valparaiso

URUGUAY £41

Buenos Aires

Montevideo

ARGENTINA £319

Over the same period, around 70 per cent of British investment was in transport infrastructure, particularly railways (some 675,000 track miles built by 1920) but also ports, shipping and other trade facilities. Colonial development also required huge investment in the urban centres, buildings, roads and infrastructure required by British settlers and administrators. British investors also financed banks and other financial institutions, commercial firms and urban utility companies.

The development of agriculture and industry continued variably throughout the Empire. In Egypt the Aswan Dam construction project (1902) and associated works allowed major agricultural

A Rhodesia Railways train crossing the Victoria Falls Bridge in the 1920s. British investment created railway networks throughout the Empire and in many other parts of the world.

expansion. The administration called on the irrigation expertise of engineers employed by the government of India, where public works had long been not only an important part of the British modernizing mission but also a way of increasing state revenues. This process was accelerated after the 1857 rebellion and by 1870 the subcontinent had absorbed £180 million of British overseas investment, around £100 million in railways alone, and this continued to increase until the First World War.

Economic Intervention

From the 1880s Britain's economic pre-eminence was increasingly challenged by the growing economies of Europe and the United States; new stratagems were introduced to protect British trade. Joseph Chamberlain (Colonial Secretary 1895–1903) promoted a new, more systematic development of Britain's tropical colonies. Many had hitherto been left to the fickle hand of free enterprise, but now active government intervention helped transform the economies of several, including British Guiana, Cyprus, the Gold Coast and Lagos, where a railway was begun in 1896 connecting the coast and Northern Nigeria. In India, the Viceroy Lord Curzon (1898–1904) placed a new and similar emphasis on commercial and industrial development, recognizing the value of the role of the state in shaping national development.

By 1914 42 per cent of Britain's overseas investment was directed towards the Empire, where it played a key part in creating increasingly modern and independently-minded countries.

Imperial Exploitation Overseas trade and resources

"The foundation of a colony is the creation of a market."

Jules Ferry, speech, 27 July 1885

As the pioneer of industrial capitalism, Britain was the prime motor behind the creation of a new network of international trade in the 19th century. The British economy grew rapidly from the 1820s, and the country became increasingly dependent on foreign markets to absorb rising industrial output.

The main feature of the new international trading system was the exchange of British (and European) manufactures for foodstuffs (25 per cent of imports by the 1850s) and raw materials from around the world. Apart from Europe, most of Britain's trade took place with the 'neo-European' economies – the USA, the

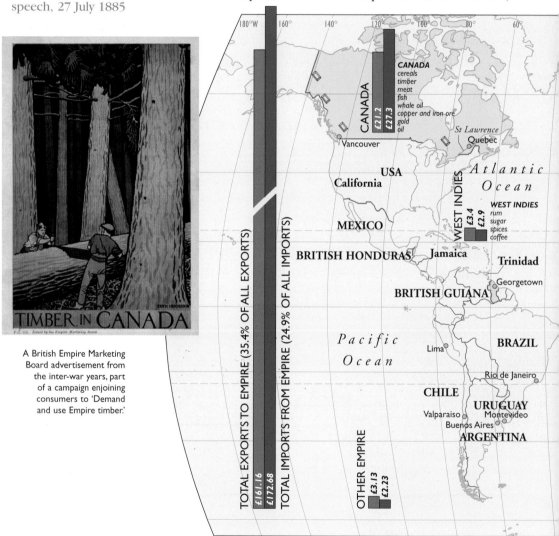

A British Empire Marketing Board advertisement from the inter-war years, part of a campaign enjoining consumers to 'Demand and use Empire timber.'

British colonies of white settlement, Argentina, Uruguay and Chile. It was Britain's migrants, expertise and capital that were largely responsible for their economic growth and for opening up vast new areas for food production and the exploitation of resources.

British exports were initially dominated by cotton manufactures, but the metal industries grew fast from the mid-century, with machinery and steam engines rising to 10 per cent of exports. British coal also formed an important return cargo for ships from all parts of the world. By 1850 the Empire was taking 30 per cent of all British exports, and from the 1870s to 1914, 35 per cent.

Early imports to Britain from the Empire benefited from tariff protection, but from the 1840s these were reduced in tacit recognition of the desirability of cheap food for a growing urban industrial population. West Indian sugar and raw cotton suffered, along with Canadian timber, but imports of other foods and raw materials from the Empire grew. Australasia and southern Africa became important as suppliers of wool, and Canada of wheat. Tropical and subtropical products came in growing quantities; cotton from Egypt and India, tea from India and Ceylon, cocoa, palm products and oilseeds from West Africa, and rub-

Imperial Exploitation

Overseas trade and resources (to 1914)

British Empire 1901

EAST AFRICA source of Imperial resources/raw materials

gold field

British Imperial balance of trade 1909–13 (yearly average, £ millions)

£7.9 exported to Empire | £5.8 imported from Empire

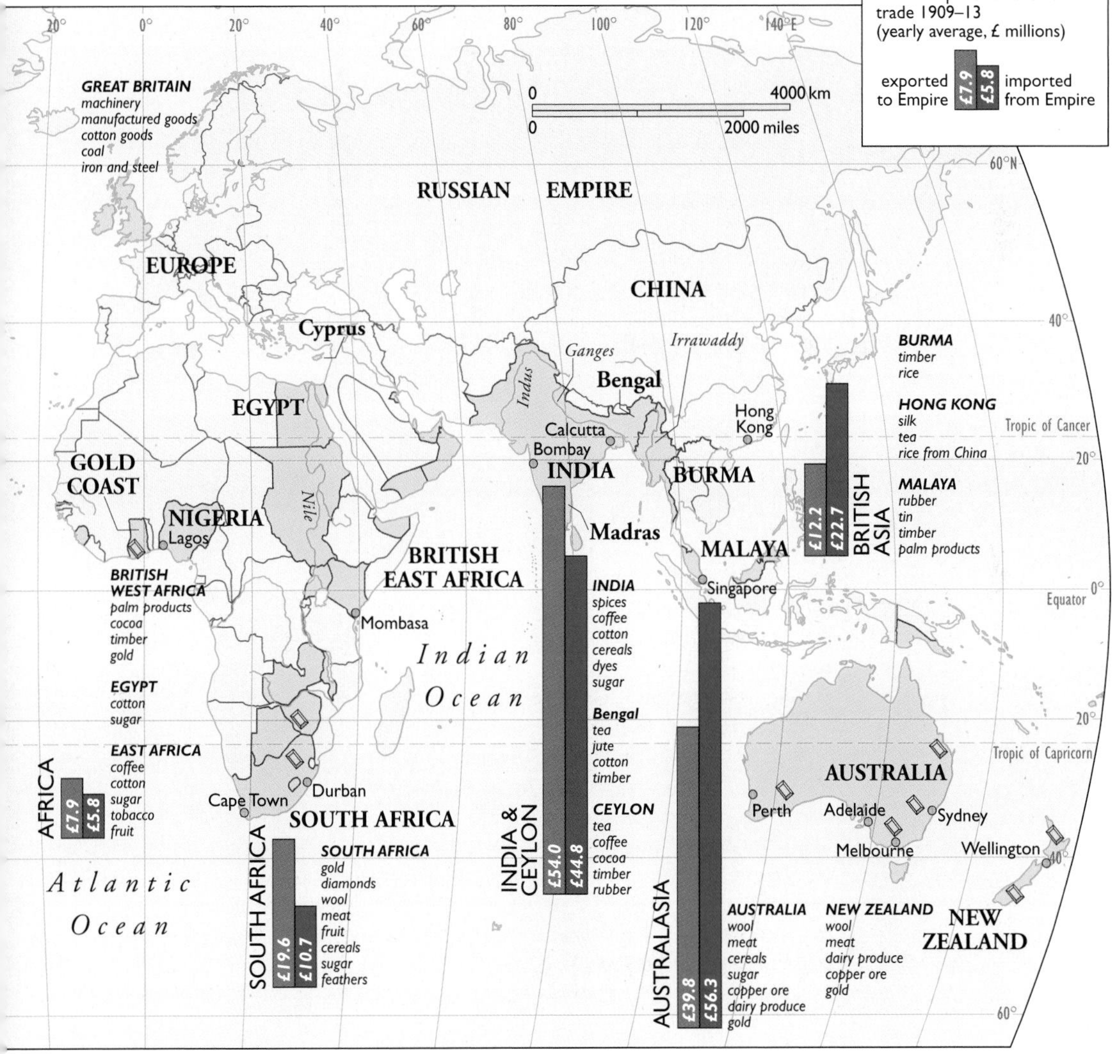

ber and tin from South East Asia. From the 1880s refrigerated shipping allowed the transportation of meat and dairy products from New Zealand and Australia.

The impact of these economic developments was fundamental in determining Britain's changing relationship with its Empire.

Exhibiting the Empire Imperial exhibitions to 1953

In the century from 1851 the phenomenon of the international exhibition – a successful combination of education, entertainment and trade fair – reflected Britain's attitudes to the Empire and helped mould national perceptions as instruments of imperial propaganda.

"The [Wembley Exhibition, 1924] overwhelmed me … its influence still lingers after all the years that have passed. "

Eric Pasold,
Ladybird, Ladybird
(1977)

The Great Exhibition of 1851, housed in the Crystal Palace erected in London's Hyde Park, was the first of a regular series of exhibitions throughout the world. As an industrial exposition it showed off Britain's technical achievements, commercial supremacy, pride and self-confidence, while exhibiting some anxiety about design values and mass-produced products. Several colonies were represented and the initial focus on industry gradually gave way to a more pronounced colonial theme by the 1880s, an accompaniment to the aggressive new imperialism in international affairs. From 1886 British exhibitions were almost entirely related to the Empire.

The British exhibitions took place in the provinces and home countries as well as London, and some exhibits also had a separate touring life. Railway travel allowed mass attendance, as at the Glasgow events (5.7 million visitors in 1888, 12 million in 1938), but attendances peaked with the British Empire Exhibition at Wembley in 1924–5 (over 27 million visitors).

Extravaganzas of Empire

The Colonial and Indian (1886) was the first official, government-backed exhibition, in a series that was to culminate in the Wembley and 1938 Glasgow events. It was designed to give a 'practical demonstration of the wealth and industrial development of the … British Empire' and was also the first to produce large amounts of printed ephemera as imperial propaganda. The Franco-British (1908), Japan-British (1910) and other exhibitions sought to encourage and justify specific diplo-

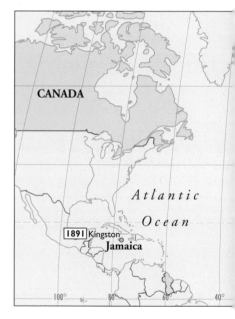

matic alliances, although they too retained a strong imperial flavour. All the exhibitions stressed the importance of imperial economic interdependence, especially those organized during the inter-war period, when Imperial self-sufficiency and limited protectionism in difficult worldwide economic conditions became government policy.

Imitative exhibitions became popular in the Empire itself, especially in the white dominions, where they were used to reflect political development and economic advance. These exhibitions also celebrated the successful creation of British settler societies, and promoted a sense of Imperial unity and developing national pride. Such events were not restricted to the white dominions, either: the Calcutta Exhibition of 1883–4 attracted over one million British and (largely middle class) Indian visitors.

An Indian elephant with howdah at the Great Exhibition of 1851 in London. From industrial trade fairs, the exhibitions developed into demonstrations of imperial pride and achievement.

London was also host to a near-annual series of exhibitions on imperial themes between the 1890s and 1914, organized at Crystal Palace, White City and Olympia by the entrepreneur Imre Kiralfy. He incorporated the spectacular British theatre tradition, with exotic orientalist architecture on a grand scale. His 1899 Greater Britain Exhibition was typical. It had not only a 'kaffir kraal' and 'Savage South Africa' spectacle with real Africans but also re-enactments of the Matabele War (1893) and Rhodesian Revolt (1896–7).

The Wembley exhibition was the ultimate imperial extravaganza, costing £12 million and including multiple extravagant pavilions covering 220 acres. Its aims were to foster the search for new sources of raw materials in the Empire, to develop inter-Imperial trade and to 'make the different races of the British Empire better known to each other'. Visitors were attracted through extensive media coverage, ephemera and a wide range of funfair entertainments and large-scale events. With Britain's Empire now at its geographical limit, the message was resolutely pro-imperial and self-justificatory. This was repeated at Glasgow in 1938.

By this time, the imperial exhibition phenomenon was running out of steam – but the imperial and racial attitudes that such exhibitions had fostered remained part of British society.

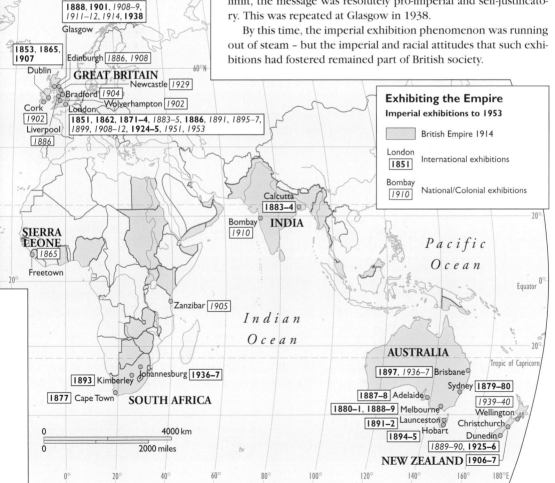

Hunting to Kill Game and exploitation

The hunting of wild animals and birds was an important feature of the colonial advance in many British (and European) territories. This was particularly true in Africa, which had the largest resource of game and – because of its rapid depletion – pioneered initiatives to protect and preserve stocks. These measures were also adopted in India and other British territories.

"When I arrived I was obsessed by an unashamed blood-lust. Hunting is man's primitive instinct, and I indulged it and enjoyed it to the full. "

Richard Meinertzhagen, *Kenya Diary 1902–6* (1957)

Throughout much of the colonial period game was important for trade, provided meat for subsistence and was used to pay for local labour. It supported explorers, missionaries and their followers, and white hunters became significant in African trade networks and politics, as well as in reconnoitring the European advance. One of the most famous, Frederick Selous, guided the British South Africa Company's Pioneer Column into Mashonaland in 1890. The focus of early white hunting activity (from the 1650s) was the Cape region, and over the following 150 years it was largely cleared of game. The hunting frontier was gradually pushed northwards; hunters, *trekboers* and other settlers cleared the High Veld and regions as far as the Limpopo by the 1890s. For the later farmers wild animals and settled agriculture were often incompatible.

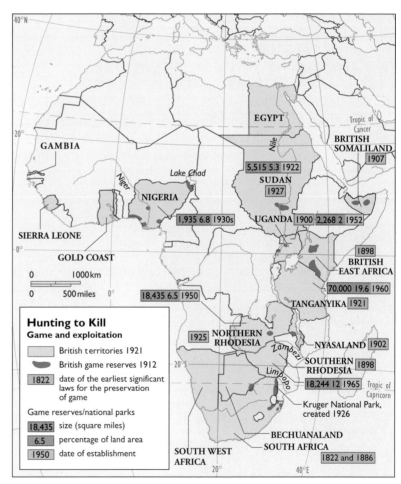

Hunting to Kill
Game and exploitation

British territories 1921

British game reserves 1912

1822 date of the earliest significant laws for the preservation of game

Game reserves/national parks

18,435 size (square miles)

6.5 percentage of land area

1950 date of establishment

The British authorities at the Cape recognized the threat to wildlife; limited game legislation was introduced as early as 1822 and subsequently extended to the Afrikaner states. But the scale of the slaughter increased throughout the 19th century as more modern guns were introduced and many more hunters appeared. Hides, horns and trophies were valuable, but the primary draw was elephant ivory, used in an increasing range of manufactured goods. Its export from the Cape, worth £60,000 in 1875, collapsed to £2,000 within ten years as a result of overexploitation. African peoples, such as the Ndebele (of later Southern Rhodesia) and the Lozi (later Northern Rhodesia), used income from hunting to strengthen their power in relation to rivals and the growing European presence, buying modern weaponry which further decimated game stocks. Between 1872 and 1874 around 45,360 kilograms (100,000 lb) of ivory (equivalent to approximately 2,000 elephants) was traded by the Ndebele, who obtained 60 per cent directly and the remainder from white hunters. The rhino, hippopotamus, buffalo and giraffe were also in retreat as far as the Zambezi.

A hand-coloured postcard showing white hunters returning with a bag of four Kudu antelope, probably in the Transvaal, in the early 1900s.

The Lure of Hunting

Later, as game stocks were depleted, African chiefs found their ability to oppose the European advance correspondingly weakened, and game assisted British penetration in other ways. It was used to provision military forces engaged in the move into Central Africa and supported labourers building railways throughout the continent, which itself allowed further hunting penetration. Improved access and pacification attracted a growing number of tourist shooting parties led by white hunters, increasingly turned safari hunters, who became famous and fabled. The romantic literary genre that developed around hunters of the African wilderness helped attract tourists and settlers to Rhodesia and East Africa, a trend that peaked between the wars.

In a further blow to game resources the cattle disease Rinderpest destroyed large numbers of wild animals from the 1890s, particularly buffalo, zebra, antelope and buck. It spurred the introduction of new protective game laws that increasingly prohibited Africans from hunting for food, a necessity for many as their cattle died from disease and periodic drought stunted their crops. Recreational hunting by Europeans continued largely unabated, and game reserves were established to ensure a healthy supply of game. In West Africa, where white elite sport hunting never really developed, such reserves were rare.

Throughout the Empire hunting, traditionally an aristocratic and royal activity, was pursued enthusiastically by the administrative and officer class. This was especially true in India where it was used to display British authority and prestige and cement bonds with Indian aristocrats. The limited extent of tourist hunting until the 20th century delayed the introduction of reserves into Asia but they inevitably followed. The international agreement of 1933 marked the transition of reserves into national parks, reflecting a concern to strengthen protection for wildlife and their habitats that further excluded indigenous peoples and, increasingly, white tourist hunters. The Kruger National Park in South Africa, converted from the Sabi reserve in 1926, was the first in the British Empire that was now devoted to tourism not hunting, and establishing the pattern of post-imperial conservation policies.

Plant Hunting The gardens of Empire

In the late 18th and 19th centuries Britain supported a diverse programme of worldwide scientific exploration. The quest for botanical knowledge, especially in identifying plants of economic value, had an important influence in determining imperial expansion.

"The King has much at heart his new botanical garden at St Vincent's; his object ... is to improve the commerce of the West-India islands, and to provide the British troops ... with medicinal plants. "

William Jones (1787)

Botanical illustration of breadfruit from Delahaye's *Plants of the Torrid Regions* (1789). The plant is believed to have originated in New Guinea and the Indo-Malay region. Europeans discovered its starchy qualities in the 1500s.

Although internationally plants and seeds were often acquired and distributed independently of government and official botanical gardens, these institutions played a crucial part in the economic development of the Empire and in transforming the environment of large parts of the world. The Royal Botanical Garden at Kew came to play a decisive role in Imperial botany, plant exploration and exploitation. Its scientific role was developed particularly by Sir Joseph Banks between 1772 and 1820, and following the appointment of Sir William Hooker as director in 1841 Kew developed a powerful influence at the Colonial (and India) Office. It was allotted an Imperial role at the centre of a new network of gardens in the colonies, to act as centres for plant hunting and the rigorous assessment of fruit, vegetables, timber and other crops for cultivation and colonial development. Kew was also promoted as the premier international centre for the exchange of plants and seeds.

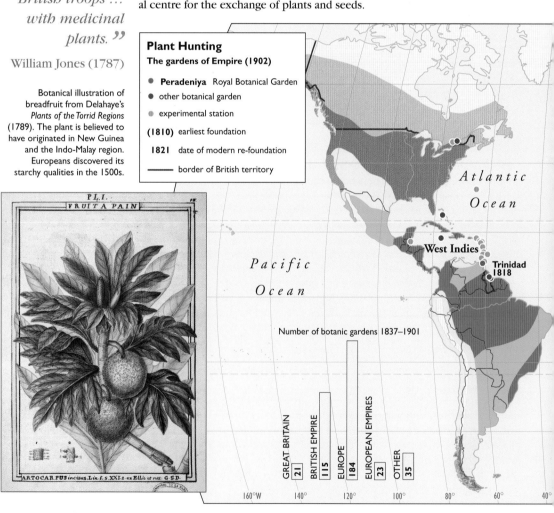

Plant Hunting
The gardens of Empire (1902)

- **Peradeniya** Royal Botanical Garden
- other botanical garden
- experimental station
- **(1810)** earliest foundation
- **1821** date of modern re-foundation
- border of British territory

Atlantic Ocean

Pacific Ocean

West Indies

Trinidad 1818

Number of botanic gardens 1837–1901

GREAT BRITAIN	BRITISH EMPIRE	EUROPE	EUROPEAN EMPIRES	OTHER
21	115	184	23	35

160°W   140°   120°   100°   80°   60°   40°

Imperial botanic gardens multiplied. There were four in 1789, around ten in 1837 and more than 100 by 1901, including the eminent Royal Botanical Gardens of Calcutta, Peradeniya (Ceylon), Pamplemousses (Mauritius) and Trinidad in addition to agricultural research stations and related institutions. The colonies appreciated the economic benefit of botanic gardens, but the new settler and expatriate communities also wanted attractions with ornamental plantings in imitation of 'home'. This was particularly so in Australia and New Zealand, where botanic gardens were likened to municipal public parks. Some were closely associated with acclimatization societies, producing British ornamentals and other plants as a part of transplanting national identity.

The impact of botanic gardens on the economics of empire, as well as nutrition and medical health, was profound. Sugar, tea, cinchona and other crops transformed the economies of many colonies. Others promoted commercial forestry, as in the Malayan states which benefited hugely from rubber cultivation. In the 1880s there was a new emphasis on economic botany, especially in the poorer tropical colonies. The need for an alternative crop to sugar in the Caribbean led to the foundation of economic gardens focused on Trinidad and Jamaica. By promoting cocoa, coffee, bananas, limes, new types of cotton and sugar cane they helped build new prosperity in the region in the early 1900s. Although the 20th century saw a decline in botany's popularity its value was proved, and it remained an essential part of the make-up of the British Empire.

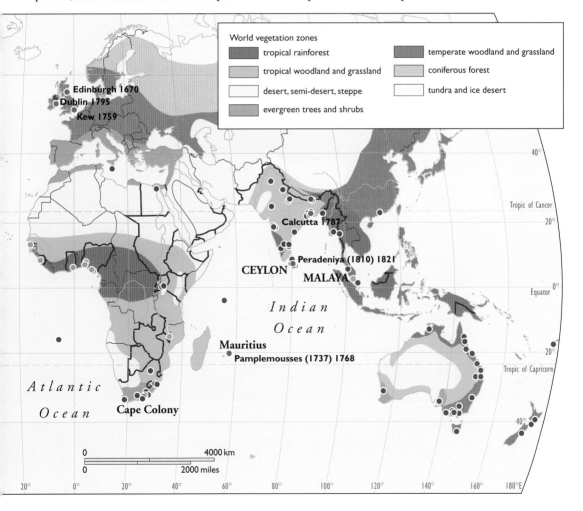

Searching for Souls Protestant missions to 1914

"[Missions] strengthen our hold over the country, they spread the use of the English language ... in fact each mission station is an essay in colonisation."

Harry Johnston (1890)

The growth of the British Empire was accompanied by an unprecedented expansion of Christian – overwhelmingly Protestant – churches and missions throughout the world. In different ways their role and influence were important in both the development of the Empire and its ultimate breakdown.

The Society for the Propagation of Christian Knowledge (established 1698–9) began the official overseas missionary work of the Anglican Church in southern India in 1728. Church organization, however, was only introduced to the Empire from the 1780s, initially in British North America (Canada) after the loss of the American colonies, where it was viewed as a buttress to state authority by a government that equated religious dissent with political radicalism. The Anglican Church thus acquired new dioceses, wealth and authority – but also came under increasing attack from other denominations. Between 1830 and 1870 exasperated and increasingly secular Imperial and colonial governments withdrew from all religious support.

Church expansion was accompanied by a wider religious revival that gave rise to new missionary endeavour. Enthusiastic lay communities established the

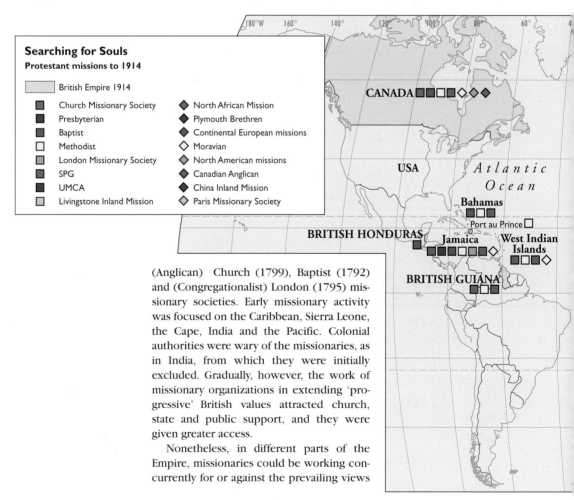

Searching for Souls
Protestant missions to 1914

- British Empire 1914
- ■ Church Missionary Society
- ■ Presbyterian
- ■ Baptist
- □ Methodist
- ■ London Missionary Society
- ■ SPG
- ■ UMCA
- □ Livingstone Inland Mission
- ◆ North African Mission
- ◆ Plymouth Brethren
- ◆ Continental European missions
- ◇ Moravian
- ◇ North American missions
- ◆ Canadian Anglican
- ◆ China Inland Mission
- ◇ Paris Missionary Society

(Anglican) Church (1799), Baptist (1792) and (Congregationalist) London (1795) missionary societies. Early missionary activity was focused on the Caribbean, Sierra Leone, the Cape, India and the Pacific. Colonial authorities were wary of the missionaries, as in India, from which they were initially excluded. Gradually, however, the work of missionary organizations in extending 'progressive' British values attracted church, state and public support, and they were given greater access.

Nonetheless, in different parts of the Empire, missionaries could be working concurrently for or against the prevailing views

An ivory plaque from the Congo depicting two missionary figures. Some Africans, once converted, became Christian missionaries themselves.

of the colonial establishment. They championed the interests of slaves against the plantocracies in the West Indies (where Baptists and other Nonconformists were prominent) while in Sierra Leone they shaped a new colony out of a heterodox community of freed slaves, immigrants and indigenous peoples through religious and civil authority, education and a common English language.

Commerce, Christianity and Civilization

Towards mid-century a new wave of missionary endeavour began, prompted by religious revival and a growing confidence in the ability of commerce to bring Christianity and civilization to the rest of the world. The writings of the immensely popular Scottish missionary David Livingstone also inspired new enthusiasm and led to the foundation of the Universities Mission to Central Africa and the Livingstone Inland Mission to the Congo.

Missionary advance took place everywhere, increasingly with the aid of local converts, and from the 1880s the interests of church and state once more ran largely in parallel. Many missionaries saw the Empire as the means of spreading Christianity, and broadly sanctioned an imperialism that, for example, obtained religious access to China in the two Opium Wars. Territorial control was often seen by well-meaning Christians as the only way to bring peace, stability and commerce to unsettled regions, especially those in Africa, where there was also a desire to counter growing Islamic influence.

The impact of religion on other peoples was ambiguous. During the years of imperial advance, missionary influence was often inimical to indigenous cultures, even when these helped to mediate the Western onslaught. Missionary influence was profound, not least through charitable works and cultural achievements ranging from (English-language) education, which underpinned the proto-nationalist movements, to the development of spelling for hitherto unwritten languages. Furthermore, under British rule colonial subjects often found missionaries to be important supporters of their rights and interests.

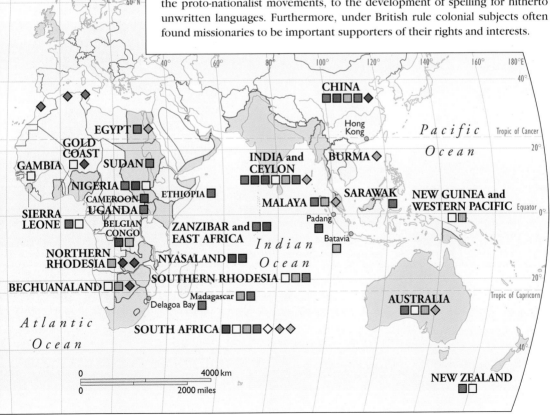

Colonial Wars The army and Imperial defence

Early British colonies relied on their own militias for defence. From the mid-18th century the British army increasingly provided garrison troops as protection from both external aggression and internal lawlessness. In the absence of a European threat, the Victorian army re-focused and became a largely imperial institution.

"War ... is the greatest purifier to the race or nation that has reached the verge of over-refinement, or of excessive civilisation. "

Field Marshal Viscount Wolseley, *Story of a Soldier's Life* (1903)

India was the British army's single largest commitment in the 19th century; its forces supplemented the huge Indian army of largely native sepoys operated by the East India Company until 1858. The Indian rebellion of 1857–8 and Russian expansion in the East, prompting several campaigns into Afghanistan and Persia, demanded ever more British regular troops to secure the Raj from within and to protect its extensive borders.

This involvement of British forces was costly in both financial and human terms, with high mortality rates from tropical diseases. In 1846, the British army's total establishment stood at 100,600, costing £10 million annually. Despite the recruitment of local forces around the Empire, the army was clearly over-stretched, and pressures were growing for the return of troops from abroad. A review of defence strategy by Earl Grey in 1846 inaugurated a period

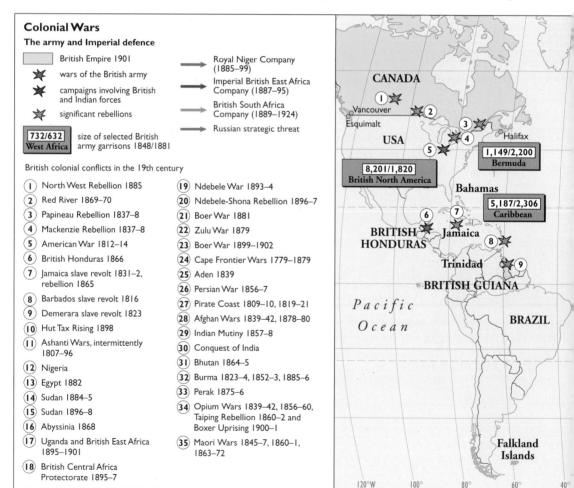

Colonial Wars
The army and Imperial defence

British Empire 1901

⭐ wars of the British army

⭐ campaigns involving British and Indian forces

⭐ significant rebellions

732/632 West Africa size of selected British army garrisons 1848/1881

→ Royal Niger Company (1885–99)

→ Imperial British East Africa Company (1887–95)

→ British South Africa Company (1889–1924)

→ Russian strategic threat

British colonial conflicts in the 19th century

1. North West Rebellion 1885
2. Red River 1869–70
3. Papineau Rebellion 1837–8
4. Mackenzie Rebellion 1837–8
5. American War 1812–14
6. British Honduras 1866
7. Jamaica slave revolt 1831–2, rebellion 1865
8. Barbados slave revolt 1816
9. Demerara slave revolt 1823
10. Hut Tax Rising 1898
11. Ashanti Wars, intermittently 1807–96
12. Nigeria
13. Egypt 1882
14. Sudan 1884–5
15. Sudan 1896–8
16. Abyssinia 1868
17. Uganda and British East Africa 1895–1901
18. British Central Africa Protectorate 1895–7
19. Ndebele War 1893–4
20. Ndebele-Shona Rebellion 1896–7
21. Boer War 1881
22. Zulu War 1879
23. Boer War 1899–1902
24. Cape Frontier Wars 1779–1879
25. Aden 1839
26. Persian War 1856–7
27. Pirate Coast 1809–10, 1819–21
28. Afghan Wars 1839–42, 1878–80
29. Indian Mutiny 1857–8
30. Conquest of India
31. Bhutan 1864–5
32. Burma 1823–4, 1852–3, 1885–6
33. Perak 1875–6
34. Opium Wars 1839–42, 1856–60, Taiping Rebellion 1860–2 and Boxer Uprising 1900–1
35. Maori Wars 1845–7, 1860–1, 1863–72

CANADA

Vancouver
Esquimalt

USA

8,201/1,820 British North America

1,149/2,200 Bermuda

Bahamas

5,187/2,306 Caribbean

BRITISH HONDURAS Jamaica

Trinidad

BRITISH GUIANA

Pacific Ocean

BRAZIL

Falkland Islands

120°W   100°   80°   60°   40°

of retrenchment. Self-governing colonies had to provide their own defence in the form of volunteer militias and regular colonial forces, and it was argued that in an age of Royal Navy domination, the telegraph and steamship would allow rapid reinforcement by regular British troops in an emergency. By the 1870s, however, growing international political tensions led to a further reappraisal in the Carnarvon Commission (1879). A more integrated system of imperial defence emerged, yet more heavily reliant on the navy. Military forces were required to protect the network of international bases and to fight the routine small wars of empire, and the British army increased from 160,000 men in 1876 to 195,000 in 1898.

The revolution in Western military technology had created a reassuring power gap between European and indigenous armies, culminating in the deployment of the machine gun and light field guns with explosive shells. In 1899, however, the Anglo-Boer War demonstrated just how deadly conflict with a similarly-equipped enemy could be, and the British military was forced again to reform and to assess the implications for potential conflict in Europe.

A hand-coloured postcard showing a platoon of Dyaks from Borneo before the First World War. The Dyaks were some of the many locally-raised troops sharing responsibility for the defence of the British Empire.

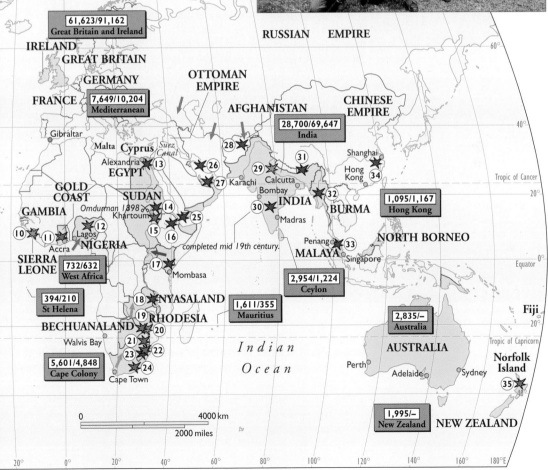

Part V: Climax and Decolonization
1901–97

At the start of the 20th century the British Empire was a colossus on the world stage. It was also incredibly diverse in its ethnic and cultural composition, which would alter yet again with the two World Wars. However, language, law, commerce, the needs of defence, and adaptable and (usually) principled government helped bind this patchwork of peoples and territories together.

The monarchy provided the symbolic leadership and was the focus of patriotic feeling throughout the British world. This was reflected in Queen Victoria's Diamond Jubilee celebrations (1897), the popular outpouring of grief at her death in 1901 and the excitement surrounding the several royal tours around the Empire. In many ways the Edwardian period was a golden age of British world dominance, prosperity and imperial unity, but its foundations were shallow. The Boer War (1899-1902) demonstrated that Britain, with all its commitments, could no longer dominate world affairs, and for several reasons.

Challenges to the Empire

Other countries were challenging Britain's global position. Germany in particular sought to attack British naval dominance, and the expense of modern armaments and commitments to the widely scattered Empire made a British response increasingly difficult. The Boer War brought a new realization of the scale of military reinforcements (up to 500,000 men) required to protect India from a feared Russian attack. The demands of being a continental and maritime power simultaneously were too great, and in 1902 Britain entered an alliance with Japan to bolster its position in the East, followed by ententes with France (1904) and Russia (1907). A further challenge was the state of British society itself and the reforms required to remedy unemployment, widespread urban poverty and poor health; such reforms were embraced at least in part to hinder the growth of working-class political radicalism and to develop a healthy resource of potential soldiery.

Fundamentally, the country's economy was in relative decline as other powers caught up with Britain's lead in industrial production. The British stake of 32 per cent of world factory output in 1870 had fallen to below 16 per cent by 1900 as the USA and Germany in particular leapt ahead. This relative decline was compounded by poor productivity, failure to invest in industry and a lack of innovation. Imports continued to increase in the early 20th century, creating a balance of payments crisis and threatening sterling's position as the world's trading currency. Tariff reform, taken up by radical politician Joseph Chamberlain and others, sought a return to a closed imperial system in which British territories provided markets for British industries and supplied essential raw materials.

These problems were addressed by the reforming Liberal government of 1906-11, which inaugurated a new, more equal British relationship with the white dominions. This was the start of the transition to a British Commonwealth which acknowledged the pressures of growing nationalism and sought ways to maintain imperial co-operation. Britain was better placed now to

British soldiers in Palestine in 1936. The British Empire acquired substantial additional territories as League of Nations mandates after the First World War, but a interwar strains on the British economy made their security and administration increasingly burdensome.

address major power tensions in Europe. The government also hoped, with only moderate success, to share more of the burden of imperial defence with the dominions. But a boom in trade, as well as increasing taxation of the wealthy, helped to finance the cost of defence and social welfare reform in Britain's Edwardian heyday. The catastrophe of the First World War brought this boom to an end, and critics of empire multiplied at home and abroad.

During and after the war, Britain was forced to devolve power and make constitutional concessions in order to counter political opposition, bolster imperial unity and reduce costs while maintaining overall control in the face of growing nationalist movements and civil unrest. The need for Indian support during the conflict led Britain to acknowledge, in the words of Secretary of State Edwin Montagu in 1917, the goal of 'responsible government in India as an integral part of the British Empire'. This re-evaluation of relative power underlay the creation of client states in the Middle East, notably Egypt, to ensure the flow of oil and the security of imperial communications. It was also behind the extension of indirect rule in Africa, whose light touch helped reduce friction. In Ireland, however, events spiralled out of control and the bitter years of conflict over Home Rule were resolved in virtual independence for the Irish Free State in 1921. The dominions, also increasingly assertive, demanded a greater role in the affairs of empire and a recognition of their independence as 'autonomous communities within the British Empire, equal in status ... united by a common allegiance to the Crown' (Statute of Westminster, 1931).

US President Franklin D. Roosevelt and British Prime Minister Winston Churchill during the Casablanca Conference in 1943. Both World Wars undermined the British Empire but the Second World War marked the beginning of its end. It weakened Britain's dwindling influence and heightened the ascendancy of the United States as the new global power.

White Empire

Nevertheless, the white Empire remained united between the wars. It was popular at home, had proved its value in the war, and the ties of blood remained strong. Skilled emigrants were in constant demand and the Empire Settlement Act of 1922 (renewed several times and, as the Commonwealth Settlement Act, finally brought to an end in 1972) assisted many British citizens to emigrate: between 1922 and 1936 they totalled 405,230. At the same time, non-white immigration in the dominions, whose identities were partly defined by race, was increasingly discouraged. South Africa developed the most overtly discriminatory policies towards its majority black population, especially after the rise of the Afrikaner Nationalist Party in the 1930s. Here Britain had lost its control, but in Kenya and Central Africa it refused to allow minority white rule.

In the Great Depression (1929–34) South Africa fared best, able to rely on gold production to insulate it from the Depression's devastating effects, but other dominions were not so fortunate. Newfoundland became insolvent, and its affairs were run by government commissioners sent from London; the experience propelled Newfoundland into the Canadian confederation in 1949. All the dominions suffered from the contraction of world markets, but they benefited from British economic leadership and the Empire's economic co-operation through the creation of an official sterling area in 1931, and protectionism adopted at Ottawa in 1932. Another factor in continued Commonwealth unity in the 1930s was the threatening international situation. The prospect of a victorious Germany and Japan was regarded with alarm throughout the individual Imperial dominions. None saw an alternative, as free and independent nations, to supporting Britain in the Second World War.

Britain emerged from the conflict with huge new areas of territory under its control, but the Empire's size was in inverse proportion to Britain's strength. The need to reduce Britain's global responsibilities became urgent. In Africa (and indeed elsewhere in the Empire) the war radicalized populations and revived nationalist movements. Discriminatory land and labour policies caused widespread discontent, and decolonization was soon driven by black ambition, complicated by white settler retrenchment; Britain was now less able and less willing, in a developing crisis of morality and purpose, to employ coercion to maintain control. The right to self-determination was soon conceded, although the British intention was nevertheless to hold on to the colonies for some time (seen as 'trusteeship'), in the belief that Africans were not yet able, through a lack of education, training, experience and suitable democratic institutions and economies, to assume independence. But in many territories the emerging African elites were impatient for change and increasingly able to harness popular support to demand independence. They also had the sympathy of the new superpowers – the USA and the USSR – while Britain's own economic recovery in the 1950s made retention of the African territories less important.

Protesters outside Marlborough House, London, in 1966 during negotiations to grant independence to Rhodesia. When Britain granted independence to Northern Rhodesia (later Zambia) in 1964, Southern Rhodesia became simply Rhodesia. In 1965 Rhodesia's white minority declared its 'Unilateral Declaration of Independence' (UDI) from the British government rather than submit to black majority rule. With the support of apartheid South Africa, the Rhodesian regime survived until 1979, when agreement was finally reached on majority rule in an independent Zimbabwe.

Independence for India

By 1939 it was clear that India would not long remain within the British Empire, and war only delayed the inevitable. But the struggle for the independence finally achieved in 1947 is remarkable both for the (largely) non-violent means by which it was attained and for the tragedy of Partition. Indian divisions were exploited by Britain to maintain control, recruiting allies among the Indian princes and landed class as well as the large Muslim minority, partly represented by the All-India Muslim League from 1906. As in Ireland, the tardy offer of home rule, and later dominion status, was insufficient to satisfy nationalist hopes, and the mainly Hindu Indian National Congress was transformed into an instrument of mass political agitation and the principal agent of change. Despite India's independence, Britain retained important interests in the East, including oil supplies from the Middle East and their protection from the perceived Soviet threat, which gave the Suez Canal ongoing strategic importance. Despite difficulties, Britain was unwilling to withdraw until the 1970s.

South East Asia had also become more and more important as a source of rubber, tin, teak and palm oil, which Britain was keen to retain, but the war's legacy was the collapse of European colonialism. Burma's path to independence paralleled growing Indian agitation and constitutional changes. Decolonization elsewhere was delayed by the developing Cold War and ethnic and economic tensions associated with the creation of new states. There was little agitation in Malaya before the war, although many Malays were concerned at the growing numbers of Chinese and Indian residents, and Chinese nationalists and communists began organizing throughout the peninsula. After the surrender of Japanese forces in September 1945 the colonies were reoccupied, a task complicated by the destruction and dislocation of war. The Japanese had also actively encouraged anti-Western nationalism while provoking nationalist and communist opposition to their own occupation. These groups were now intent on pursuing their own aims.

Between 1945 and the late 1960s the British Empire effectively disappeared. The remaining colonies and mandated territories gained their independence in two main bursts, between 1945 and 1948 (India, Burma, Egypt and Palestine) and from 1957 (Malaya and colonies in Africa and the West Indies). After 1945 Britain was forced to realize the limits of its own power and the nature of the changing world order. This was starkly brought home in the debacle of Suez in

Protestant Orangemen parade in Drumcree, Northern Ireland, in 2000. Ireland became a republic and severed its residual links with Great Britain in 1949, but Northern Ireland, retained as a part of the United Kingdom, was riven by the long, bloody, sectarian conflict between the Catholic republican and Protestant unionist communities known simply as 'the Troubles'.

1956. Empire remained popular at home, but Britain had lost interest in the imperial mission and the end came swiftly. By the 1960s Britain had come to see Europe and the developed world, not the Empire, as its economic future, and decolonization accelerated.

Some scattered territories remain, and many have prospered. In the British Indian Ocean Territory, however, in a throwback to the worst practices of imperial autocracy, some 2,000 inhabitants were systematically removed by the British government through subterfuge, dishonesty and force to facilitate the lease of the island of Diego Garcia to the USA as a military base in 1966.

Empire's Legacy

Queen Elizabeth II on a visit to Nigeria in 2003 which coincided with a Commonwealth Heads of Government meeting. It was the Queen's first state visit to Nigeria since 1956.

Elsewhere, it is Britain's withdrawal that has left a legacy of conflict and bitterness, particularly in those former dominions where indigenous peoples were subject to territorial dispossession and economic impoverishment. Restitution and compensation remain live issues in many countries. Ethnic divisions were also exacerbated in many territories, including Sri Lanka (Ceylon). But one of the most remarkable features of British decolonization has been the free association of former imperial territories in the Commonwealth of Nations. This diverse group, joined by historical accident and working together through common interest, is unique in world politics. It remains the most obvious link with the Empire while providing a range of support to its members for their future social and economic development.

The positive legacies of the Empire today lie in the community of peoples who enjoy the benefits of a shared cultural relationship through the medium of the English language in education, literature, sport, science and industry, technology and architecture. From the British perspective, law and parliamentary democracy have often been cited as great contributions to the world. But whatever moral judgement one makes on the Empire, the British imperial phenomenon largely created both the international economy and many of today's nation-states. Its impact has been profound.

Climax of Empire Trade and resources to 1942

In the Edwardian period the British Empire appeared confident and formidable. It would shortly incorporate the Afrikaner republics of South Africa and go on to greater territorial gains in the two World Wars of the 20th century. But even at the moment of climax Britain's economic and international weakness was increasingly apparent.

"On the wall at school hung a great map with large portions of it coloured red. It was an intoxicating vision for a small boy....We believed in our great imperial mission."

Earl Attlee, Chichele Lectures (1960)

The idea of empire as a partial remedy for Britain's economic problems gained ground from the late 19th century, but imperial protectionism remained hugely controversial and led to the defeat of the Conservatives in the General Election of 1906. Nonetheless, the concept of empire as a storehouse of goods became increasingly popular and Britain sought to promote the economic development of the dependent, largely tropical territories concentrated in Africa by exploiting their primary products. During the First World War the colonies prospered, but the Depression undermined colonial incomes, and investment in economic, infrastructure and social projects fell away.

In 1931 Britain was forced off the gold standard, and established the Empire (except Canada) as a 'sterling zone', where the pound was made the monetary standard, helping the Commonwealth to develop as an economic bloc. The Empire Marketing Board and other

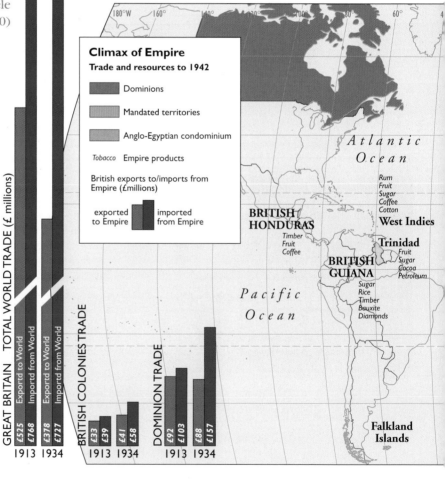

Climax of Empire
Trade and resources to 1942

- Dominions
- Mandated territories
- Anglo-Egyptian condominium

Tobacco Empire products

British exports to/imports from Empire (£millions)

exported to Empire — imported from Empire

GREAT BRITAIN TOTAL WORLD TRADE (£ millions)

Exportd to World £525
Importd from World £768
Exportd to World £378
Importd from World £727

1913 1934

BRITISH COLONIES TRADE

£33 £39 £41 £58
1913 1934

DOMINION TRADE

£92 £103 £88 £157
1913 1934

Atlantic Ocean

Pacific Ocean

BRITISH HONDURAS
Timber
Fruit
Coffee

BRITISH GUIANA
Sugar
Rice
Timber
Bauxite
Diamonds

West Indies
Rum
Fruit
Sugar
Coffee
Cotton

Trinidad
Fruit
Sugar
Cocoa
Petroleum

Falkland Islands

organizations had been established to promote intra-imperial trade. It was further helped by 'Imperial Preference', effectively old-style protectionism, introduced with the Ottawa agreements between Commonwealth members in 1932, designed to protect markets and secure cheap food and raw materials. Britain's trade with the Empire grew, doubling as a proportion of total trade between 1913 and 1938.

In much of the dependent Empire after the Second World War the long-standing economic strains, monetary inflation and trade controls fuelled nationalist sentiment. At home there was a renewed emphasis on the economic value of empire during the post-war readjustment. In 1950 it absorbed over 40 per cent of British exports in return for food and raw materials, and Britain again looked particularly to Africa to remedy shortages of goods and maintain the nation's morale. Attlee's Labour government (1945–51) represented the last gasp of the 'new imperialist' concept of colonial development, but with British economic recovery in the early 1950s the tropical colonies became less important. The Commonwealth sterling bloc remained central to Britain's financial planning and an important residual link with the Empire, but it succumbed to imperial dissolution and contracted sharply after 1973, when Britain joined the EEC (European Economic Community). The age of empire had passed.

An Empire Marketing Board (EMB) poster encouraging trade with the African sector of the Empire. The EMB (1926–33) was established in the inter-war period to develop and market food and goods produced in the Empire. It organized press and poster campaigns, exhibitions, 'shopping weeks', lectures and radio talks.

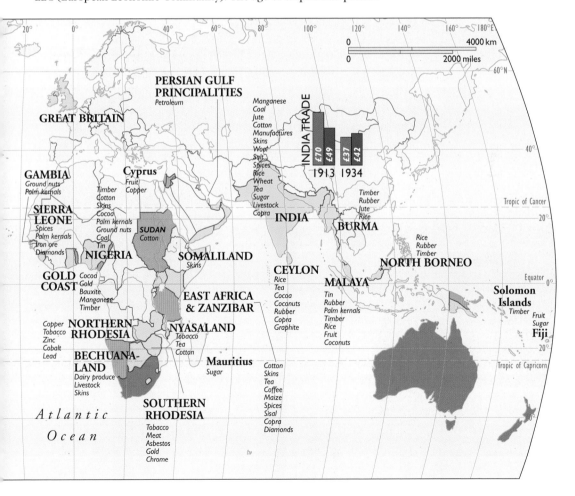

Imperial Defence 1 The First World War

Britain declared war on Germany on 4 August 1914, and in addition to more than eight million men ultimately called upon to fight in the name of the British king, George V, many Indians, Chinese, Africans, Egyptians and others served in labouring and ancillary units in all the theatres of war. The Empire's financial and material support was equally invaluable.

"The Empire stands on a pinnacle built by her own tenacity and courage – never did our reputation stand as high."

Sir Charles Monro, Commander-in-Chief India, December 1918

During the war Britain continued to receive supplies of food and other commodities from around the world thanks to the supremacy of the Royal Navy, whose units quickly destroyed the German commerce-raiders. The threat posed by such raiders, however, necessitated the early conquest of Germany's overseas empire, which provided wireless intelligence and support to German naval units and threatened Britain's imperial communications.

Campaigns in Africa and the Middle East

By early 1916 British and French forces had overrun Togoland and Cameroon, and South Africa had won control of German South West Africa. German East Africa was a greater problem; an early British-Indian assault on Tanga was badly defeated. Despite an Allied force of 100,000 British, South African, Indian and other troops, General Paul von Lettow-Vorbeck's colonial army (a maximum of 15,000 men) remained in the field until the German surrender in 1918. The cost of these campaigns to Africans included the death through famine and disease of 10 per cent of the estimated one million porters and labourers employed by both sides, in addition to civilian casualties and widespread destruction. Elsewhere, Australia took German New Guinea, New Zealand occupied Samoa, and allied Japan acquired various Pacific islands and Tsingtao on the North China coast. The German empire was completely destroyed.

In the Middle East the Ottoman empire sided with the Central Powers and Britain sent additional troops to protect Egypt and the Suez Canal. At first the 'sick man of Europe' appeared to be in rude health: in 1916 the Allied Dardanelles campaign ended in defeat; and the British thrust into Mesopotamia from Basra was stalled by the capitulation of an Anglo-Indian army at Kut. But the tide soon turned and, with Arab support, the British advance into the Ottoman provinces saw the occupation of Baghdad and northern Iraq. From Egypt, General Sir Edmund Allenby's army entered Jerusalem in December 1917 and continued through Syria, forcing the Ottoman surrender on 30 October 1918.

Post-war World

At the end of the war the world was partitioned anew. Britain was authorized by mandate of the League of Nations to administer Palestine, Transjordan, Iraq, Tanganyika (German East Africa), as well as Togoland and Cameroon divided with France. As the price for Italy's entry to the war on the Allied side in 1915, Britain ceded Jubaland in East Africa to Italian rule. The Dominions were also confirmed in their respective occupied territories, but the cost of the war and the heroism and sacrifice of the imperial troops, notably the ANZACs at Gallipoli (from April 1915), contributed to a growing proto-nationalism. In South Africa too, divisions over the war led to a reaction afterwards by more nationalist-minded Afrikaners under J B M Hertzog. Elsewhere on the continent new opposition arose and nationalist discontent encouraged by the war also led to pressing problems in India, Egypt, Mesopotamia and Ireland, which were now addressed by both coercion and conciliation.

The prestige of the Imperial armed forces throughout the war is evoked in this advertising card for Scotch whisky distillers MacDonald, Greenlees & Williams Ltd.

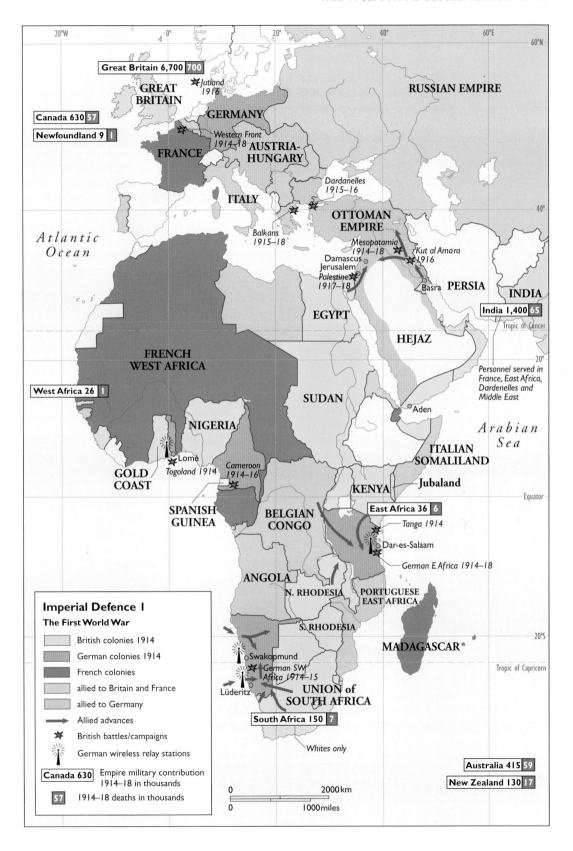

Great Britain 6,700 **700**

GREAT
BRITAIN

❋ *Jutland
1916*

Canada 630 **57**

Newfoundland 9 **1**

GERMANY

RUSSIAN EMPIRE

FRANCE

*Western Front
1914–18* AUSTRIA-
HUNGARY

ITALY

*Dardanelles
1915–16*

OTTOMAN
EMPIRE

*Atlantic
Ocean*

*Balkans
1915–18*

*Mesopotamia
1914–18* ❋ *Kut al Amara
1916*

*Damascus
Jerusalem
Palestine
1917–18* ❋ *Basra* PERSIA

EGYPT

INDIA

India 1,400 **65**

Tropic of Cancer

HEJAZ

FRENCH
WEST AFRICA

20°

*Personnel served in
France, East Africa,
Dardanelles and
Middle East*

West Africa 26 **1**

SUDAN

Aden

*Arabian
Sea*

NIGERIA

*Lomé
Togoland 1914* *Cameroon
1914–16*

GOLD
COAST

ITALIAN
SOMALILAND

Jubaland

KENYA

Equator

SPANISH
GUINEA

BELGIAN
CONGO

East Africa 36 **6**

Tanga 1914

Dar-es-Salaam

German E Africa 1914–18

ANGOLA

N. RHODESIA PORTUGUESE
EAST AFRICA

Imperial Defence 1

The First World War

S. RHODESIA

20°S

MADAGASCAR

Tropic of Capricorn

	British colonies 1914
	German colonies 1914
	French colonies
	allied to Britain and France
	allied to Germany

Swakopmund

*German SW
Africa 1914–15*

Lüderitz

UNION of
SOUTH AFRICA

⟶ Allied advances

❋ British battles/campaigns

German wireless relay stations

South Africa 150 **7**

Canada 630 Empire military contribution
1914–18 in thousands

57 1914–18 deaths in thousands

Whites only

0		2000 km
0	1000 miles	

Australia 415 **59**

New Zealand 130 **17**

Imperial Defence II The Second World War

Despite new stresses and divisions, the Empire was still remarkably coherent and united in 1939. The Dominions again came to Britain's aid against Germany, Italy and Japan, but the Allied cause was also generally supported by opinion in the colonial Empire, and the peoples of these territories were put to work once again.

"In that dark, terrific and also glorious hour we received from all parts of His Majesty's Dominions ... the assurance that we would all go down or come through together."

Winston Churchill, speech, 30 June 1943

The Second World War was much more of a global conflict than had been the case in 1914–18, and Empire and Commonwealth forces served in all theatres, including 15,000 colonial seamen in the merchant navy, where casualties, mainly from U-boat action, were disproportionately high. The war saw enemy campaigns directed against imperial territories as well as Britain itself. Egypt was a major battleground in the Allied struggle against Germany and Italy, while Japan quickly overran British territories in East and South East Asia, and threatened both India and Australia. In all these territories – but particularly in Australia – the realization that a Britain hard-pressed at home lacked the means to defend distant imperial territories prompted both a deep (though initially covert) re-examination of the imperial relationship and an urgent reappraisal of the importance of self-reliance as a national strategy.

An Overstretched Empire

The First World War had established that Britain was no longer able to rule the waves, and inter-war naval treaties reflected this decline. It was compounded by Britain's refusal to renew the 1921 alliance with Japan in the East, and with the loss of naval power the foundation of British imperial rule was seriously undermined. No longer able to exert worldwide dominance, the Royal Navy came to rely more on colonial and allied support even in 'home' waters – especially the Royal Canadian Navy in the North Atlantic, and later the USA.

Anthony Eden (1897–1997), Secretary of State for the Dominions, inspects Indian troops at their Egyptian camp near the pyramids in February 1940. Throughout the Second World War British units were supported by forces from the Empire and Dominions.

Much British naval and military effort was concentrated on the defence of Egypt (an independent kingdom since 1922, but effectively commandeered for the war with the installation of a pro-British government) and the vital Middle East oil supplies. Securing the latter necessitated the invasion of Vichy French-ruled Syria and pro-German Iraq and Iran in 1941. Italy had joined the German war effort in June 1940 and invaded British Somaliland, but its forces were cleared from North East Africa (including occupied Abyssinia) the following year. In May 1942 Vichy French Madagascar was seized and passed to Free French administration. The defeat of the Axis powers in North Africa was finally secured after the Battle of El Alamein (August 1942). With the allied advance from Morocco, the way was cleared for the invasion of Italy (1943) and the re-establishment of Britain's primary artery of communication with its eastern empire through the Mediterranean. One cost, however, was the resentment felt by Egyptians and other Arabs at the way their countries had been treated by Britain during the war; this was to take a tangible form in the Suez crisis of 1956.

The campaign in the East was more difficult. From 1941 Britain suffered a series of ignominious defeats at the hands of Japan in Hong Kong, Malaya, Borneo and Burma. The loss of the key naval base of Singapore, with 132,000

British subjects taken prisoner, including 32,000 Indian, 16,000 British and 14,000 Australian troops, was particularly shocking: British prestige in the East was fatally wounded. The Japanese advance was finally halted, and reversed, at Kohima and Imphal in North East India (mid-1944) by British forces over-whelmingly reliant on Indian troops.

Japanese expansion had brought the USA into the war, and now Britain and the Empire had to adjust to the new global power with anti-(European) imperi-al sentiments. Much of Britain's post-war national debt of £3.5 billion was owed to the USA. Dominion ties were further loosened, with Canada, Australia and New Zealand all developing closer defence links with the United States. Adjust-ing to the new climate, Britain began to address post-war imperial policy, with ideas of partnership and colonial development seen as the route to self-govern-ment within the Commonwealth.

Across the colonial Empire growing nationalism, unrest and social and eco-nomic change made the Second World War the apotheosis of British power. India was the first to go, with independence in 1947 effectively promised as the price of wartime support. In Malaya and elsewhere, Britain had supported anti-Japanese nationalist and communist guerrillas; their capabilities were now turned against Britain itself. Although the Empire was ostensibly united in con-flict, the cost of the World Wars of the 20th century was its nemesis.

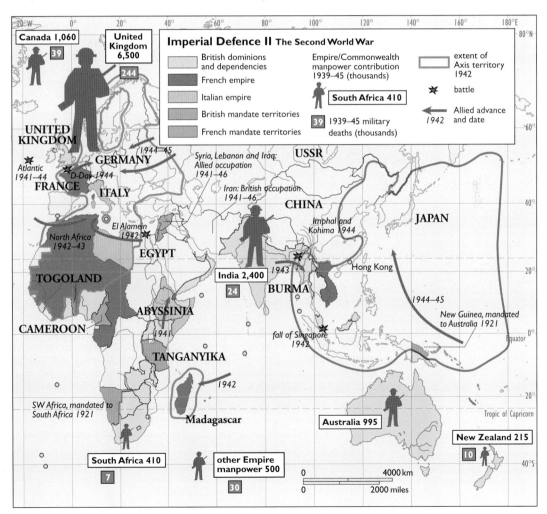

Securing the Canal The Middle East to 1945

In the 19th century Britain's interest in the Middle East intensified, spurred especially by the desire to protect Imperial communications with India. The central policy was to uphold the territorial integrity of the weak Ottoman Empire against acquisitive European powers. To the east, Britain was also concerned to restrict Russian influence in Persia, and later to defend British oil interests in the region.

"[Britain supports] the establishment ... of a national home for the Jewish people [as long as] nothing shall be done which may prejudice the ... rights of existing non-Jewish communities. "

Balfour Declaration, 2 November 1917

When the Suez Canal opened in 1869, Egypt acquired an even greater strategic importance for the British Empire. Britain gained control of Cyprus in 1878, in return for aiding the Ottoman Empire against Russia, as a useful additional military base in the eastern Mediterranean; then in 1882 the collapse of Egypt prompted what was initially seen as a 'temporary' British occupation. When war broke out in 1914, the Ottoman Empire joined the Central Powers; Britain declared Egypt a British protectorate and annexed Cyprus, but the established policy of maintaining the unity of the Ottoman Empire was in ruins.

Britain had a well-defended main line of communications based on naval power, strongpoints from Gibraltar to Aden and control of adjacent territories. British forces in the Sinai fended off Ottoman attacks on Egypt, then advanced through Palestine and Syria (1917–18) under General Sir Edmund Allenby, while an Indian expeditionary force moved up through Mesopotamia (1915–18). In Nejd, the British encouraged Ibn Saud's opposition to the Ottoman Empire. In the Hejaz, they actively assisted the Arab Revolt (1916) under Hussein, Emir and Grand Sharif of Mecca, aided by T. E. Lawrence, with deliberately vague promises of an independent pan-Arab state. This later conflicted with British support in the Balfour Declaration (1917) for a Jewish national homeland in Palestine.

These undertakings were also at variance with the Sykes-Picot agreement (1916) in which Britain and France settled the post-war partition of the Ottoman Empire. The British agreed to French control of territory to the north as a buffer against expected Russian gains in eastern Turkey, thus maintaining Russia's exclusion from the Mediterranean. With the collapse of Russia in the 1917 Revolution, the security of Britain's Mediterranean route was confirmed.

Control by Treaty

The fall of the Ottoman Empire in October 1918 made Britain's position unassailable. But pressures at home and in the Empire, and the problems of administering a volatile region, prompted modification to schemes for creating a 'greater' British Middle East that excluded France altogether. Arab aspirations were ignored, and Ottoman territory was parcelled out between Britain and France in the Treaty of Sèvres (1920) under mandate from the League of Nations. Britain was later forced to accept Turkish independence (Treaty of Lausanne, 1923) under Kemal Atatürk, and abandoned plans to establish a protectorate over Persia. Nonetheless, Britain's strategic interests were largely secure.

At the end of the war, Egyptian nationalism exploded in revolt (1919). To overcome the difficulties and expense of direct rule, Britain created a system of control by treaty, allowing independence (1922) but retaining a key role in Egyptian foreign affairs and defence. A treaty of 1936 arranged for the withdrawal of British troops, except from the Canal Zone, which was recognized as a vital British interest. In Iraq, a major nationalist revolt occurred in 1920–1 and Faisal, son of Hussein, Sharif of Mecca, was made king, supported by British

Field Marshal Sir Edmund Allenby (1861–1936) with his servant on the verandah of his Cairo residency in 1918. Allenby led the Egyptian Expeditionary Force in the conquest of Palestine and Syria in 1917–18. He was High Commissioner of Egypt (1919–25) during the explosion of Egyptian nationalism that threatened Britain's imperial influence in the region and led to Egypt's independence.

power. In exchange, Britain received privileges confirmed by a treaty that remained in force after full Iraqi independence in 1932. In Britain's client state of Transjordan, Faisal's brother Abdullah was made Emir and was bound to Britain by a security treaty (1928). Palestine was more of a difficulty. Arab nationalist aspirations were denied and increasing Jewish immigration exacerbated intercommunal tensions, culminating in an Arab revolt against British rule (1936–9) and the parallel development of Zionist terrorism.

At the start of the Second World War, Britain was powerfully positioned in the Middle East, but lacked Arab support in the impending contest with Germany and Italy. British interests, which included essential oil supplies, were secured only through widespread military occupation (in Iraq following a pro-Axis coup in 1941). At the end of the war, local resentment was even greater, and Britain's authority soon suffered a series of challenges, due to come to a climax in the disaster of the Suez invasion of 1956.

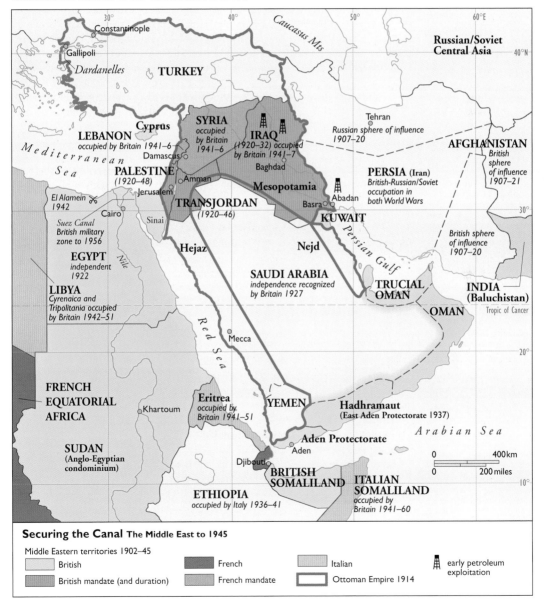

Securing the Canal The Middle East to 1945

Middle Eastern territories 1902–45

British	French	Italian	early petroleum exploitation
British mandate (and duration)	French mandate	Ottoman Empire 1914	

A Free Ireland Ireland's long road to independence

Ireland was an early object of British conquest, and pursued the most intractable and persistent struggle for self-determination. National feeling fed off the insensitivity displayed by British rule, encouraging both the republican, or revolutionary, strand in the Irish opposition and the constitutional or parliamentary tradition.

> *"You cannot conquer Ireland, you cannot extinguish the Irish passion for freedom."*
>
> Patrick Pearse, following the Easter Rising, 1916

The main aim of the proponents of peaceful reform for Ireland was Home Rule. This meant repealing the Act of Union (1800) that had abolished the Irish Parliament, transferred legislative power to Westminster and created a system of imperial rule headed by viceroys based at Dublin Castle. Early political discontent successfully centred on Catholic emancipation, but failure to achieve repeal of the union led to an unsuccessful 'Young Ireland' revolt in 1848. Ireland's contribution to the European 'year of revolutions' took place during the great famine (1846–9) caused by the failure of the potato crop, on which many in Ireland were entirely dependent. Death and emigration caused a population of nearly 9 million to collapse to only 6.6 million in 1851. The government's inability, and even unwillingness, to provide enough relief further embittered relations and eroded British legitimacy in Ireland.

Crowds march through the streets of Dublin in April 1939 to commemorate the Easter Rising (1916) of Irish nationalists against British rule in Ireland. A banner of the National Association of the Old IRA can be seen. The name Irish Republican Army (IRA) has been used to refer to a number of paramilitary groups in Ireland's history. 'Old IRA' refers to the army of the Irish Republic around the time of the Easter Rising, when Irish volunteers and the Irish Citizens' Army merged, rather than to later claimants to the name.

Irish Grievances

The famine and the violent activities of the Irish Republican Brotherhood (IRB), the Fenians (established 1858), drew attention to the need for land reform. William Gladstone's Liberal party began to address national grievances from 1868, but in the meantime support for Home Rule in Ireland was growing. Leadership of the movement was assumed by the charismatic politician Charles Stewart Parnell of the Home Rule League. During the 'land war' of 1879–82 Parnell skilfully exploited the grassroots activism of the Irish Land League (formed 1879) and used parliamentary disruption to focus British minds on Irish grievances. After the 1885 British general election his 85 MPs held the balance of power in Parliament and their leverage helped persuade Gladstone to support the Home Rule crusade.

Republican Divisions

However, on the very eve of victory, nationalist ambitions were frustrated – and remained so for the next two decades – by their own divisions and by the parliamentary opposition of Liberal unionists and Conservatives allied with the Ulster Protestants. The Ulster Protestants were strongly opposed to rule from Catholic Dublin and feared a threat to their economic prosperity. Gladstone's two Home Rule Bills (1886 and 1893) were defeated, but Ireland remained solidly in favour of self-government, and in elections between 1885 and 1912 Home Rule candidates won at least 80 of the 103 Irish seats.

When a third Home Rule Bill was finally introduced by the Liberals, with Irish support, in 1912 it provoked passionate unionist opposition in Ulster, led by Sir Edward Carson. The Ulster Volunteer Force, a private army of up to

100,000 men, was organized, and in response nationalists created the Irish Volunteers and the (socialist) Irish Citizens' Army. Civil conflict was only averted by the outbreak of the First World War, and although the Home Rule Bill was passed, it was shelved until the return of peace.

The Easter Rising

This stratagem, and Irish parliamentary support for the British war effort, enraged the revolutionary element in Ireland. In the Easter Rising of 1916 a radical core of around 1,000 volunteers and members of the Citizens' Army, led by Patrick Pearse of the IRB and James Connolly of Sinn Féin, took over the main public buildings in Dublin and proclaimed an Irish republic. The rising's brutal suppression radicalized popular opinion in Ireland. The constitutional Home Rule party lost support, and it declined further still with the prospect of conscription in Ireland. At the 1918 elections the party was largely displaced by the revolutionary republican party Sinn Féin, whose 73 parliamentary representatives established an independent national parliament – the Dáil Éireann – in Dublin in January 1919.

Political developments were accompanied by a developing guerrilla offensive (1919–21) by the Irish Volunteers, now called the Irish Republican Army, led by Michael Collins. In 1920 the British government passed a Government of Ireland Act, allowing for Home Rule on equivalent terms in both Dublin and Ulster, within the United Kingdom of Great Britain and Ireland. Both sides sought an end to hostilities and, after a truce, a treaty was agreed in December 1921. This recognized the Irish Free State not as a republic but as a dominion of Britain, subject to the Crown, and also the autonomy of Northern Ireland (whose own Home Rule parliament was established in 1921). It also preserved the status of three British naval bases in Ireland.

The agreement was sharply divisive in Ireland, but it was accepted by most of the country. Die-hard republicans were defeated in a short Irish civil war (1922–3), after which their opposition was directed through the Fianna Fáil party, which came to power under Eamon de Valera in 1932. He set about breaking Irish constitutional ties with Britain, and negotiated with Prime Minister Neville Chamberlain the return to Irish control of the treaty ports in 1938. Eire remained neutral during the Second World War, became a full republic in 1949 and left the Commonwealth. The separation was complete.

Belfast City:
3 Unionist,
1 Liberal Unionist

Lough Swilly
Londonderry City
Donegal
Londonderry
Antrim
NORTHERN
IRELAND
Belfast
Tyrone
Down
Fermanagh
Monaghan
Armagh
Sligo
Leitrim
Cavan
Louth
Mayo
Roscommon
Longford
Meath
Galway
West Meath
Dublin
Galway City
Dublin
Offaly
Kildare
IRISH FREE STATE
(EIRE from 1937)
Leix
Wicklow
Clare
Carlow
Tipperary
Kilkenny
Wexford
Limerick
Kerry
Waterford
Dublin: 4 Nationalist;
University: 1 Unionist,
1 Liberal Unionist
Cork
Queenstown
(Cobh)
Berehaven

0   100 km
0   50 miles

A Free Ireland

Ireland's long road to independence

Parliamentary representation, 1900

Nationalist

Unionist

Liberal Unionist

—— Northern Ireland border, 1920

● British treaty ports 1921–38

Protestant composition of county populations, 1926

0–20%

20–40%

40–60%

60–80%

Independent Dominions

Canada, Newfoundland, Australia and New Zealand were officially designated dominions in 1907 as a mark of their growing status, and were joined later by South Africa and the Irish Free State. As the century progressed, their relationship with Britain changed.

As the dominions became more involved with the world, and in fighting Britain's wars, they demanded more of a say in policy and decision-making. The First World War did much to change the outlooks and ambitions of this proto-Commonwealth. It brought international recognition of their contributions, and they both signed the post-war peace treaties and joined the League of Nations in their own right. Some emerged from the war with their own mandated territories, and Australia and New Zealand would continue an imperial path of their own in the Pacific and Antarctic.

> *"By the end of [the Second World War] the status of the white colonies had changed. No longer could they be ruled from Whitehall. They had become nations. "*
>
> Earl Attlee, Chichele Lectures (1960)

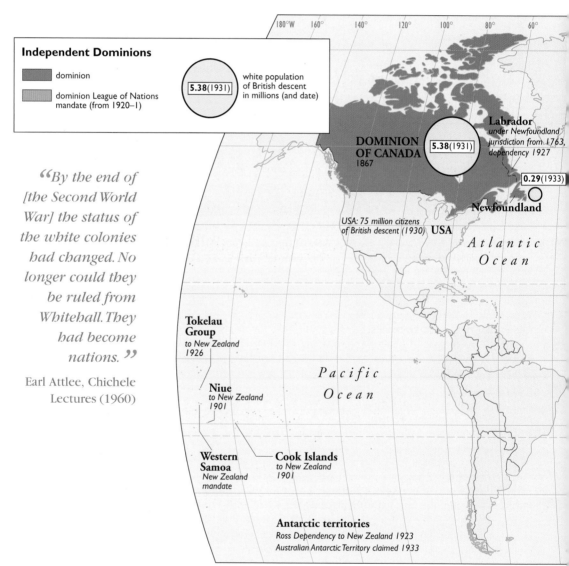

Independent Dominions

- dominion
- dominion League of Nations mandate (from 1920–1)

5.38(1931) — white population of British descent in millions (and date)

DOMINION OF CANADA 1867

5.38(1931)

Labrador *under Newfoundland jurisdiction from 1763, dependency 1927*

0.29(1933)

Newfoundland

USA: 75 million citizens of British descent (1930) **USA**

Atlantic Ocean

Tokelau Group *to New Zealand 1926*

Niue *to New Zealand 1901*

Pacific Ocean

Western Samoa *New Zealand mandate*

Cook Islands *to New Zealand 1901*

Antarctic territories *Ross Dependency to New Zealand 1923 Australian Antarctic Territory claimed 1933*

Their new independence was recognized at the 1926 Imperial Conference and confirmed in the Statute of Westminster in 1931. But the ties of empire held strong. Race remained a major unifying factor, and was reinforced by emigration from Britain; the Empire (overwhelmingly the dominions) was the destination of 43 per cent of British emigrants in 1900, rising to 83 per cent in the late 1930s. The total number of emigrants fluctuated but remained significant well into the late 20th century.

The economic Depression from 1929 forced the dominions to fall back on British leadership and support. At the 1932 Imperial Economic Conference in Ottawa, free trade was temporarily abandoned in favour of 'Imperial Preference' (protectionism). The dominions realized, however, that Britain was no longer to be relied upon as the engine of their own economic growth.

In the threatening international climate of the 1930s the dominions recognized imperial solidarity as the best form of defence, and gave firm backing to Britain in Second World War, but the same cold calculation operated afterwards. Britain's economic and military weakness was apparent to all, and the dominions adjusted to the post-war dominance of the USA as the arbiter of international affairs. Imperial ties were loosening.

A family enquiring about emigration to Australia at Australia House, London, in 1953. British emigration to the white dominions increased from the beginning of the 20th century. The Second World War was a major trigger for large-scale migration to Australia. Many Europeans were displaced by the war and Australia was suffering from an acute labour shortage. A significant proportion of Australia's overseas-born population today originates from Britain.

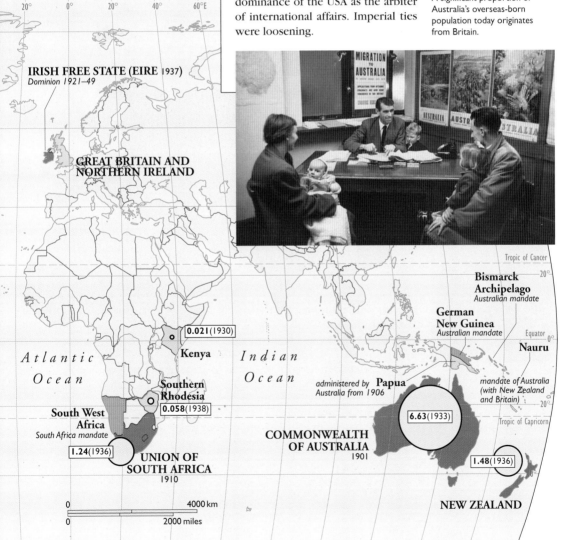

IRISH FREE STATE (EIRE 1937)
Dominion 1921–49

GREAT BRITAIN AND NORTHERN IRELAND

Bismarck Archipelago
Australian mandate

German New Guinea
Australian mandate

Nauru

Tropic of Cancer

0.021(1930)

Kenya

Atlantic Ocean

Indian Ocean

administered by **Papua**
Australia from 1906

mandate of Australia
(with New Zealand and Britain)

Southern Rhodesia

0.058(1938)

6.63(1933)

Tropic of Capricorn

South West Africa
South Africa mandate

COMMONWEALTH OF AUSTRALIA
1901

1.24(1936)

UNION OF SOUTH AFRICA
1910

1.48(1936)

0   4000 km
0   2000 miles

NEW ZEALAND

Colonial Revolts Decolonization and confrontation

Nationalism gained in strength during and after the First World War, but Britain managed potential conflict effectively. Persuasion and coercion were used to suppress nationalist ambitions, to counter ethnic and economic tensions and to maintain imperial control until the costs became too great.

"Not only is India going, but [also] Malay[a], Ceylon and the Middle East ... with a tremendous repercussion on the African territories."

Ernest Bevin, Foreign Secretary, speech, 1 January 1947

A statue of Archbishop Makarios (1913–77), first president of the Republic of Cyprus. The British gained control of Cyprus in 1878, and the island was formally annexed in 1914. From the 1940s some Cypriots demanded union with Greece and this political struggle erupted into guerrilla activity in 1955. Cyprus finally gained its independence in 1960.

Britain pioneered the use of air power for colonial control in Iraq, where the RAF helped defeat a revolt in 1920 and later quash an insurgency in the north. Disturbances throughout the Indian subcontinent (and Burma) required massive military and police resources. An Afghan invasion was defeated in 1919, and operations on the North West Frontier throughout the 1920s absorbed 50,000 troops by 1937. Opposition to British rule erupted more fiercely after the Second World War, when Britain was in even weaker economic circumstances, had additional responsibility for territory captured from the Axis powers, and could no longer afford to maintain two million men under arms. The USA, now the dominant power, also restricted Britain's ability to use of force to maintain imperial control.

Britain now conceded the principle of self-determination to certain territories, notably India, although here communal divisions led to the partition of the country and a hurried departure in 1947. Similarly, British forces were withdrawn from the quagmire of Arab-Jewish conflict in Palestine in 1948. This episode embittered British relations with the whole of the Middle East, particularly Egypt, where assaults on the Suez garrison intensified from 1951. Britain had hoped to preserve Egypt and India as close allies, but events ran quickly out of control, gravely weakening British authority.

Britain sought to extricate itself from Egypt while protecting its economic interests – particularly oil – in the Middle East from the growing Soviet threat. But an agreement with the Egyptians allowing the withdrawal of Britain's 80,000-strong garrison by 1956 was followed by the nationalization of the Suez Canal by President Nasser, and a British invasion to re-establish control over the

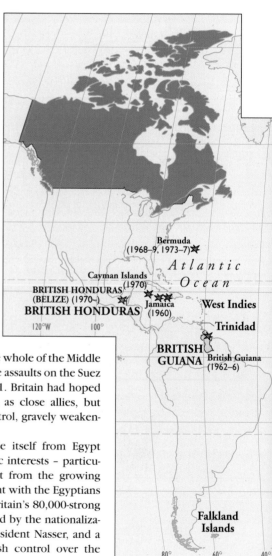

Bermuda (1968–9, 1973–7)

Cayman Islands (1970)

BRITISH HONDURAS (BELIZE) (1970–)

BRITISH HONDURAS (1960)

Jamaica

Atlantic Ocean

West Indies

Trinidad

BRITISH GUIANA

British Guiana (1962–6)

Falkland Islands

strategic waterway. The failure of this expedition ended any hope of continued world power status for Britain. British influence was undermined in Jordan, which expelled British advisers, and Iraq's pro-British regime was overthrown in 1958. Aden and the South Arabian Federation succumbed to a sustained guerrilla war from 1963 to 1967 when, lacking sufficient internal support, Britain finally withdrew.

Elsewhere, Britain's exhausted post-war finances encouraged further economic exploitation of the remaining African and Asian colonies. Some of these were valuable assets – notably Malaya, where Britain determined to resist the communist insurgency of 1948–60. Here Britain conceded self-government, and retained sufficient local support to defeat the opposition and maintain economic and strategic co-operation.

Other imperial emergencies were relatively small-scale, with the exception of the Mau Mau insurrection in Kenya, suppressed by police and 12,000 troops during 1952–6. Whites in Southern Rhodesia unilaterally declared independence in 1965, which Britain was able to counter with a trade embargo that helped end the illegal regime only in 1980. British postwar governments were loath to withdraw armed forces from 'East of Suez', but continuing economic weakness dictated an eventual retreat from the Indian Ocean and Persian Gulf in 1971. British troops continued to be sent to scattered remnants of the Empire in order to preserve order and oppose external threats, but at last ambition and resources were reconciled.

Colonial Revolts
Decolonization and confrontation

- dominions
- mandated territories 1945
- Anglo-Egyptian condominium
- British bases and date of withdrawal
- emergencies and policing duties from 1945
- defensive operations from 1945
- main inter-war policing operations

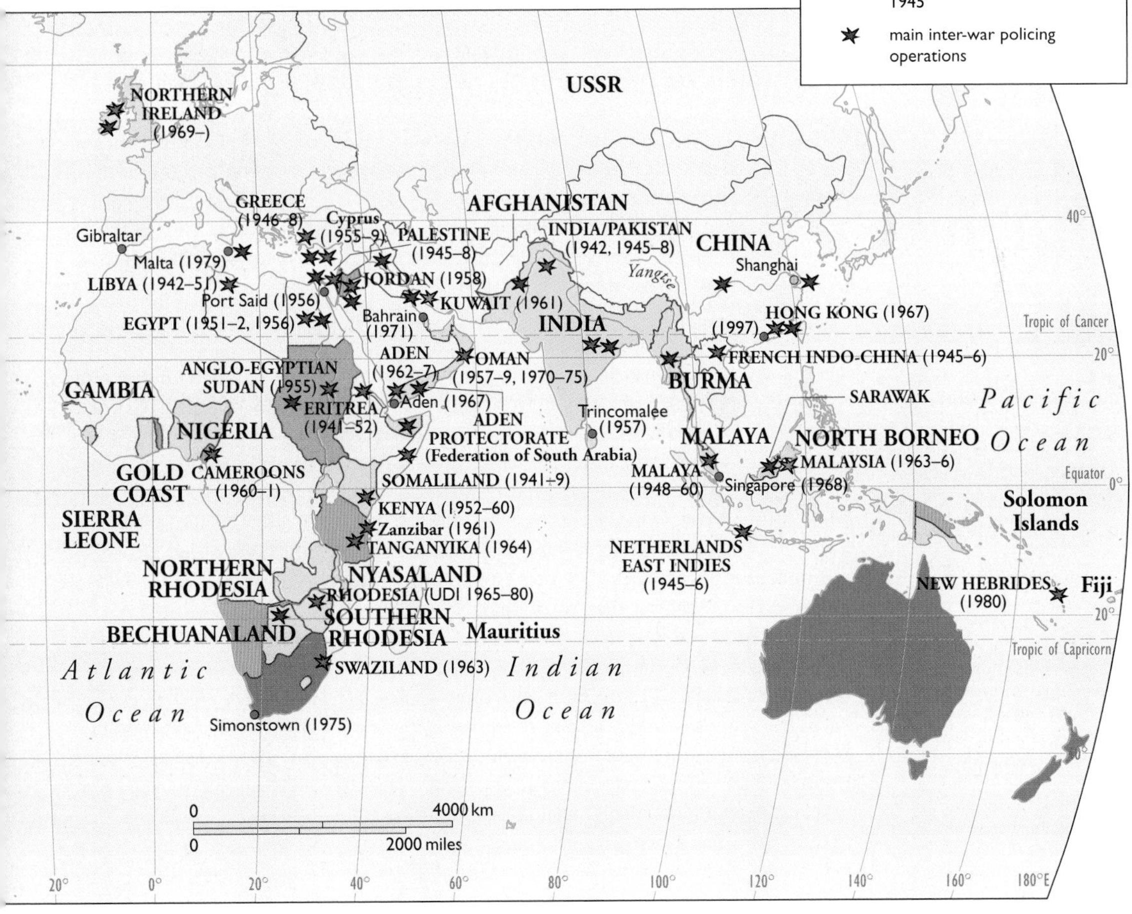

The Road to Suez The Middle East 1945–56

After 1945 Britain balked at the cost of maintaining a formidable military presence in the Middle East and Mediterranean. It had also lost the battle for Arab (and Iranian) opinion, and new threats to British dominance emerged in the developing Cold War world. The USA was hostile to British primacy in the region and keen to vie for oil and influence.

"Particularly since Suez ... in the Middle East we have lost confidence in our ability to deal with situations."

Sir Charles Johnston, Governor of Aden, 16 March 1961

In British-mandated Palestine, the arrival of increasing numbers of Jewish immigrants from post-war Europe aggravated existing communal conflict with the Arab population; Jewish terror groups also intensified their attacks on the British administration. Faces with US support for Zionist ambitions and widespread Arab hostility, Britain resigned the United Nations mandate in May 1948 and left the warring parties to arrive at their own solution. This led to the foundation of the state of Israel and the first Arab-Israeli War (1948–9). It also fatally weakened Britain's position in the Middle East. Arab nationalists, although heartened by the withdrawal, blamed Britain for betraying the Palestinians, and anti-Western radicalism gained ground everywhere.

The first bombshell came from Iran, where Mohammed Mosaddeq nationalized the Anglo-Iranian Oil Company. Britain was unable to respond with military action for fear of the US response. The latter's new influence in the region was further apparent when the CIA engineered a military coup in Iran (1953) which promoted US oil companies at Britain's expense. The Iranian actions resounded throughout the Middle East. Even conservative Saudi Arabia stepped up its territorial claims to the British-protected Gulf states and their potential oil reserves. But the main flashpoint was Egypt. Palestine and the disputed future of Anglo-Egyptian Sudan had soured relations and dashed Britain's hopes of a treaty allowing the withdrawal of troops. In July 1952 a revolution removed King Farouk, one of the monarchs in the Middle East broadly favourable to British interests; his pro-British inclinations had proven an important factor in his downfall.

Egyptian citizens being searched by a British soldier during the Suez Crisis of 1956. The crisis marked the conclusion of the shift in the global balance of power from Britain to the USA and the Soviet Union.

Nasser's Egypt

Colonel Gamal Abdel Nasser seized power in Egypt in 1954, and agreed terms for the evacuation of British troops by mid-1956. But a clash was approaching. Nasser, a strong pan-Arab nationalist who was hostile to the British presence throughout the Middle East, sought to end British influence altogether and attain the leadership of the Arab world. Nasser also regarded the Baghdad Pact for regional (anti-Soviet) security, established in 1955 with Britain as a member, as inimical to Arab interests and to his own ambitions. When Britain attempted to recruit Jordan to the pact, Nasser exploited Jordanian internal discontent. After serious riots in Amman in 1956, King Hussein dismissed his British advisers, abrogated the 1946 Anglo-Jordanian treaty and adroitly moved towards aligning his country with Egypt.

In the end Britain fell victim to Egyptian hostility and US antipathy. Nasser's anti-Western stance forced him to purchase arms from the Eastern Bloc, which in turn prompted the cancellation of US (and later British) funding for the huge Aswan Dam construction project. As an alternative source of funding, Egypt nationalized the Anglo-French Suez Canal Company in July 1956. British interests and prestige were at stake, and Prime Minister Anthony Eden was determined to recover control of the Canal. The USA was little affected by the Egyptian move and its government was not unhappy at the erosion of British influence in the region. It now opposed British military intervention, but Eden gambled on ultimate US acceptance, and ordered the invasion of the Canal Zone (October), in collusion with France and Israel. But the USA, and international opinion, demanded the allies' withdrawal, and they had little choice. The British evacuation began in December 1956.

The Suez debacle ended any pretence of continued British primacy in the Middle East. In 1958 an Iraqi revolution disposed of the pro-British monarchy in that country, and the Gulf princedoms and Aden began to agitate for their own independence. The hope of creating a British commonwealth in the Middle East was at an end.

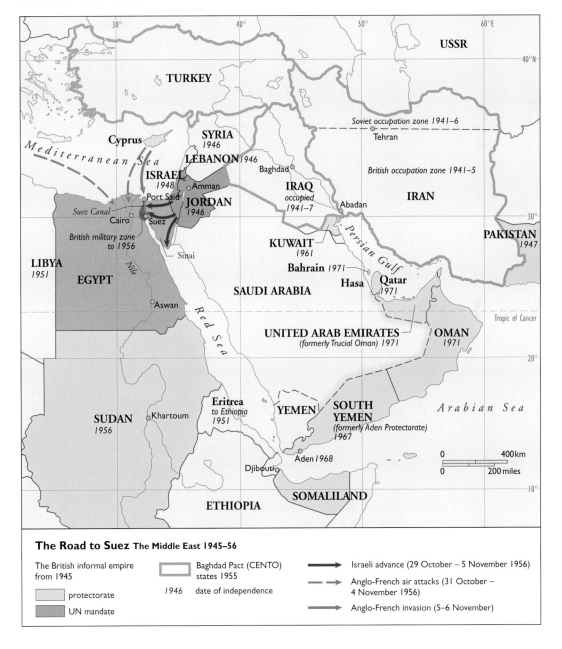

The Road to Suez The Middle East 1945–56

The British informal empire from 1945

- protectorate
- UN mandate

Baghdad Pact (CENTO) states 1955

1946 date of independence

→ Israeli advance (29 October – 5 November 1956)

⇢ Anglo-French air attacks (31 October – 4 November 1956)

→ Anglo-French invasion (5–6 November)

The End of the Eastern Empire

The military disasters of 1941 ultimately proved fatal to British efforts to restore its South East Asian empire after 1945. First Burma and then Malaya and the Borneo territories proved impossible to hold in the face of nationalist opposition, the changing international order and domestic pressure for economic retrenchment.

"The British Empire in the Far East depended on prestige. This prestige has been completely shattered."

Christopher Thorne, *Allies of a Kind ... 1941-45* (1978)

Britain's armed forces had proven inadequate to meet the onslaught of Japan in December 1941. For Prime Minister Winston Churchill, Malaya was 'the worst disaster and largest capitulation in British history'. It was also the most humiliating, and invigorated nationalists everywhere in the region.

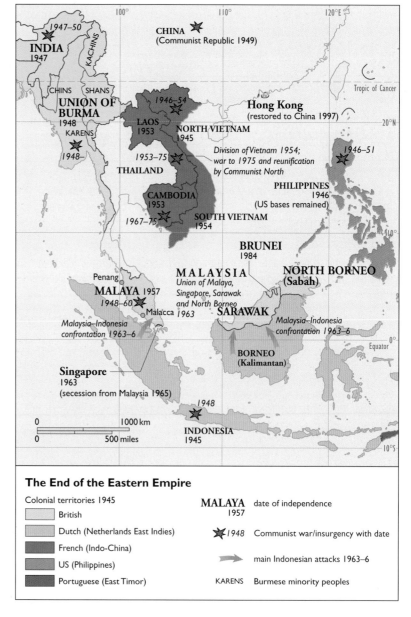

The End of the Eastern Empire

Colonial territories 1945

- British
- Dutch (Netherlands East Indies)
- French (Indo-China)
- US (Philippines)
- Portuguese (East Timor)

MALAYA 1957   date of independence

⭐ *1948*   Communist war/insurgency with date

➤   main Indonesian attacks 1963–6

KARENS   Burmese minority peoples

The war's legacy was the collapse of European colonialism in Asia. In 1944–5 British forces re-took Burma, aided by Aung San's Burma National Army and the Burma Communist Party. With limited military resources available, Britain had no choice but to grant independence; the British government also balked at the cost of post-war reconstruction. In January 1948 the Union of Burma was established, and all ties with Britain and the Commonwealth were broken. An insurgency by the Communist Party and Karen separatists followed, and Burma lapsed into traditional isolation.

In Malaya British attitudes were different. The country was an important trade and strategic asset, rich in tin and rubber, and Britain was keen to entrench its position in the territory and create a more efficient and united colony. The Malay states, Penang and Malacca were combined into a stronger Malay Union (1946), with the future prospect of dominion status and the incorporation of other British territories. To many Malays, however, this simply meant the weakening of their ethnic dominance. Britain relented and in February 1948 the Union was replaced by the Federation of Malaya, but the issue aggravated inter-communal tensions, particularly with the Chinese community.

Communist Insurgency

In June 1948 the Chinese-dominated Malayan Communist Party's Malayan People's Anti-British Army launched an insurgency, which lasted until 1960. Britain was determined to protect its economic interests and increasingly, in alliance with the USA, to contain the communist threat in the region. The Malayan Emergency was finally resolved by effective counter-insurgency techniques, the failure of the communists to gain popular support (particularly from the Malay community) and by Britain's commitment to independence, which was granted in 1957.

A British soldier lights a cigarette for a Dyak irregular in Malaya in 1950. The Dyaks, or Dayaks, played an important part in Britain's successful campaign against communist insurgency in the region.

In the post-war period the USA's anti-colonial stance was modified to oppose the threat of communism, particularly after the creation of the People's Republic of China (1949). Conflicting priorities occasionally led to Anglo-US friction, such as over Britain's recognition of China in 1950 (undertaken partly to preserve the security of Hong Kong). With its own regional commitments, Britain was also reluctant to become too closely involved in US wars in Asia, especially Vietnam, although a loose security pact (SEATO) was agreed in 1954. This soon proved ineffectual, and the USA turned instead to Australia and New Zealand (the ANZUS pact), reflecting the new power alignment in the region.

Britain recognized the inevitability of decolonization in South East Asia, and sought to retain influence through the Commonwealth, defence agreements and the sterling area. It backed Malaya's incorporation of Singapore (until 1965) and northern Borneo (except Brunei) in the Federation in 1963 for added mutual security. British and Commonwealth forces supported the new state of Malaysia in a three-year war with Indonesia (1953–6) which asserted claims of its own to British Borneo.

In 1967 the sterling crisis forced Britain to reconsider its commitments 'East of Suez', and the following year the decision was taken to withdraw. Britain could no longer afford the status of a regional power in South East Asia. The defence agreement with Malaysia was replaced by the Five-Power Treaty sharing the burden with Australia, New Zealand and Singapore, where Britain's main Far East naval base and permanent presence in the region was abandoned for the second and last time in 1971.

Wind of Change Nationalism and white rule in Africa

Britain recognized that growing African national consciousness, famously described by Prime Minister Harold Macmillan in 1959 as a 'wind of change' blowing through the continent, would inevitably lead to decolonization. The challenge was to manage this process while preserving British interests.

"I had become conscious of myself as a Kenya African, one among millions whose destinies were still in the hands of foreigners."

Waruhiu Itote, Mau Mau General, 1967

West Africa was seen in Britain as the region with territories best suited for independence. In 1957, the Gold Coast, renamed Ghana, became the first independent state in sub-Saharan black Africa, under the moderate nationalist Kwame Nkrumah. Britain's divestment of its African colonies accelerated after 1959 with the beginning of French decolonization and the growing realization that Britain's economic future lay with Europe. West Africa posed few obvious problems, and the old mandated territories were shaken off at the same time.

Multiracial Interests

Other British colonies in eastern, central and southern Africa, such as Nyasaland and the High Commission territories, were regarded as too undeveloped or small for independence, and more suited to gradual incorporation within larger federal states. The violent nationalist Mau Mau revolt in Kenya (1952–60), confined largely to the Kikuyu peasantry, tended to confirm British prejudices. The movement towards independence was inexorable, however, and Britain opposed simply handing power to the small white settler communities, whose attitudes, abilities and local policies successive British governments generally disdained. The interests of Africans were viewed as paramount, and the ideal was multiracial development and universal suffrage with safeguards for minorities, even where this was opposed by the white communities.

The proposal for an East African Federation of Kenya, Uganda and Tanganyika (with a combined population of 18 million in 1950, with 44,000 whites) was therefore abandoned in the face of widespread opposition from Africans, who saw it as a way of entrenching white settler power. Kenya became independent under Jomo Kenyatta in 1963.

Kenyan nationalist leader Jomo Kenyatta (1894–1978) dressed in traditional robes. This picture was taken at about the time of his arrest for his alleged involvement in the Mau Mau rebellion of 1952. He became the first prime minister (1963–4) and then president (1964–78) of independent Kenya. Under his leadership Kenya became one of the most stable and prosperous of the African states.

Rhodesia

Similar nationalist opposition to British plans for federation had deepened with the creation of the Central African Federation in October 1953, amalgamating Nyasaland and Northern and Southern Rhodesia. The Federation had been favoured by Britain in part as a counterweight to the regionally dominant power of South Africa which, under General Jan Christian Smuts (prime minister 1939–48), had visions of territorial expansion to the north. South Africa retained the mandated territory of South West Africa, making it in effect a fifth province of the Union of South Africa. But Britain's colonies opposed Afrikaner nationalism and its developing racial policies (*apartheid*), and refused incorporation. After the electoral victory of the Afrikaner National Party in 1948, British relations with South Africa became strained, and the latter withdrew from the Commonwealth in 1961.

Opposition to the Central African Federation, particularly in Nyasaland and Northern Rhodesia where there were few white settlers, led to its collapse. It was dissolved in 1963 and Britain introduced non-racial constitutions as the basis for independence in Malawi and Zambia in 1964. Like the white South Africans, the settlers in Southern Rhodesia were fearful of black majority rule. They had dominated power since achieving self-government in 1923, although

40 years later they still numbered only around 200,000 in a population of several million black Africans. Supported by South Africa, white Rhodesian leader Ian Smith issued an illegal 'Unilateral Declaration of Independence' (UDI) in 1965. It was followed by 15 years of international isolation, British-backed sanctions and guerrilla war, and white Rhodesia came to an end with Britain's transfer of title to create the independent black state of Zimbabwe in 1980.

By 1968 the surge of decolonization had culminated in the half-reluctant independence of Botswana, Lesotho and Swaziland, Britain's other remaining African colonies. Their fate was to be dominated by South Africa, whose own adjustment to majority rule would have to wait a little longer.

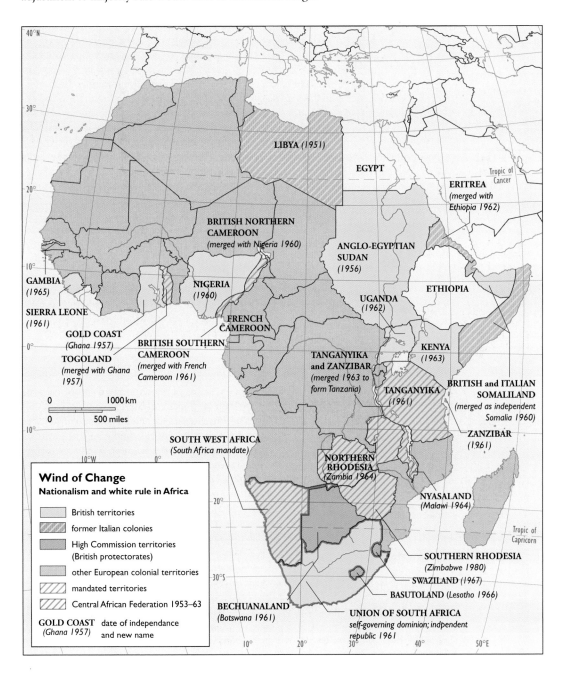

Wind of Change

Nationalism and white rule in Africa

- British territories
- former Italian colonies
- High Commission territories (British protectorates)
- other European colonial territories
- mandated territories
- Central African Federation 1953–63

GOLD COAST date of independance
(Ghana 1957) and new name

LIBYA (1951)

EGYPT

ERITREA (merged with Ethiopia 1962)

BRITISH NORTHERN CAMEROON (merged with Nigeria 1960)

ANGLO-EGYPTIAN SUDAN (1956)

GAMBIA (1965)

NIGERIA (1960)

ETHIOPIA

UGANDA (1962)

SIERRA LEONE (1961)

FRENCH CAMEROON

GOLD COAST (Ghana 1957)

KENYA (1963)

TOGOLAND (merged with Ghana 1957)

BRITISH SOUTHERN CAMEROON (merged with French Cameroon 1961)

TANGANYIKA and ZANZIBAR (merged 1963 to form Tanzania)

TANGANYIKA (1961)

BRITISH and ITALIAN SOMALILAND (merged as independent Somalia 1960)

ZANZIBAR (1961)

SOUTH WEST AFRICA (South Africa mandate)

NORTHERN RHODESIA (Zambia 1964)

NYASALAND (Malawi 1964)

SOUTHERN RHODESIA (Zimbabwe 1980)

SWAZILAND (1967)

BASUTOLAND (Lesotho 1966)

BECHUANALAND (Botswana 1961)

UNION OF SOUTH AFRICA self-governing dominion; indpendent republic 1961

Tropic of Cancer

Tropic of Capricorn

0   1000 km
0   500 miles

India and Partition

Britain's efforts to contain nationalist unrest in India in the early 20th century succeeded only in increasing opposition. The Second World War brought matters to a head, and partition between Hindus and Muslims emerged as the only workable option.

> *"It is a dream that the Hindus and Muslims can ever evolve a common nationality."*
>
> Muhammad Ali Jinnah, presidential address to the Muslim League (1940)

In the years before the First World War, Indian nationalist agitation, seriously aggravated by the partition of Bengal (1905-11), drew limited reforms from the Raj. The Government of India Act (1919) failed to satisfy Indian demands for home rule, and other grievances led to the government's repressive Rowlatt Acts (1919) which intensified civil unrest and Indian opposition.

In 1920 troops under General Sir Reginald Dyer fired on demonstrators at Amritsar, killing 379 and injuring 1,200. The episode provoked widespread anger, which was exploited by nationalists, especially the Indian National Congress leader who came to direct the movement, Mohandas Karamchand Gandhi (1869-1948), known as Mahatma (great soul). His first major campaign of non-violent non-co-operation lasted from 1919 to 1922 and captured the imagination of the Indian public. In an attempt to mollify nationalist feelings, the viceroy Lord Irwin acknowledged in 1929 a British desire to see India achieve dominion status. Gandhi's second mass campaign of 1930 was halted for the duration of the abortive Round Table Conference in London in 1931, but when it was eventually revived Britain reacted by suspending civil liberties and imprisoning Gandhi and the main Congress leaders.

The Path to Partition

In 1935 a new Government of India Act introduced a constitution designed to divide the nationalist opposition. It granted autonomous government for the Indian provinces, with protected Muslim representation, with the aim of a federal India of provinces and princely states. It was to be organized as a diarchy, with defence and other major policy areas reserved for the viceroy. Congress,

Indian leader Mahatma Gandhi reading as he sits cross-legged next to a spinning wheel, the symbol for India's fight for independence. Gandhi led popular campaigns of non-violent non-cooperation that helped make Britain's role as colonial administrator increasingly untenable.

aiming for a unitary Indian state, participated in the elections of 1936 but campaigned against the plan. Congress won control of most of the provinces, but its success alarmed the Muslim League, whose ambitions began to move towards a separate Muslim state.

The provincial governments resigned in 1939 in opposition to India's entry to the war on Britain's side without consultation or concession. Faced with an imminent Japanese invasion in 1942, London was forced to be more flexible to gain nationalist support, and promised full dominion status (effectively independence) after the war. But by now Congress had begun to demand complete and immediate independence. Gandhi launched a 'Quit India' campaign which provoked a major government crackdown; INC leaders and 90,000 followers were arrested and 1,000 died.

The withdrawal of Congress from government allowed the Muslim League to extend its influence and gain control of Bengal, Assam, Sind and the North West Frontier Province. The elections of 1945-6 were a triumph for the League and showed the extent of polarization. A cabinet deputation was sent to India in 1946 to help reconcile the two parties and allow Britain to hand over power to

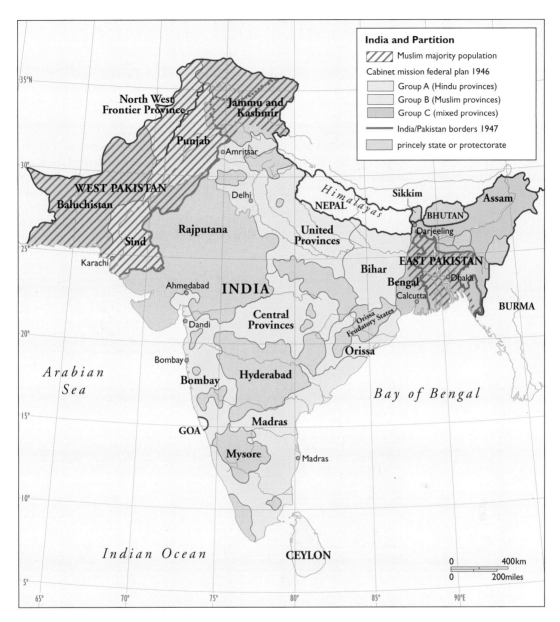

a united country which might be retained as a major strategic ally. It envisaged provinces autonomous in most matters but grouped for issues of common interest (defence, foreign affairs and communications). Equal administrations representing Group A (Hindu-majority provinces), and Groups B (Muslim-majority) and C (mixed provinces), would co-operate as a central government.

The plan soon unravelled in the face of Congress hostility and was overtaken by Muhammad Ali Jinnah's call for direct action by Muslims on 16 August 1946. From Calcutta, severe intercommunal violence spread across the sub-continent; it continued for 18 months, leaving one million dead and ten million cross-border refugees. The only solution left was partition, overseen by the last viceroy, Lord Louis Mountbatten. Two boundary commissions worked hurriedly to fix the borders of an independent Hindu India and Muslim East and West Pakistan, which came into being at midnight on 14–15 August 1947.

The Commonwealth and the Rump

The Commonwealth evolved from Britain's acknowledgement of the increasing independence of the states in its empire. Over time, a larger, looser free association of countries has emerged.

"This British Commonwealth of Nations ... stands for a fuller, richer, and more various life among all the nations that compose it. "

General Jan Christian Smuts, speech 15 May 1917

The origins of the Commonwealth lay in the relationship of Britain with the white dominions. This favoured group of territories was known the 'British Commonwealth of Nations', united in a common allegiance to the Crown. In 1946 the adjective 'British' was dropped as the association was redefined in the light of Indian decolonization in 1947. India's insistence on its own republican constitution, a precedent accepted by the Commonwealth, allowed other newly independent former colonies to join while choosing their own heads of state. The British monarch was recognized instead as Head of the Commonwealth and 'symbol of the free association of the independent Member Nations'. Other states continued as monarchies, notably Canada, Australia and New Zealand among a total of 17 in 1988.

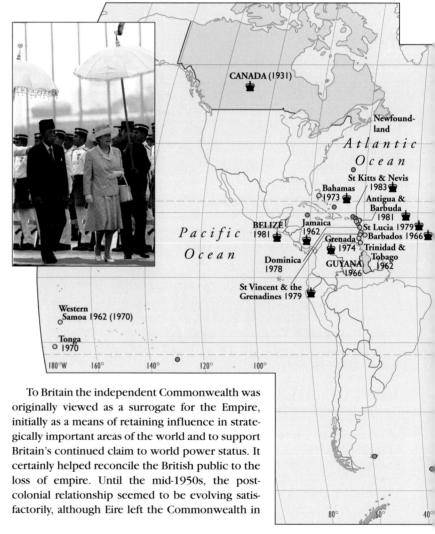

Queen Elizabeth II on a Commonwealth visit to Malaysia in 1998. The Queen travels the world widely and many of her trips are to Commonwealth countries. She takes her role as Head of the Commonwealth seriously and always attends the biannual Commonwealth Heads of Government Meetings.

CANADA (1931)

Newfound-land

Atlantic Ocean

St Kitts & Nevis 1983
Bahamas 1973
Antigua & Barbuda 1981
BELIZE 1981
Jamaica 1962
St Lucia 1979
Grenada 1974
Barbados 1966
Trinidad & Tobago 1962
Dominica 1978
GUYANA 1966
Pacific Ocean
St Vincent & the Grenadines 1979

Western Samoa 1962 (1970)

Tonga 1970

180°W   160°   140°   120°   100°

To Britain the independent Commonwealth was originally viewed as a surrogate for the Empire, initially as a means of retaining influence in strategically important areas of the world and to support Britain's continued claim to world power status. It certainly helped reconcile the British public to the loss of empire. Until the mid-1950s, the post-colonial relationship seemed to be evolving satisfactorily, although Eire left the Commonwealth in

80°   60°   40°

1948 and Burma refused to join at independence (1948). Continued association was backed by ties of sentiment or kinship, economic and financial co-operation, favoured access to British markets, and technical assistance.

The relationship soured for Britain with the Suez Crisis of 1956, which prompted widespread criticism and attracted little Commonwealth support. British governments also found it difficult to accept the new dominance of independent African and Asian states, many of which were more sympathetic to the Eastern Bloc and to non-aligned values. Further conflict arose over Britain's colonial policies and attitudes towards apartheid South Africa (which left the Commonwealth in 1961) and Rhodesia from 1965. The issue of race and sanctions was immensely divisive over three decades.

Shifting Interests

With the growing attraction of European Economic Community membership (from 1973) and the strategic alliance with the USA, Britain's interest in the Commonwealth has dwindled. It continues to be a useful organization encouraging co-operation and discussion between developed nations and Third World countries. Even states with a slender claim to historic ties have actively sought membership, namely Mozambique and Cameroon (1995). All that remains of Britain's empire, however, is a rump of minor dependencies, either too small or unwilling to relinquish their direct ties with Britain.

The Commonwealth and the Rump

- Commonwealth members and date of independence (membership date in brackets if different)
- former British territories not members of Commonwealth and date of independence
- ♔ countries with the British monarch as head of state
- ● British dependencies

Imperial Legacies

The historical political, economic, social and cultural legacies of the British Empire are still very much alive in the modern world. In some regions decolonization left behind intractable conflicts. Some disputes have been resolved but others remain as tensions and shared memories to dictate future conflict.

> **"*[Colonial peoples] are able by our service to make a contribution to the larger life of mankind. "***
>
> Arthur Creech Jones, Secretary of State for the Colonies, speech, 29 July 1947

The remnants of Britain's empire today consist mainly of territories that are too small and unsuited to independence. Sometimes, responsibility for these territories has proven onerous, as in the case of the Falklands, which involved Britain in a war to recover the disputed islands following the Argentinian invasion of 1982. Gibraltar remains a source of tension with Spain, and although Hong Kong was satisfactorily returned to China in 1997, the hand-over agreement guaranteeing its distinctive way of life and political autonomy within China has the potential to cause of friction in the future. At the other extreme is Bermuda, a territory whose benign economy and political system generate no incentive to seek independence.

Economic interest and strategic considerations influenced Britain's decision to fight the Malayan insurgency and Indonesian claims on Malaysia in the 1960s. They also dictated British policy towards Kuwait, part of the Ottoman empire until detached as a British protectorate (1899–1961). The Iraqi invasion of 1992, justified through its inherited Ottoman claims, culminated in the US-led Gulf War, with British participation, to re-establish Kuwaiti independence. Continuing military assistance was also provided to Belize from 1981 in order to deter any invasion by Guatemala in pursuit of its territorial claim to the Central American state.

The most serious conflict accompanying decolonization arose in India, where intercommunal divisions led to partition; the lingering hostility between India and Pakistan is now focused on the divided territory of Kashmir. The former Palestine mandated territory also remains bitterly divided between Israelis and Palestinians and a source of international tension.

Communal Strife

Racial tensions have sometimes prevailed in regions of the world where (predominantly) British settlers colonized the lands of indigenous peoples. British settlement of Ireland has bequeathed a bitter historical legacy and continued division

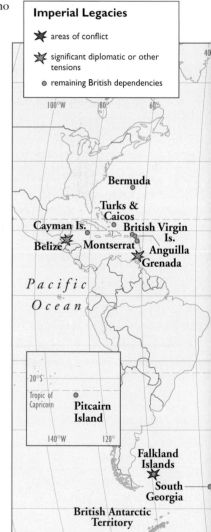

Imperial Legacies

- ✹ areas of conflict
- ✹ significant diplomatic or other tensions
- ● remaining British dependencies

Bermuda

Turks & Caicos

Cayman Is.

British Virgin Is.

Belize Montserrat Anguilla Grenada

Pacific Ocean

Pitcairn Island

Falkland Islands

South Georgia

British Antarctic Territory

between the Catholic/nationalist and Protestant/unionist communities in the North, where paramilitary campaigns continued from 1969 until the IRA ceasefire of 1994.

In Africa – in particular – European imperialism has often created modern states whose borders ignore older ethnic, linguistic and religious boundaries. This has contributed to internal conflicts, including attempts to reduce or maintain the power and influence of dominant groups.

A predominant characteristic of the British Empire was large-scale economic migration; this too has sometimes left an aftermath of ethnic hostility, particularly in Sri Lanka where open warfare between Tamils and Sinhalese commenced in 1983. Significant numbers of migrants from South Asia and the Caribbean began arriving in Britain itself at the end of the Second World War, and by 1991 these communities formed 5.5 per cent of the British population (some three million people). Despite some racial tensions the general effect has been to broaden cultural life and understanding in British society.

Chris Patten, the last Governor of the Crown Colony of Hong Kong, accepts the folded Union Jack at ceremonies marking the end of 156 years of British rule on 30 June 1997.

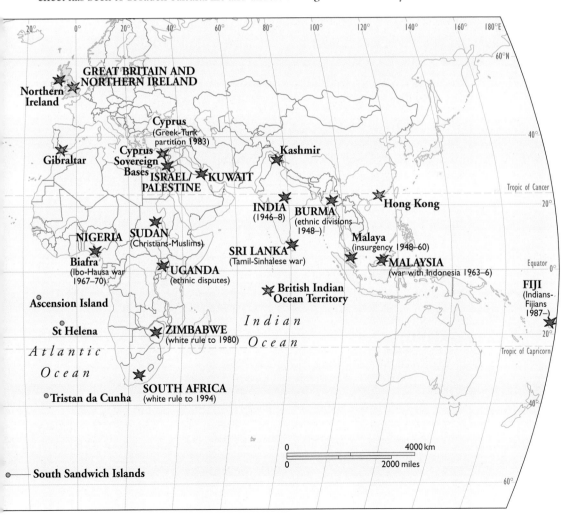

Main Territories of the British Empire

Territory	Date of acquisition	Independence
Aden (South Yemen)	1839	1967
Anguilla	1650	*British dependent territory*
Antigua (Antigua and Barbuda)	1632	1981
Australia, Commonwealth created 1 Jan. 1901 from the colonies of: New South Wales *1788*, Van Diemen's Land (Tasmania) *1825*, Western Australia *1829*, South Australia *1836*, Queensland *1859*, Victoria *1851*	1770 Eastern Australia (New South Wales) claimed; settled 1788. Whole of Australia claimed 1829	1907 dominion; independence recognized 1931
Bahamas	1629	1973
Bahrain	1861, 1880 protectorate treaties	1971
Barbados	1624	1966
Barbuda (Antigua and Barbuda)	1628	1981
Basutoland (Lesotho)	1868	1966
Bechuanaland (Botswana)	1885	1966
Bermuda	1609	*British dependent territory*
British Antarctic Territory	From 1819	*British dependent territory*
British Guiana (Guyana)	1796–1815	1966
British Honduras (Belize)	1638	1981
British North Borneo (Sabah, Malaysia)	1881 British North Borneo Company; protectorate 1888	1963 joined Malaysia
British Somaliland (Somaliland)	1884–7	1960
British Togoland (Ghana)	1914 occupied; mandate 1920	1956 joined Gold Coast
British Virgin Islands	1666 occupied; annexed 1672	*British dependent territory*
Brunei (Sultanate of)	1888	1984
Burma (Myanmar), created from:		1948
Arakan, Assam, Manipur and Tenasserim	1824–6	
Pegu	1852	
Upper Burma and Karenni	1885	
Canada, federation created 1867 from: Canada East (Lower Canada, Quebec) *1763*, Canada West (Upper Canada, Ontario) *1763*, New Brunswick *1763*, Nova Scotia *1713* including Cape Breton Island Later incorporated: Newfoundland *1497–1713*, Prince Edward Island *1763*, British Columbia *1849–66*	1497 English claim to Newfoundland. From 1670 Hudson's Bay Company claims Rupert's Land and Northwest Territories (sold to Canadian government 1869) 1759–60 acquisition of French North America	1907 dominion; independence recognized 1931
Cayman Islands	1670	*British dependent territory*
Ceylon (Sri Lanka)	1795–6	1948
Chagos Archipelago (British Indian Ocean Territory)	1810	*British dependent territory*
Cyprus	1878	1960
Dominica	1761	1978
Egypt	1882, protectorate 1914	1922
Falkland Islands	1766 first settlement	*British dependent territory*
Fiji	1871 first settlement; Crown Colony 1874	1970
Gambia	1661 earliest foothold	1965
Gold Coast (Ghana)	1621 earliest foothold	1957
Gibraltar	1704	*British dependent territory*
Grenada	1762, ceded 1763	1974
Hong Kong	1841, ceded 1842	1997 to China
India (India, Pakistan, Bangladesh)	Cession of Bombay 1661 (effective 1665) but commonly regarded as 1757 with the acquisition of Bengal	1947 as India and East and West Pakistan
Iraq	1915 occupied; mandate 1920	1932
Ireland (Eire and Northern Ireland)	From 1169	1922 dominion (Irish Free State); Eire independence recognized 1931
Jamaica	1655	1962
Kenya	From 1887 (lease of coast from Zanzibar)	1963
Kuwait	1899	1961
Labuan (Malaysia)	1846	1963 joined Malaysia

Territory column: Dates in italics refer to dates of foundation of colonies/ provinces/ states.

Territory	Date of acquisition	Independence
Malaya (Malaysia)	From 1786 with the acquisition of Penang	1957; joined with Sabah, Sarawak, Labuan and Singapore as Malaysia 1963
Malta	1798–1800	1964
Mauritius	1810	1968
Montserrat	1632	*British dependent territory*
Mosquito Coast (Nicaragua)	1658	1894
Muscat and Oman (Sultanate of Oman)	1861; de facto protectorate extended 1891	1971
Nauru	1914 Australian occupation; mandate 1920	1968
Nevis (St Kitts and Nevis)	1628 first settlement	1983
New Hebrides (Vanuatu)	1887 Anglo-French condominium	1980
New Zealand	1769 claimed by Captain James Cook; annexed 1840	1907 dominion; independence recognized 1931
Newfoundland (Canada)	1497 claimed for England; annexed 1583	1907 dominion; joined Canada 1949
Nigeria	1861–1914	1960
Northern Rhodesia (Zambia)	1889–1900	1964
Nyasaland (Malawi)	1889	1964
Palestine (Israel/Palestinian Territories)	1917 occupied; mandate 1920	1948
Papua (Papua New Guinea)	1884 Papua (British New Guinea); 1914 conquest of German New Guinea, joined with Papua 1945 as Papua New Guinea	1975
Qatar	1868	1971
St Helena	1651 occupation by East India Company	*British dependent territory*
St Kitts (St Kitts and Nevis)	1623 first settlement	1983
St Lucia	1605 first settlement; permanent control 1803	1979
St Vincent (and the Grenadines)	1627	1979
Sarawak (Malaysia)	1841 ruled by Brooke rajahs; British protectorate 1888	1963 joined Malaysia
Seychelles	1794 occupied	1976
Sierra Leone	1787	1961
Singapore	1819 ceded to Stamford Raffles; to Britain 1824	1963 joined Malaysia; independent 1965
Solomon Islands	1893	1978
South Africa, Union of, formed 1910 from:		1910 Dominion. Independence recognized 1931
Cape Colony	1806	
Natal	1824, re-established 1843	
Orange Free State	1900	
Transvaal (South African Republic)	1900	
South West Africa (Namibia)	1915 occupied by South Africa; mandate 1921	1990 independent from South Africa
Southern Rhodesia (Rhodesia, Zimbabwe)	1888	1965 UDI; black majority rule 1980
Sudan	1898	1956
Swaziland	1890–3	1968
Tanganyika (Tanzania)	1916 occupied; mandate 1920	1961
'Thirteen Colonies, The' (USA): Massachusetts *1620* Connecticut *1639* Maryland *1632* Delaware *1704* Georgia *1732* New Hampshire *1623* New Jersey *1665* New York *1664* North Carolina *1729* Pennsylvania *1681* Rhode Island *1636* South Carolina *1729* Virginia *1607*	From 1607, first permanent English settlement of North America at Jamestown, Virginia	1776 declaration of independence as United States of America
Tobago (Trinidad and Tobago)	1762	1962
Transjordan (Kingdom of Jordan)	1917–18	1946
Trinidad (and Tobago)	1797	1962
Trucial States, or **Trucial Oman** (United Arab Emirates)	From *c.*1820 informal protectorate; extended 1892	1971
Turks and Caicos Islands	1678	*British dependent territory*
Uganda	1890	1962
Western Samoa	1914 occupied by New Zealand; mandate 1920	1962
Zanzibar, Sultanate of (Tanzania)	1862	1963

Further Reading

1. GENERAL

Brown, Judith (ed.), *Oxford History of the British Empire, Vol. IV: The Twentieth Century* (Oxford, 1999)

Canny, Nicholas (ed.), *Oxford History of the British Empire, Vol. I: The Origins of Empire. British Overseas Enterprise to the Close of the Seventeenth Century* (Oxford, 1998)

Judd, Denis, *Empire: The British Imperial Experience, 1765 to the Present* (London, 1996)

Marshall, P. J. (ed.), *The Cambridge Illustrated History of the British Empire* (Cambridge, 1996)

Marshall, P. J. (ed.), *Oxford History of the British Empire, Vol. II: The Eighteenth Century* (Oxford, 1998)

Porter, Andrew (ed.), *Oxford History of the British Empire, Vol. III: The Nineteenth Century* (Oxford, 1999)

Samson, Jane (ed.), *The British Empire* (Oxford, 2001)

2. MILITARY AND POLICING

Anderson, David M., and Killingray, David (eds.), *Policing the Empire* (Manchester, 1991)

Black, Jeremy, *The British Seaborne Empire* (New Haven and London, 2004)

Lenman, Bruce, *Britain's Colonial Wars 1688-1783* (Harlow, Essex, 2001)

MacKenzie, John M. (ed.), *Popular Imperialism and the Military* (Manchester, 1992)

Omissi, David E., *Air Power and Colonial Control* (Manchester, 1990)

3. TRANSPORT AND TECHNOLOGY

Harcourt, Freda, *Flagships of Imperialism* (Manchester, 2006)

Headrick, Daniel R., *The Tools of Empire: Technology and European Imperialism in the Nineteenth Century* (Oxford, 1981)

Headrick, Daniel R., *The Invisible Weapon: Telecommunications and International Politics 1851-1945* (Oxford, 1991)

4. CULTURE AND RELIGION

Greenhalgh, Paul, *Ephemeral Vistas: Exhibitions and Expositions Universelles* (Manchester, 1988)

MacKenzie, John M., *Propaganda and Empire* (Manchester, 1985)

MacKenzie, John M. (ed.), *Imperialism and Popular Culture: The Manipulation of British Public Opinion 1880-1960* (Manchester, 1986)

Porter, Andrew (ed.), *The Imperial Horizons of British Protestant Missions, 1880-1914* (Grand Rapids, Michigan and Cambridge, 2003)

Richards, Jeffrey (ed.), *Imperialism and Juvenile Literature* (Manchester, 1989)

Pickles, Katie, *Female Imperialism and National Identity: Imperial Order Daughters of the Empire* (Manchester, 2002)

Ward, Stuart (ed.), *British Culture and the End of Empire* (Manchester, 2001)

5. EMIGRATION AND INDIGENOUS PEOPLES

Constantine, Stephen (ed.), *Emigrants and Empire* (Manchester, 1990)

Richards, Eric, *Britannia's Children: Emigration from England, Scotland, Wales and Ireland since 1600* (London and New York, 2004)

Russell, Lynette (ed.), *Colonial Frontiers: Indigenous-European encounters in Settler Societies* (Manchester, 2001)

6. ENVIRONMENT

Drayton, Richard, *Nature's Government: Science, Imperial Britain, and the 'Improvement' of the World* (New Haven and London, 2000)

McCracken, Donal P., *Gardens of Empire: Botanical Institutions of the Victorian British Empire* (London, 1997)

MacKenzie, John M. (ed.), *Imperialism and the Natural World* (Manchester, 1990)

MacKenzie, John M., *The Empire of Nature: Hunting, Conservation and British Imperialism* (1988)

Index

Acknowledgements

PICTURE CREDITS

Pages: 8 The Bridgeman Art Library, London; 9 The Art Archive; 14 The Bridgeman Art Library, London; 15 The Bridgeman Art Library/National Portrait Gallery; 16 The Art Archive; 17 AKG, London; 18 The Bridgeman Art Library, London; 20 The Art Archive; 23-28 The Bridgeman Art Library, London; 31 Corbis/Werner Forman Archives; 32-9 The Bridgeman Art Library, London; 40 The Art Archive; 41 The Bridgeman Art Library, London; 43-4 The Art Archive; 46 The Bridgeman Art Library, London; 47 National Maritime Museum, Greenwich; 48-52 The Bridgeman Art Library, London; 54 Corbis; 56-60 The Bridgeman Art Library, London; 61 The Art Archive; 62 Advertising Archives; 63 The Bridgeman Art Library, London; 64 Advertising Archives; 66-69 The Bridgeman Art Library, London; 70 Scala, Florence; 75 Getty Images/Hulton Archives; 76 Scala Archives, Florence; 78-84 The Bridgeman Art Library, London; 85 Mary Evans Picture Library; 86 The Bridgeman Art Library, London; 87 The Art Archive; 89 The Bridgeman Art Library, London; 91 The Art Archive; 93-4 Author's collection; 97 The Art Archive; 99 Author's collection; 100 The Art Archive; 103 The Bridgeman Art Library, London; 105 Author's collection; 106 Getty Images/Hulton Archives; 107 Corbis; 108 Corbis/Hulton Archives; 109t Corbis/Alan Lewis/Sygma; 109b Corbis; 111 Scala Archives, Florence/HIP; 112 Author's collection; 114 Corbis/Hulton Archives; 116-18 Getty Images; 121 Corbis/Hulton Archives; 122 The Art Archive; 124-7 Getty Images; 128 Corbis/Bettmann Archive; 130 Getty Images; 132-5 Corbis.

Conceived and produced by John Haywood and Simon Hall
Designed by Darren Bennett
Edited by Fiona Plowman
Picture research by Veneta Bullen
Cartography by Pam Baldaro, Lyn Ertl and Bob Smith, Cartographic Unit, University of Southampton
Index prepared by Gerard M.-F. Hill

… a Haywood & Hall production for Penguin Books